T0358810

WHAT IS MY LEGACY?

Realizing a New Dream of Connection, Love and Fulfillment

MARTIN LUTHER KING III
ARNDREA WATERS KING
MARC KIELBURGER
CRAIG KIELBURGER

WITH A FOREWORD BY HIS HOLINESS THE DALAI LAMA

FLASH
POINT

Scripture quotations from the Authorized (King James) Version. Rights in the Authorized Version in the United Kingdom are vested in the Crown. Reproduced by permission of the Crown's patentee, Cambridge University Press.

LEGACY+
imprint

A collaboration with Legacy+
legacyplus.org

FLASH POINT

Published by Flashpoint™ Books, Seattle
www.flashpointbooks.com

Produced by Girl Friday Productions

Cover design: Lisa McCoy
Interior design: Rachel Marek
Production editorial: Abi Pollokoff
Project management: Kristin Duran

Cover image credits: UP LT, Drum Major Institute; UP RT, Flip Schulke Archives/Getty Images; CTR LT, WE Charity; CTR RT, Legacy+; LO, WE Charity; back flap, courtesy of Legacy+. Insert pages image credits: 1 (ALL), Michael Ochs Archives/Getty Images; 2 (UP), 7 (LO), 8 (ALL), Bettmann/Getty Images; 2 (LO), TPLP/Getty Images; 3 (ALL), Don Uhrbrock/Getty Images; 4 (UP), Marvin Koner/Getty Images; 4 (LO), 5 (ALL), 6 (UP), Flip Schulke Archives/Getty Images; 6 (LO), Robert Abbott Sengstacke/Getty Images; 7 (UP), Santi Visalli/Getty Images; 9 (ALL), 17 (LO), 18 (ALL), 22 (LO), 23, 24 (ALL), Drum Major Institute; 10 (ALL), 11 (UP, LO LT), 12 (ALL), 13 (UP), 14 (ALL), 15 (ALL), 16 (UP), 19 (ALL), 20, WE Charity; 11 (LO RT), Kielburger Family; 13 (LO), WE Charity via Canadian Living; 16 (LO), Toronto Star Archive; 17 (UP), Martin Luther King III and Arndrea Waters King; 21 (UP), Dennis Reggie; 21 (LO), courtesy of Martin Luther King III; 22 (UP), SAUL LOEB/Getty Images; 25 (UP), Arndrea Waters King; 25 (LO), 26 (ALL), 27 (ALL), 28 (ALL), 29 (UP), 30, 31, 32 (ALL), Legacy+; 29 (LO), Kevin Sabitus/Getty Images

ISBN (hardcover): 978-1-964721-09-5
ISBN (ebook): 978-1-964721-10-1

Library of Congress Control Number 2024919066

First edition

To our beloved children, Yolanda, Lily-Rose, Violette, Hilson, Arthur James and Lachlan. Your boundless curiosity and limitless potential remind us of the beauty and possibility in the world. You are the inspiration behind Living Legacy, and it is our deepest hope that you will grow up in a world where Dr. King's dream and the Beloved Community are ever closer to reality.

CONTENTS

FOREWORD

THE DALAI LAMA

IT IS A SIMPLE TRUTH that every human being wants to be happy and does not want to suffer. Living in an increasingly interdependent world, we need to realize that if we do good to others, we benefit, too, while if we cause others harm, we also end up harming ourselves.

We are well into this new century, and there is growing awareness of the value of love and compassion. Developing these feelings entails transforming our hearts and minds. The path to peace will open to us if we embrace the oneness of humanity.

For inspiration, we can look to the legacies of Dr. Martin Luther King Jr. and Mahatma Gandhi. They taught that nonviolence does not mean passive acceptance of things as they are, but rather acting every day of our lives to bring about change for the better. Fundamentally, this means if you can, help others, but if you cannot do that, at least do them no harm.

We must rebuild our connection with the world around us. The idea of distinguishing between "us" and "them" is now out of date because, in today's reality, we are all interdependent. Therefore, we should embrace the notion that the entire population of over eight billion human beings is part of "us" and we must share this planet—our only home—with the entire human family.

I understand this book about Dr. Martin Luther King Jr. is being published in conjunction with a movement called Realize the Dream, whose goal is to provide one hundred million hours of voluntary service by the time of the one hundredth anniversary of Dr. King's birthday in 2029. I hope that, inspired by his example, readers may be moved to make their own contribution to realizing that dream.

His Holiness the Fourteenth Dalai Lama

INTRODUCTION

On Dreams Unfulfilled and Hopes for a New Understanding of Legacy

Martin Luther King III

ON AUGUST 28, 1963, IN front of a crowd of nearly 250,000 people spread across the National Mall in Washington, DC, my father, the Baptist preacher and civil rights leader Reverend Dr. Martin Luther King Jr., delivered his famous "I Have a Dream" speech from the steps of the Lincoln Memorial. That speech now stands out as one of the twentieth century's most unforgettable moments and celebrated speeches.

After laying bare the brutal facts of racism in America, my father offered up a dream of an America in which people of all races and faiths live together in harmony and mutual respect, free of economic and employment inequalities. Among the most quoted lines of the speech are "I have a dream that my four little children will one day live in a nation where they will not be judged by the color of their skin but by the content of their character."

I was five at the time, too young to attend. Instead, I stayed at home in Atlanta. But I have since listened to his dream many times over the years. Every time, it brings tears to my eyes. His message of hope is something that I've continued to share throughout my life. My father's dream is not just a speech he gave or an idyllic view of what could be. His dream is something we must all choose each day to work toward. What my father was asking for all those years ago was to create a world where every person can realize their dreams.

That is something I also want for each of us. My father's dream remains unfulfilled, but it is still very much alive.

After leading the March on Washington, he went on to win the Nobel Peace Prize, the youngest person awarded the honor at that time. Then when I was ten years old, in 1968, my father was assassinated. He was frozen in time at the height of his influence as a vital, passionate civil rights leader who has inspired millions of people to take nonviolent action for peace and social justice.

My dad will always be larger than life. And for me, the struggle of my life has been, first and foremost, growing up without him. As a boy, I longed to shoot hoops, wrestle, and ride bikes with my dad, as we used to do before he was killed. As a man, I wish he'd seen me graduate from college, marry the love of my life, the incredible Arndrea Waters King, and raise a fierce daughter—his only grandchild—Yolanda Renee King, with his oratory gifts running through her veins.

My mom, the incomparable Coretta Scott King, who died in 2006, would sometimes tell me, "Your father would be so proud of you." This would bring tears to my eyes. I would almost melt into the moment, wanting so badly to hear those very words from his mouth and feel the warmth of his approval.

As you can imagine, I have thought more about legacy than

most people. My father passed a huge legacy to me, and so did my mother—combating hate, racism, violence and poverty while trying to build the Beloved Community with room for us all. An important part of my life has been furthering their work. What a great honor it is to pursue this mission, in the hopes that my efforts—on the wings of their legacy—will help create a better world.

Even so, I've grappled with my parents' legacies and my role in them. I've spent my life in the shadow of my dad's accomplishments, and I've often struggled to figure out how to emerge from my father's vast shadow to define my own legacy. Many times, I have asked myself whether the purpose of my life will be defined by my father or by me.

MY FATHER'S DREAM REMAINS UNFULFILLED, BUT IT IS STILL VERY MUCH ALIVE.

In recent years, I've found a new relationship with legacy that isn't about trying to live up to someone else's reputation or even follow in someone's footsteps. Rather, I've come to believe that a legacy should be alive and evolving; it's not just something stagnant to be passed on to the next generation after we're gone. It's really about the impact and purpose we live every day.

What if we started living today the way we hope to be remembered and shared our unique talents, passions and resources with the world now? Not tomorrow, but now? I want to show you how you can live your legacy every day. I also want to share with you how your purpose and impact infuse your daily actions and benefit your family, community, faith and work. It is how you use your unique talents, passions and resources to make the world a better place that truly counts, not just what you leave behind.

And this is in part why I am a coauthor of this book that you hold in your hands. This book explores an entirely new and empowering way to think about legacy. Not in the sense of what you leave to others in your will, but the impact you can make today. And it is written by four authors, including me.

My first coauthor is my amazing wife, Arndrea Waters King. In Arndrea, I've found a partner who is equally committed to human rights and combating hate and racism as I am, especially through her long-standing efforts with the Center for Democratic Renewal. At the center, she played a key role in mobilizing the Georgia hate crimes legislation and preparing major reports and publications, including *When Hate Comes to Town: Faith-Based Edition*. She organized marches and rallies that led to the building of a major multiracial collaboration known as the Southern Coalition Against Racism and Bigotry. She investigated the Ku Klux Klan, neo-Nazis, skinheads, various white supremacists, and the burning of Black churches. She started a national hate crimes summit and was one of the first people to bring together all factions of all communities who were impacted by hate crimes. Before that the NAACP, gay and lesbian communities, Jewish communities, Asian Americans and Pacific Islanders, Arab communities, Indigenous American communities and other groups all did their monitoring separately. She recognized the importance of intersectionality to combat hate crimes long before it was a widely known approach to human rights work. Currently, Arndrea is leading the Drum Major Institute to continue advancing the King legacy.

My wife possesses a maturity, mental prowess and calming

strength that brings out the best in me. She's also beautiful and reminds me of my mother in so many ways. And she is an amazing mother to our daughter, Yolanda. Arndrea is helping her explore all the options open to her as the grandchild of Martin Luther King Jr. and Coretta Scott King. Of course, if Yolanda wants to be a biologist, actor or teacher, we will support her. But already, at age sixteen, she is drawn to speak out for voting rights, gun control and other causes.

In a roundabout way, Yolanda's passion for youth activism is how we cemented our friendship with the other coauthors, our close friends Marc Kielburger and Craig Kielburger, cofounders of Legacy+, an organization supporting partners building movements and legacy projects. Those of you who live in the US may not have heard of Marc and Craig, but in Canada, they are renowned human rights activists and global movement builders. Their story begins in 1995, when the younger brother, Craig, was twelve and read a newspaper story about a boy named Iqbal Masih who had been forced into slavery and was murdered after his escape, presumably because he became an activist against child slavery. Craig was horrified to think of children being enslaved, and the more he learned, the more he felt compelled to do something to help them. That was the origin of how Marc and Craig started their first charity, called Free the Children, when they were teenagers.

A few years later, in addition to their work in the Global South, and eventually under a new name, WE Charity, they launched national service programs in the US, Canada and the UK, engaging tens of thousands of schools. To encourage youth to care and contribute, they rewarded youth service with giant celebrations called WE Day. At more than 130 events, from New York to Los Angeles, Toronto to London, some 1.5 million youths came together. They earned their entry by contributing a collective total of forty million hours of community service on issues such as homelessness, the environment, racism and inequality. At WE Day, they were celebrated by world leaders and renowned humanitarians, such as the Dalai Lama, Malala Yousafzai, Mikhail Gorbachev, Elie Wiesel, Jane Goodall and Magic Johnson, and countless entertainers.

SO, IN ANSWER TO THE QUESTION "HAVE I DONE ENOUGH?" THE ANSWER CAN ONLY BE "THERE IS SO MUCH MORE TO BE DONE."

This is where Yolanda and I come into the story. I was impressed with how Marc and Craig created transformative social change and future-ready global citizens. I believed strongly—and stated publicly—that if my father were still alive, he would be involved in this movement to raise compassionate, engaged young people. For these reasons I signed on to speak to youth at WE Days on three continents to commemorate the fiftieth anniversary of my father's "I Have a Dream" speech, crisscrossing Canada and the US and visiting the Caribbean and the UK.

When Yolanda was five, she attended her first WE Day with me. She was mesmerized by the incredible youth who spoke with boundless passion about the issues they cared about. I remember her saying, "I want to do that."

In 2018, when Yolanda, then age nine, was presented with the opportunity to speak at March for Our Lives in Washington, she seized the moment, speaking passionately for gun control. I believe her exposure to the amazing youth at WE Day inspired her to do that.

A friendship grew between Arndrea, me, Marc and Craig. We've come to love them and value their humanity and unwavering belief that we can make the world a better place. We also admire how they are nonpartisan and draw support from all ends of the political spectrum to come together to do huge things in service of humanity.

This explains why, in 2021, I asked Marc and Craig to meet Arndrea and me in Atlanta.

People were struggling. All around me, there had been deaths and job losses due to Covid. It was also a tumultuous but pivotal time in the world, particularly in North America. Many of us were moved to action by the heinous May 2020 murder of George Floyd, the growth of the Black Lives Matter movement, and the disenfranchisement of Black voters across the US. And I was at a crossroads. I was about to turn sixty-five; the one hundredth anniversary of my father's birthday was approaching in 2029; and my daughter was emerging as a future leader. Although I was proud of my work as an elected politician, human rights leader, and advocate on issues of social justice, nonviolence and equality, I wondered if I'd left my father and mother's legacy in good shape for my daughter and future generations.

Through the efforts of my family and other supporters, my father's name is known throughout the world, bestowed upon thousands of streets, parks, schools, libraries and even a national holiday in the US. But the legacy of what he stood for is lesser known and more elusive, including his vision of building a Beloved Community where people of all races and walks of life belong. More so, he envisioned the Beloved Community as the society so many of us are still yearning for: a society built on justice, nonviolence, and equal opportunity, and—this last part is especially important for Arndrea and me—a world built on love and compassion for one's fellow human beings. Arndrea has been on the front lines of investigating some of the worst evils perpetrated by humans, and yet she always says, "You stand up against the evil act, but you never destroy the human."

While there were times in my life when I lived in the shadow of my father's legacy, the truth is that inheriting my father's name and legacy has been a privilege and a deep honor. So, in answer to the question "Have I done enough?" the answer can only be "There is so much more to be done."

During our lunch with Marc and Craig in Atlanta, I laid out my hopes—and dare I say, dreams—of building a movement across the US and around the world, leading up to the anniversary of my father's one hundredth birthday. Together, we agreed that we wanted to truly fulfill my father's vision. We aim to do more than commemorate my father; we want to create sustainable change so that his legacy will endure for all future generations.

Our mission is to build the Beloved Community. We want to unite all peoples, creeds and races in fulfilling their potential for themselves and others. The greatest unifying forces are a common set of beliefs combined with a shared goal. This book outlines our beliefs. And love is our shared goal. Our campaign is called Realize the Dream, and we are mobilizing people to build unity and love through service with one hundred million hours of volunteerism by the one hundredth anniversary of the birth of my father in January 2029. This equates to $2.9 billion in social value for communities across America. We will also support two hundred thousand teachers with free resources that are vital to support thousands of underfunded schools and districts, impacting over six million students. We aim to promote awareness around diversity, equality and inclusion in schools, NGOs, places of worship and workplaces. No matter the color of our skin, our religion, who we love or our socioeconomic status, we can all come together around service.

This movement needs you, and this book is an invitation to join the movement to help us celebrate the King legacy and achieve your dreams in your own way. How? By living your own legacy to create a positive and lasting impact.

WE WANT YOU TO LIVE YOUR LEGACY EVERY DAY—WITH DEEP PURPOSE AND GOALS GREATER THAN YOURSELF.

In these pages, we will talk about some of the very real crises we are still struggling with globally and personally. And we will share why we believe Living Legacy is an answer to solving the world's—and humanity's—critical problems. We need to create a new dream for ourselves and the world, and it starts by shifting our thinking about legacy.

We want you to turn the idea of legacy on its head, and instead of amassing wealth and good deeds to pass on to others, we want you to live your legacy every day—with deep purpose and goals greater than yourself. We ask you, What if we started living, today, in the way we hope to be remembered, and shared our unique talents, passions and resources with the world?

We need this fresh perspective and this visionary approach to address the contemporary challenges facing ourselves and our world. There is a need for a new dream: a new relationship with ourselves, others and our world. This book provides a path to fulfillment by focusing on contribution, connection and love. This is what Living Legacy represents. Through a series of questions we pose in this book, interwoven with our personal stories and observations, we will help you take the first steps on your own legacy journey.

We will help you take stock of where you are now, what you want for your life, and how you got where you are. Each of us is the product of many legacies—family, culture, nation. We look at those legacies that shaped us to make a choice about which ones we carry forward because they empower us, and which to leave behind because they hold us back. We also help you identify your beliefs and values and define your purpose. We show you how to put your Living Legacy into practice by developing and synchronizing your Inner Purpose and Outer Purpose.

THERE IS A NEED FOR A NEW DREAM: A NEW RELATIONSHIP WITH OURSELVES, OTHERS AND OUR WORLD.

We must change how we think about legacy and move beyond the focus on end-of-life decisions about what property or family memorabilia to leave loved ones, and instead grow toward crafting our legacy in the present moment. As you can imagine, with four authors of such different backgrounds, it was challenging to pull this book together. We are different colors and genders and come from different countries and perspectives. Our differences are our strengths. Yet, we share a common passion for making the world a better place. My wife and I are devoted to furthering the King legacy through our words and actions. Marc and Craig advise countless individuals and empower them to live their legacies. Together, we want to support others to live a legacy of positive impact and build a better world.

We can do this together. My mother, Coretta, once said that "the greatness of a community is most accurately measured by the compassionate acts of its citizens." She was referring to the power of ordinary, everyday citizens to make a difference for the better. Too many people go through life feeling helpless to change things. But God put us here for a greater purpose than that. We know it's a constant struggle, but it is a challenge we must meet if we want our lives to have meaning and purpose.

Your Living Legacy is more than the material possessions you bequeath to others; it's an ongoing and timeless gift you share with those around you. And it's both a path to your own fulfillment and a way to fulfill our vast dreams for a better world.

CHAPTER 1

A New Legacy on the Horizon

WALTER CRONKITE'S CALM VOICE ECHOED through the Kings' Atlanta home, delivering the heartbreaking news to ten-year-old Martin: his dad had been shot on the balcony of the Lorraine Motel in Memphis, Tennessee, where he'd gone to support striking African American sanitation workers. Upon hearing the announcement, Martin recalls running to his mom's bedroom with his brother and sisters, hoping beyond hope it wasn't true. Her TV was on low. Coretta Scott King had been on the phone with Andrew Young, Dr. King's top lieutenant, who witnessed the shooting. *Martin was shot in the neck,* he'd told her. *It's pretty bad. Bring someone with you.*

As Martin's mother raced to the airport, their home filled with friends anxiously waiting for more news, hoping for the best, expecting the worst, which would come soon enough.

The next special bulletin that cut through the chaos of the King home shattered a nation and devastated young Martin. Cronkite again on CBS: "Dr. Martin Luther King, the apostle of nonviolence in the civil rights movement, has been shot to death in Memphis, Tennessee."

Martin felt like he was dreaming. *I hoped and prayed I would wake up and Dad would be there, and it was just a bad dream.* Everyone surrounding him was crying. He can't remember if he cried, too, but sometimes, all these years later, he weeps when he remembers that day. He was only a boy, and he'd never felt more alone, more detached. He looked for his mom for comfort, but she'd already left the house on her futile mission to reach her dying husband's side. At the airport, Coretta heard her name echoing over the public address system and knew he was dead. Atlanta mayor Ivan Allen Jr. confirmed the devastating news that the assassin's bullet had killed her husband. She'd heard the threats, seen him stabbed, and was home when their house was bombed. All this to say, Coretta knew the cost of trying to make America better. She had made peace with the fact that her husband could be killed. Her four children, of course, had not.

When she returned home that night with a police escort, never having left Atlanta, Coretta found Martin sitting alone in his bedroom and she gathered him into her arms. He remembers her words as a gift: *Your father has been killed and he's going home now to live with God,* she said. *When his servants like your father have served, sometimes God brings them home to be with him. One day, you will see him again.*

Martin had no idea how to act in the moment, or the days that followed. He wanted to cry until he couldn't cry anymore, but he took cues from his stoic mother. Be strong and do not break—because the world is watching. Just four days later, Martin, his sister Yolanda and younger brother, Dexter, silently marched with Coretta and forty thousand people through the streets of Memphis to honor his dad.

There would be more special news bulletins in Martin's life that would make him fearful. That's how the mysterious drowning of his dad's brother, Rev. Alfred D. King, was announced in 1969. So, too, the assassination of his grandmother Alberta Williams King in 1974, while she was playing the organ at Ebenezer Baptist

Church in Atlanta. Martin was a high school student that summer, working as a page for Senator Edward Kennedy in Washington, DC, when once again he learned about the murder of a beloved family member from a special news bulletin. For years, Martin's pulse quickened and he became overwhelmed by dread when an unexpected announcement would come over the television or public address system. In these moments Martin, now the elder statesman, sometimes feels like the ten-year-old boy listening to Walter Cronkite delivering the news that broke his world.

BE STRONG AND DO NOT BREAK—BECAUSE THE WORLD IS WATCHING.

The eldest son and namesake of Dr. Martin Luther King Jr. inherited both the aftermath of his family's traumatic legacy and the tremendous legacy of his parents' monumental impact on the world, which reached far beyond the civil rights movement. Dr. King chose courage and determination in the face of oppression, ignorance and violence. Despite imprisonment, brutal attacks and the threat of death, he never swayed from his end goal of achieving rights for all through nonviolent protests. During a time when rights were withheld from people of color and hatred was expressed through beatings and killings, Dr. King led marches for the right to vote, desegregation, labor rights and other civil rights. He was one of the leaders of the 1963 March on Washington, where he delivered his iconic "I Have a Dream" speech. His efforts led to pivotal legislative gains in the Civil Rights Act of 1964, the Voting Rights Act of 1965 and the Fair Housing Act of 1968.

Martin's mother, Coretta, was a lifelong advocate for African American equality, as well as a trained musician and singer who incorporated her talents into her civil rights work. After her husband's assassination in 1968, she helped lead the struggle for racial equality, became active in the women's movement, fought apartheid in South Africa and advocated for LGBTQ rights. She founded the Martin Luther King Jr. Center for Nonviolent Social Change in Atlanta and succeeded in making her husband's birthday a national holiday, with President Ronald Reagan signing it into being in 1983. Coretta's life's work was building the Beloved Community, carrying her message of love and connection to almost every corner of the globe.

From his mother, Martin inherited a legacy of advocacy and public service. She also instilled in him an abiding dedication to family, which he's carried into his marriage with Arndrea and the raising of their daughter, Yolanda. From his father, he inherited his name, as well as his accomplishments as a champion of civil rights and nonviolence. And from them both, Martin inherited the unfulfilled legacy of the Beloved Community. Fulfilling that legacy is at the core of this book's purpose.

Given the enormity of the legacies he's inherited, Martin has thought about legacy throughout his life. He's also had to privately work through the trauma, fear and isolation he simultaneously inherited. And at the same time, he's had to find his authentic voice and way of carrying his magnificent inheritance forward. Martin will be the first to tell you how crucial it's been for him to learn how to claim and live his own unique legacy. Here, too, is a core incentive for his writing and sharing the book.

In the pages to come, you'll see that Martin has devoted his life to public service, first as an elected official and then as a human rights leader and advocate of nonviolence. Like his parents, throughout his adult life, he's stood up against the injustices of the world and been arrested numerous times for leading and participating in nonviolent protests. He's met with every president since Jimmy Carter and has a long history of working with the Congressional Black Caucus. He's led numerous marches, some with over two hundred thousand people, on behalf of civil rights. He travels the world, meeting with leaders and the public, speaking to issues especially important to him, including nonviolence, voting rights and protecting democracy. He was invited to help monitor the election of Nelson Mandela and was there when he was inaugurated. Because of his worldwide humanitarian work, he's won numerous global awards.

Even with all his accomplishments, Martin was still struggling with carrying the name of his famous father when he met his future wife, Arndrea. From their first meeting, a beautiful and seemingly fated love story emerged. In Arndrea, Martin found a partner who'd already built an impressive career in public service and human rights activism. But more significantly, Arndrea's life had been deeply inspired by the convictions and dreams of the King family, beginning with her work at the Center for Democratic Renewal, originally founded as an anti-Klan network. She was mentored early on by Dr. C. T. Vivian, a lieutenant of Dr. King's who believed strongly in the promise of the Beloved Community and instilled in Arndrea an even deeper respect and desire for the dream.

Together Martin and Arndrea explored what it means to inherit a legacy as glorious, profound and complex as the King family's and specifically what it meant for their lives going forward. They have since chosen to join forces in revitalizing the Drum Major Institute, launching the Martin Luther King III Foundation, and dedicating their life's work to fulfilling the King family's dream of a Beloved Community. This dream with all its promises for humanity speaks to them both on the most profound, soulful levels. The Beloved Community is a world where all are welcome and all are accorded dignity, respect and equal rights. A world that values peace, justice and dignity for all.

Yet, with each passing year, they've come to see that without your help and the help of others, the Beloved Community is growing further and further out of reach.

A WORLD IN PERMACRISIS

Each year on the King national holiday, Martin and Arndrea are called upon to explain Dr. Martin Luther King Jr.'s legacy. Martin's father was born on January 15, 1929, and the holiday in his honor falls on the third Monday of every January. It's a day that Martin's mother, the late Coretta Scott King, long fought to be recognized. To honor Dr. King's legacy, the United States has a national day of civic, community and service projects. It's a "day on, not off," so people across the country can serve their community and take steps to achieve Dr. King's dream of the Beloved Community.

On one recent King national holiday, the four of us authors were gathered in Washington to commemorate Dr. King. Throughout that day, big-name journalists, like Jim Acosta of CNN, John Yang of PBS, the *Morning Joe* squad at MSNBC, and so many more, vied for Martin and Arndrea's time and insights. But it didn't matter who was holding the mic, the questions were almost all the same: "Are Americans living up to Dr. King's legacy?" Martin said to John Yang, "Every year, I'm asked the question 'Have we achieved the dream that your dad envisioned?' And my answer unfortunately, every year, is 'We didn't achieve it last year, but every January we have an opportunity to start anew.'"[1]

Ever the optimist, Martin tried to hit a note of hope, even as he was worn down by the acrimonious times we live in. "We are at the most divided time, probably, that we've ever been in the history of our nation," he responded. "He wanted to eradicate the triple evils of poverty, racism and violence from our society, and clearly there is a lot of work that we have to do for those things to be eradicated. So, I hope that people are renewed and get engaged in a way that they maybe have not been engaged in the past."[2]

But truth be told, Martin knew it then and knows it now—the King Dream is in a fragile state.

Instead of moving closer toward eradicating what ails our world and coming together in the spirit of love and interconnection, we are engulfed in one crisis after another. And all around us, there is more and more to feel afraid of.

Hate crimes in America, which Arndrea spent a great deal of her career investigating, are at their highest level since the FBI began documenting them in the 1990s.[3] More than 1,225 different hate groups and extremist political organizations exist across America.[4] Gun violence especially remains an overwhelming constant in our nation. Martin and Arndrea's daughter, Yolanda, has spoken out about the need for better gun control on numerous occasions. Yolanda, like many of us, is heartbroken about the rise in school shootings that plague our country. Many parents are afraid to send their children to school; many of us do not feel safe leaving our homes.

We are a world in crisis. Climate crisis. Crisis of war. Crisis of violence. Mental health crisis. Opioids crisis. Cost of living crisis. Crisis of purpose. Crisis of faith. Crisis of loneliness. Crisis of meaning. There are simply too many to name. "Permacrisis" topped the Collins Dictionary's 2022 list of words of the year.[5] It's defined as an "extended period of instability and insecurity"[6] that has us stumbling from slag heap to car crash to multiple-vehicle pileup.

We believe there are two types of crises: *inner crisis* and *outer crisis*. Inner crisis is a crisis of self. Inner crisis is manifested, for example, in loneliness, emotional disconnection, unhealthy relationships and mental health challenges, as well as addiction and suicide. Outer crisis is a crisis within society. Outer crisis is manifested, for example, in highly divisive politics, media that stoke fear and anger, an environment on the verge of irreparable harm and a broken education system. The challenge is that inner crises create more outer crises. Similarly, more outer crises result in more inner crises. These two kinds of crises reinforce and perpetuate one another, and we become captured in a state of permacrisis.

So many of these inner and outer crises intensified during the isolating, confusing time when Covid shuttered our world in 2020. As the virus swept the globe, killing loved ones, we were consumed by fear. People were dying alone in hospitals. We lived under lockdown. We couldn't even hug our loved ones. The pandemic supercharged the disconnection many of us were already feeling. Then George Floyd was murdered, a collective breaking point, and Black people and their allies poured into the streets to protest.

MARTIN KNEW IT THEN AND KNOWS IT NOW—THE KING DREAM IS IN A FRAGILE STATE.

Amid all this anger and unrest, Martin recalls feeling the same anguish and fear he felt as a boy, in the aftermath of his father's murder. As Martin wrote in the introduction to this book, it was in the second year of the pandemic, in 2021, that the authors of this book joined together to help fulfill the dream of the Beloved Community. Since that day the four of us have come together often and asked ourselves many hard questions, in particular: Why do we have such a broken, disconnected world?

It's complicated, of course, but we think it's mostly because so many among us are struggling. Millions of us have become disconnected from ourselves. Millions more have become disconnected from others and the world. We will explain more about the state of disconnection throughout this book. So of course, we then asked ourselves, What is the primary source fueling this disturbing escalation of human disconnection? And the answer we all agreed upon was . . . *fear*.

We've all seen it from our life experiences, but science even affirms what happens to us when we feel afraid or threatened by the troubled world around us. Instead of making altruistic choices out of love and connection, we let fear cause us to revert to a self-preservation mindset, leading to us acting in ways that are survivalist, protective and often divisive. This of course fuels further inner crisis.

But fear also perpetuates the staggering amount of outer crises in the world right now. When our fear tells us to disconnect from others and the outer world, our inner world also suffers. We disconnect from our innate need for love, human connection and community—our fundamental sense of belonging. To manage the fear and overwhelm that we feel in the throes of permacrises, we often try to numb and distract ourselves and isolate, which in turn leads to more inner crises, manifested by seclusion, depression and loneliness.

And the cycle continues over and over and over.

Embracing Nonviolence: My Journey of Faith, Leadership and Change

Rev. Al Sharpton

From my earliest days in Brooklyn as a boy preacher, I felt a pull toward the nonviolent movement of Dr. King. Yet, where I come from, it was seen as a Southern, weak approach that didn't work in the North. But I delved into the teachings of the church I grew up in; from the Exodus of the slaves to Saint Paul's letters, I found a powerful alignment with my own beliefs.

Despite the popularity of other paths among my peers, I chose to follow Dr. King's philosophy wholeheartedly.

The true test of my commitment came in 1989 when I was thirty-five. I was responding to the tragic death of Yusef Hawkins, a young Black man killed in Bensonhurst, a predominantly Italian neighborhood in Brooklyn. He was mistaken for someone else and murdered. To combat this blatant racism, I organized nonviolent marches every Saturday for a year despite the hateful and violent reactions we received from the locals.

One January day in 1991, as I led the march, I was stabbed in the chest. The attack only strengthened my resolve. Lying on a gurney in Coney Island Hospital, unsure of the severity of my injury, I made a vow: if I survived, I would continue to march, to fight nonviolently.

After my recovery, I returned to holding our rallies. When a fellow organizer attempted to exclude white participants, I stood firm in my belief in inclusivity, a core tenet of Dr. King's teachings. This led me to found the National Action Network in Harlem, marking a new chapter in my journey for justice.

Reflecting on my journey, I saw nonviolence not as a sign of weakness but as a powerful form of protest. It resonated with my religious teachings and the civil rights movement's strategic use of economic boycotts and mass mobilization.

My commitment to nonviolence was solidified through these events. It was a commitment not just in theory but proven in the face of adversity, embodying the teachings of Dr. King and the ethos of the civil rights movement. Embracing nonviolence—even when it wasn't a popular approach in the North—came when I took stock of my beliefs and what was required to defuse the violence.

A few years later, in 2000, I had another opportunity to evaluate my path and make a change. It was during a poignant conversation with Coretta Scott King.

Martin Luther King III and I had become very friendly through our shared dedication to activism and nonviolence. He wanted his mother to get to know me. I thought, *I've been around her a million times,* and he said, "I want her to really get to know you."

I guess she had an agenda. Mrs. King expressed her support for our planned March on Washington against racial profiling. But she also gently questioned my use of divisive language, including the N-word.

At first, I said, "Mrs. King, that's how we talk in the North, and I try to relate to the people in the street." She challenged me to consider the impact of my words and the responsibility I had to elevate others and set an example through our language.

This exchange was transformative. It wasn't a reprimand but an opportunity for self-reflection, guided by the wisdom of the civil rights movement's matriarch. Mrs. King's insights prompted me to shift my approach to leadership. Leadership entails upholding certain standards, including the language we use and a deeper sense of accountability.

***Rev. Al Sharpton** is a social justice activist, Baptist minister, radio talk show host and TV personality. As a disciple of the teachings of Dr. King, in 1969 Sharpton became the youth director of the Southern Christian Leadership Conference's Operation Breadbasket, NY chapter. In 1991, he founded the civil rights organization the National Action Network (NAN).*

Our beautiful, challenging, resilient world is literally and met-aphorically on fire, and, in many ways, so are we. Is there really no way to douse these flames?

To borrow a phrase from one of our mutual friends, Oprah Winfrey, here's what we know for sure: Tempting as it may seem to turn away and shut the door on the world of hate, violence and poverty, a world spiraling in permacrisis, it's not going to make us feel any better. In fact, turning away often makes us feel worse. It ends up leaving us alone with our anxious selves, stewing in our own despair, disconnection and fear.

Here's what else we know for sure: There's a better way to re-spond. One that will have an undeniable impact on our world and help us find true fulfillment along the way. This is where your leg-acy and its power to heal the permacrisis comes in.

We would like to share our journey to this realization. In some ways, our human voyage hasn't been that different from others. Even for Martin and Arndrea, being members of a family with as much history as the Kings doesn't separate them from our funda-mental humanity.

We've all faced disappointments and failures. We've each had to dust ourselves off and get back up again. We've built friendships and community. We've all fallen in love. We've married. We've had children. Some of those children have turned into teenagers who suddenly see us as ridiculous and embarrassing. We've cared for aging parents. We've lost beloved family members. We've seen mental illness ravage loved ones. We've struggled with self-doubts; we've ached in the face of our own and others' suffering. We've sought ways to feel connected to something greater than our-selves, and have found that connection in different ways, through God, a higher power, or communing with the natural world. We all love dogs, but two of us also love cats. We all love to laugh. We all find awe in sunrises and sunsets. Only one of us likes to dance, and the others just wish they were better at it.

In other ways, our human journeys have been unique. Because each of us was called into human service from an early age, we've collectively spent 130-plus years trying to address and heal the major social issues of our lifetimes. We've been mentored by human rights activists and civil rights leaders, and we've been inspired by thousands of dedicated teachers and tens of thousands of remarkable students. We've met with and shared the stage with iconic global leaders, heads of state, and Nobel laureates. Equally and especially, we've met children living in poverty and parents who have lost children at a young age at home and abroad.

We've all traveled to multiple war zones. We've each borne firsthand witness to major humanitarian crises, including the horrors of violence, famine and natural disasters. We have collectively traveled to over one hundred countries, mainly spending time doing humanitarian aid work in Africa, Asia and Latin America. We've dedicated ourselves to personally knowing and honoring the Indigenous people of all countries, including those who live in our homelands of Canada and America.

We say all this not to separate us from you, but to say all these experiences, conversations and travels have informed our understanding of humanity and inspired us more and more greatly to serve and help this troubled world. Everywhere we have gone we have seen the earth cry for help. We have heard the cries of mothers and babies. We have equally seen pure love, instances of joy and contagious eruptions of laughter. We have seen the power of love, freedom and even what could be described as miracles of faith. We have experienced many instances of breaking down with tears of sorrow and equally being broken open with those tender tears of joy.

From all of these experiences, we have only seen one true solution to what we are facing as individuals and what the world is facing as our home. This solution is the reason we wrote this book. This solution is how we reach the Beloved Community that Dr. King dreamed of. And the solution is embedded in the question Martin is asked every year about whether we are living up to his father's legacy. The solution resides in legacy. But not the typical way most of us think about legacy. Rather, an entirely new way of seeing legacy's impact on our lives and an entirely new way to live a legacy rather than leave one.

THE DEATH AND REBIRTH OF LEGACY

We have a term that we developed that explains our solution, it is called "Living Legacy." What do we mean by Living Legacy? We think of it as a philosophy and a way of life. *Living Legacy involves making daily choices to live in a way that leads to connection, purpose and meaning. It provides a path to healing ourselves and to achieving what is often the most elusive human desire: fulfillment.*

Once we discover how to live our legacies every day rather than focusing on just leaving them, we are able to live more fully in the present, as opposed to being stuck in the past or fretting about the future.

We've seen firsthand that this philosophy has the power to change your life. It provides us with the means to heal ourselves and our families. And it has the power to change the world. In the coming pages, we will break it down more for you and show you how you can be your own Living Legacy architect.

But for now, we want to share how we came to our understanding of the transformative potential of Living Legacy.

Martin came to this with an ingrained understanding of the

conventional ways we think of legacy. How it can be something left to people—a reputation, a huge accomplishment, a defining moment—or it can be the more commonly accepted definition of passing on wealth, property or family heirlooms. But through years of reckoning with the blessings and complexity of his family legacy, Martin has come to reject the conventional notions of legacy. For instance, he doesn't like the idea of treating his father as an idol. An idol is something that's removed from a shelf once a year, dusted off and returned to the shelf. It is a memory, past tense, to be admired, but lives outside of us. Instead, Martin experiences his father's legacy as alive, continuing to be felt and engaged with. He feels the same about the legacy of his mother and all his ancestors. Their legacy lives within him and continues to influence and guide Martin. And though there was a time when the King family legacy sometimes felt too large and overwhelming to fill, Martin has found a way to define and live his own legacy, his own impact on the world, and he does so every day by incorporating the Living Legacy methods we share in the ensuing pages.

Arndrea, too, has given much thought to legacy and is ever mindful about raising their daughter within the King family legacy. She's putting her heart and soul into making sure that Yolanda, the only grandchild of Dr. Martin Luther King Jr. and Coretta Scott King, is raised with loving-kindness and a sense of history, but also helping her be known for what she uniquely has to offer the world.

Arndrea knows how easily each of us can be impacted by the legacies of racism and slavery. She poignantly remembers investigating the suspected lynching of a Black boy, seventeen-year-old Raynard Johnson, who was found hanging from a pecan tree in Kokomo, Mississippi, in 2000, and the opposition she faced from the locals who didn't want her there asking questions. At times

Arndrea feared for her life, as she felt the legacy of sanctioned lynchings that dwelled in the region's history.

The way she chooses to live her legacy every day is by acknowledging how the legacies from the past still rise within her. For instance, Arndrea is open about the ways the legacies of racism and sexism sometimes make it hard for her to stand in her power and claim her voice. But Arndrea has come to realize that those legacies can and must be transformed within her. Not only for her sake and Yolanda's sake but also for the world's sake. Harnessing the tools that she will share in these pages, Arndrea chooses the legacy she wants to live now by steadying herself in her core convictions and spiritual strength and speaking out even when the legacies of fear tell her she shouldn't. In this way, Arndrea's chosen legacy—her wisdom, voice and enormous compassion for humanity—can be lived and known in the world.

On the surface Marc and Craig's connection with legacy seems obvious: they are well known as "legacy architects," helping civic leaders, entrepreneurs, entertainers, sports figures and visionaries build large-scale movements and make a positive impact in the world. But on a personal level, they began their journey into understanding the impact of legacy when they were still teenagers who became famous for fighting modern slavery, human trafficking and child labor in forgotten pockets of our world.

When twelve-year-old Craig read a newspaper article about the life and murder of an enslaved child in Pakistan, he earnestly approached various international humanitarian organizations, but the only thing they wanted from a teenager was his parents' credit card numbers. The awfulness and injustice of the story inspired him to raise funds to travel to South Asia and join activists kicking down doors to free children enslaved in carpet factories, brick kilns and fireworks factories. He was still only a young teenager when he appeared on the world stage, including *Oprah*, *60 Minutes*, CNN and the BBC, asking hard questions about the plight of child laborers and what world leaders would do to protect them. Marc and Craig soon founded Free the Children together to address the extreme poverty that led to child slavery and other forms of human suffering. They began partnering with impoverished communities around the world, asking them what they needed to break the cycles of poverty. Their charitable work became enormously successful as they helped to not only build but also operate and maintain thousands of schools and schoolrooms educating two hundred thousand children, small businesses serving thirty thousand women, as well as hospitals, farms, water projects and college training programs.

Their early activism once earned them an invitation to spend a week with the Dalai Lama in Stockholm, Sweden, in 1997, along with a small group of notable philosophers, historians, teachers and religious leaders. They'd gathered to consider a profound question: What is the greatest challenge facing our time? The deeply wise Dalai Lama suggested it wasn't weapons of mass destruction or terrorism or ethnic cleansing. Instead, he said it was that "we are raising a generation of passive bystanders." He worried that instead of raising their voices against injustice, young people were remaining silent, and this did not bode well for the future of the world.

WHAT IS THE GREATEST CHALLENGE FACING OUR TIME? . . . "WE ARE RAISING A GENERATION OF PASSIVE BYSTANDERS."

Dr. Martin Luther King Jr. Changed My Life

Dan Rather

I have been very lucky during my more than nine decades on this earth. I was lucky to find a wife willing to put up with me. And I was lucky to choose a career, journalism, that allowed me to be a lifelong learner. One of my first and best teachers was Dr. Martin Luther King Jr.

I began at CBS News in the early 1960s. In 1962, my first major regular week-in, week-out assignment was to cover Dr. King in what was then the emerging civil rights movement in the Deep South. "Eye-opening" does not convey the depths of what that experience taught me.

I was born and raised in Texas in the 1930s, a place mired in institutionalized racism. We had separate schools, separate restaurants and separate drinking fountains. It wasn't as dark as Alabama or Mississippi at the time, but there is no question about it; it was legalized racism. Then, as a young reporter, I was cast in with this heroic figure. When I first met Dr. King, I had no idea who he was, nor did much of the country. At the time, Dr. King and his movement were struggling to gain traction and garner news coverage. He faced constant danger but was determined not to give up, never to give in.

I quickly came to admire him tremendously because he walked on the razor's edge of lethal danger every minute of every day. There was no thought in my mind other than *He will not live a long life.* Anybody who was around him and witnessed his calm resolve would have reached the same conclusion.

Dr. King had what I've called "quiet at the center." I'm sure he had his fears. He even spoke with me about them at times. But the more chaotic and dangerous things became, the more he seemed to draw on some inner spiritual resolve, to become quieter and more determined.

The first time I covered a Ku Klux Klan rally, I remember the sheer horror that prevailed from Black people, and I thought to myself, *What must that be like? To have this hanging over you every day, every night?* There I was, a privileged white reporter operating on the edges of this Klan rally, a gathering meant to terrorize. I was deeply affected by seeing Dr. King's courage in the face of such stunning hatred. His response was to rise above and say, "I, Dr. King, and my movement, we're dedicated to non-violent protests."

Dr. King spoke candidly with me about news coverage of the civil rights movement. He was surprisingly savvy about this fledgling media, television news. And he was concerned that Southern affiliates would persuade the network to tone down coverage. I wasn't concerned. My bosses in New York were rock-ribbed when it came to reporting the news without fear or favor to anyone. However, King's concerns were not unfounded. The CBS Atlanta affiliate refused to carry some of the reports in 1962.

By 1964, I had become the network's chief White House correspondent. As such, I had a front-row seat as Dr. King's efforts helped drive historic civil rights legislation through Congress and into federal law. By then, he could see clearly how much remained to be done and how many perils lay ahead. He pressed on, although an early death would be his destiny.

As a white Southern man, I always felt during those turbulent times that I had a dog in that fight. In my gut, I knew as all reporters should know, that dehumanizing others is immoral. We are the champions of the little guy. But Dr. King wasn't the little guy. He was the champion of us all. He changed me as a person and as a professional, and I'm forever thankful for it.

Dan Rather is an author, journalist and former anchor of the CBS Evening News. He has covered some of the most significant events of the modern age, including the civil rights movement, Vietnam, the fall of the Berlin Wall and September 11. Rather has received countless honors and awards, including multiple Peabodys and news Emmys.

The Dalai Lama's concerns added a second element to Marc and Craig's mission: raising children to care and contribute. Through WE Charity, they built service programs in multiple countries, engaging millions of students. In the US, they partnered with the College Board to launch AP with WE Service, integrating service learning into the Advanced Placement (AP) coursework. The program is available in all fifty states and is America's only on-transcript recognition of service when applying to college. Twelve years after their meeting in Stockholm, the Dalai Lama agreed to attend one of their WE Day events in Vancouver to address more than fifteen thousand middle and high school students being celebrated for their service. Marc and Craig will never forget His Holiness walking past the empty chair they'd placed on stage for him, and instead going to the very edge of the stage so he could better see into the faces of all the youth gathered there. He told the young crowd about making the twenty-first century one of peace: "That is what young people must do. Strive for peace." The legacy of his wise words once shared in Stockholm was now living in all the youth before him that day.

A third chapter in their social entrepreneurship journey traces its roots to another incredible early supporter of their work, Oprah Winfrey. In the late '90s, when Craig was a guest on her show, she spontaneously pledged to establish one hundred primary schools in developing countries in partnership with the brothers. The early charity did not have the capacity for such a large gift. Over the years that followed, Oprah provided regular mentorship and millions in early-stage funding to help the organization build best-in-class systems. Years later, Oprah would ask the brothers for a favor. She dreamed of creating her own large-scale impact program. The brothers and their team designed and quietly operated the backend for Oprah's namesake O Ambassadors program providing service-learning programs to over two thousand American schools. The brothers realized that even someone as successful as Oprah needed support to maximize impact. They gathered a team of experts to assist in building large-scale movements and legacy projects. Over the years Legacy+ has supported many of the foremost visionaries, foundations, corporations, as well as people from all walks of life, creating enormous impact. All this is to say, Marc and Craig, like Martin and Arndrea, have come to care less about the legacies we are *leaving*, and more about the ones we are *living*.

REVERSING THE CRISIS

We will show you how living your legacy every day will move us ever closer to keeping Dr. King's legacy alive and advancing his dream of the Beloved Community. By reframing legacy into something active and alive, we not only help heal the world but also offer a path to meaning and purpose. In doing so, we find the fulfillment so many of us are seeking. The solution to our crises lies within each of us. It's not something we need to find or invent. It's already right here inside us.

We believe when Dr. King spoke about the Beloved Community, he envisioned a community that, at its core, was truly and deeply connected. As authors, we believe that we are all truly connected—to each other, to nature, to the universe. From the moment we are born, we are hardwired in our need to feel connected to something or someone on a deep and meaningful level. Unfortunately, in our culture, we are more "connected" than ever through technology, but lonelier than ever as these "connections" are often not real, satisfying or deep. We need something much more meaningful. We need to love and be loved.

As Arndrea reminds us often with a smile, "love" is literally in the word "beloved" of Dr. King's inspiring vision of the Beloved Community. Love is what happens when you feel a deep sense of connection with someone or something higher than yourself. It could be your children, your family, your best friend, your God, your spiritual self, nature or the universe. It could be your pet. Marc, for example, loves his 120-pound Bernese mountain dog, named Daisy, so much that her photo is his smartphone's wallpaper (much to the amusement of his wife and his two daughters).

Love is within us all and love is how we rid the world of the triple evils that we are working to eradicate. If we could distill all that we've come to believe and all that we hope you infuse into your Living Legacy, it would be this: Love is how we heal the world. And love is how we heal ourselves. This may seem trite or like a platitude, but trust us, love is the most powerful force in the universe, and it is the salvation for humanity.

You can see how hopeful we are, despite the permacrisis that envelops so many of us. We are writing this book out of a profound desire to help ourselves heal, as well as to collectively heal the world around us. We want to help you move from disconnection to connection, emptiness to fulfillment, and especially from fear to love, so we can fulfill the dream of the Beloved Community.

LOVE IS HOW WE HEAL THE WORLD. AND LOVE IS HOW WE HEAL OURSELVES.

Let us return to the day we joined together at the nation's capital on Dr. King's birthday. After Martin and Arndrea finished their news interviews, we waded through a sizable crowd of people surrounding the King Memorial near the Washington Mall to lay a wreath at the feet of the towering granite sculpture of Dr. King's likeness. It was a cold, blustery day and most of us were wearing warm coats, necks wrapped with scarves to shield us from the wind. The majority of those who were there were African American. Many were families. Moms and dads taking their children to stand before the memorial to the man who'd fought so courageously for their civil rights. We noticed how reverence and gratitude filled the eyes of many who made the pilgrimage to the memorial that day.

We also noticed how many took time to read the words, once spoken by Martin's father, inscribed in the statue's stone. One passage from his 1963 "I Have a Dream" speech was especially poignant: "Out of the mountain of despair a stone of hope." In direct sight from where we stood is the Lincoln Memorial, where Dr. King delivered his most famous speech, which resounds today and is at the heart of this book's mission.

It was impossible not to feel the magnitude of Dr. King's vision and the hope among those gathered to heal the unrest gripping the nation. For Arndrea and Martin, it deepened their desire to use whatever skills and resources they could muster to help heal the broken world and its inhabitants. For Marc and Craig, they also felt deeply honored to join the King family in this moving experience and in their mission to heal the world and its people through rededicating themselves to building the Beloved Community.

We truly believe this vision is possible. And with your help, maybe one day soon, Martin can provide a different answer when journalists ask him to reflect on whether we have fulfilled his father's legacy. Living Legacy is our stone of hope. Together we can live our legacy day by day. And together, we will show you how.

From Legacy to Disconnection: Getting to the Source

LATE ONE AFTERNOON, A GROUP of villagers gathered by the riverside. Some were fishing, others washing clothes, but all looked up when they heard a cry. A ways upstream and moving fast, they could see a child's head bobbing in the current, her arms waving and splashing desperately. A villager quickly dove in and managed to grab the child before the swift waters could sweep her away, towing her back to land with the help of the others. No sooner had they reached land when two more flailing children appeared upriver. The people on the bank shouted in alarm, and more came running from the village. Together, linking arm in arm, they made a human net to catch the drowning children as they passed. But already, yet another child was visible, thrashing and trying to stay afloat.

A woman broke from the chain of villagers and began to run up the riverbank. "Where are you going?" the others cried. "You must help us save these children!"

"We can't just keep pulling them out," the woman said. "I'm going upstream to find out why they're falling in!"

Archbishop Desmond Tutu shared this parable with Marc and Craig, illustrating a profound lesson. Tutu, alongside Nelson Mandela, guided South Africa from the oppressive darkness of apartheid to democracy and global leadership. Tutu was an irreplaceable statesman, a powerful storyteller and one of the wisest men we've had the privilege of knowing. His guidance and mentorship are dearly missed. Today, Tutu's parable of the river is more relevant than ever. The river represents the state of permacrisis, and we—all of us, every person in the world—are drowning in it, in one form or another.

But what will we find if we look upstream? Every river is fed by tributaries—a multitude of streams flowing into it. When we went upstream to investigate the river of permacrisis, we discovered the tributaries of countless legacies. Rivulets of historical legacies flow, merge and shape the world around us and each of us as individuals. Indeed, we found that legacy is embedded in the physical, mental and emotional structure of who we are and in the culture we live in.

Whether we're facing an outer crisis or an inner one, we rarely step back to recognize the role legacy has played in shaping the world and us as individuals. But this is what we invite you to do now as we travel upstream together.

THE WEIGHT OF HISTORY AND FAMILY WOUNDS

One of the best ways we've found to understand how we arrived at this state of inner crisis and outer crisis is by breaking legacy down into two overarching types: collective legacies and familial legacies. Let's start with collective legacies.

Collective legacies are the powerful forces, the great events and tides of the past that continue to influence us year after year. People often cry, "Stop dredging up history!" But historical legacies are like waves in the ocean. On the surface, when we see a wave crash, it seems to crest and then cease to matter. Yet every wave creates a powerful, unseen force—an undertow. Stronger and more lasting than a wave, an undertow is what causes people to drown, not the wave that birthed it.

We see the undertow of historical legacies in ancient and modern wars, oppressive class systems, and the lingering effects of colonialism, racism and patriarchal structures that harm women—and men as well—in many societies. These sweeping collective legacies flow insidiously through everything around us and within us, powering the global and social conflicts that grip the world tighter every day.

As we write this, the wars in Ukraine and the Middle East have seen children die by the tens of thousands. Yemen, Sudan, Myanmar, Haiti, the Democratic Republic of the Congo, and the Sahel region of West Africa—all are experiencing horrific violence. Each of these conflicts is the undertow of historical legacies: colonialism, the Cold War, ancient ethnic feuds, and grudges. Driven by these legacies, nations feed their citizens and their future into the atrocities of pointless wars.

Tightening our gaze on these widespread collective legacies, we can see how they have shaped the crises we face in any nation or community. For instance, in the United States, the multiple crises we face are rooted in the legacies of racism, slavery, colonialism, patriarchy, materialism, homophobia and the idolization of rugged individualism, among others.

We all know the legacies of slavery and racism didn't just disappear when Abraham Lincoln signed the Emancipation Proclamation. Because these legacies were never fully addressed and healed, they remanifested in the Jim Crow laws, which enforced racial segregation for almost a hundred years until Dr. King and the civil rights movement began to dismantle them. Even after that, the legacies of racism and slavery did not fade away. They continue to shape our world through the systemic racism experienced by Black Americans—multigenerational cycles of poverty; the lack of property ownership, equitable education, and health care; and ongoing vulnerability to violence.

Recognizing and understanding the impact of historical legacies is crucial for addressing the root causes of our current crises.

THE KING FAMILY JOURNEY UPSTREAM

When Dr. King started his journey upstream in the 1950s, he wanted to heal the source of the painful racial divide that plagued the United States. He began his vocation as a civil rights crusader by taking on the manifestations of America's racist legacies— segregated buses, stores, and schools and the denial of voting rights. Yet, these were symptoms of a deeper problem, not the source. While he could end segregation and install voting rights for Black Americans, it wouldn't completely mend the divide in American society.

During the 1967 National Conference for New Politics, Dr. King delivered a speech he titled "The Three Evils of Society." In that address, he identified three social ills at the root of America's problems: racism, poverty and violence. This was Dr. King traveling upstream, seeking the source of the issues.

Martin now carries his torch. Rather than following in his father's footsteps as a minister, Martin chose a political career, believing he could further his father's dream of healing the legacies that harmed so many Americans. However, as he worked to advance legislation to protect civil liberties and oppose bills aimed at curtailing voting rights for Black Americans, he realized he was fighting the same battles his father had waged half a century earlier. And while these were important battles, even winning them didn't heal the underlying legacies.

Almost sixty years after Dr. King marched from Selma to Montgomery alongside religious leaders from many different faiths to demand voting rights for Black citizens in Alabama, states are still passing laws intended to disenfranchise minority communities.[7] Over half a century since segregation was banned by law, the number of children attending predominantly Black schools is rising.[8] The number of Black families living in extreme poverty remains double that of white Americans.[9] Meanwhile, the American justice system continues to incarcerate Black Americans at a disproportionate rate.[10] Why? Because the legacies of racism and slavery are still pulling people under.

BUT WHAT WILL WE FIND IF WE LOOK UPSTREAM? EVERY RIVER IS FED BY TRIBUTARIES—A MULTITUDE OF STREAMS FLOWING INTO IT.

For Arndrea, her journey upstream was the crusade against hate crimes. In her study of this dark world of hatred and violence, Arndrea found that the toxic ideas and attitudes leading to such crimes rarely had a basis in personal experiences. Occasionally, hate crimes were committed because someone had been hurt by an individual, so they developed a hatred for that person's race or sexual identity because of that. But more often than not, the perpetrators of hate crimes were driven by inherited legacies of biases that they never even questioned.

They Called Me Marty

Martin Luther King III

My father was named after my grandfather. Since I was my dad's firstborn son, he hoped that I, too, would carry the name Martin. My mother objected.

In 1957 I arrived on the scene. Dad was rising to prominence as a civil rights leader. Amid the late 1950s civil unrest, he was expected to be a messiah, a diplomat, a punching bag for white supremacists and a political prisoner. In all circumstances, he was to rise above the fray with eloquence and dignity. My mom, Coretta, sensed that naming me after him might be a crushing burden to shoulder. She worried I might grow up to try to match or better his achievements or be hobbled by the weight of the public demands that came with his name.

After much discussion, I was named Martin Luther King III. Marty, for short. My parents hoped that diminutive would shield me somewhat from the pressure of being my father's namesake. Martin III or Marty, no matter what I'm called, I've struggled to emerge from my father's historic legacy to define my own. I was ten when he was assassinated at age thirty-nine. After he died, my mom encouraged me to be my own man. She told me I didn't have to attend Morehouse College, or become a minister, or a civil rights leader like Dad. She only insisted on one thing: "Just be your best self," she said. Mom gave me freedom to make my life my own.

Still, a country's expectations followed me. Mike Wallace of *60 Minutes* came to our home before Christmas in 1968 to find out how we were holding up eight months after Dad was killed. My brother and sisters (Dexter, Yolanda, Bernice) and I sat in our Sunday best next to a Christmas tree. Mom introduced me as Martin Luther King III, and then added, "We call him Marty."[102]

Wallace asked me: "I imagine, of course, that you bear your name with great pride, your father's name. But are there ever any difficulties because you are Martin Luther King?" I was eleven. I told him, "Well, sometimes there are difficulties, but most of the time there aren't any . . . but sometimes . . ." I trailed off without confiding anything.

> ## *I wish I could hug that younger version of me and assure him that one day, he would proudly grow into his father's name.*

Wallace, the hard-nosed newsman, pressed me. "What kind of things?"

"Well, sometimes people ask me my father's name and sometimes they tease me about my name . . ." I didn't reveal any more details to Wallace. He didn't need to know that I'd sometimes lie about my identity. I'd tell people who asked that I didn't know my own name just to avoid their unwelcome commentary about Dad or my imagined destiny. Wallace then asked what I wanted to be when I grew up. "I want to be a preacher like my father," I said shyly. I knew that was what was expected of me. I envied my older sister, Yolanda, who proudly proclaimed to Wallace that she wanted to be an actress.

I wish I could hug that younger version of me and assure him that one day, he would proudly grow into his father's name. It's been a challenging journey to escape his shadow. My father was the most famous alumnus of Morehouse, the Atlanta college both he and my grandfather attended. Dad enrolled at fifteen and was a standout student. My grandfather, a sharecropper's son, walked barefoot every day from Stockbridge to Atlanta, where he worked odd jobs while putting himself through high school. He was thirty-two when he worked his way through Morehouse, becoming a prominent preacher and civil rights leader. (He was heavily influenced by his father-in-law and my great-grandfather A. D. Williams, the pastor at Ebenezer Baptist

Church and the founder and president of the Atlanta chapter of the NAACP in 1918.)

On my first day as a legacy student, the assembled first-year students at Morehouse were told the late Martin Luther King Jr. had been a student and the college was proud to have his son as a freshman. I slid down in my seat for fear they would single me out. Fortunately, they didn't. I did not want to be treated differently because of who I was. I introduced myself as Marty to the other students.

> *Instead of worrying I'd be saddled with the weight of his name, I've wondered how I can build on his legacy of love and forgiveness and creating community.*

Morehouse turned out many fine professionals, including doctors, lawyers, teachers, administrators, community leaders and ministers. And I think Dad would have wanted me to be a minister, just as he wanted me to carry his name. But the ministry was not my calling. I graduated with a BA in political science. At age twenty-two, I was considering the Peace Corps or law school. I believed God, in His wisdom, would show me the right path. For a time, I marched, led peaceful rallies, and went to jail for protesting South Africa's apartheid and other injustices. I came to believe the best way to change the system was from within. In 1987, at age twenty-nine, I won a seat on the Fulton County Board of Commissioners. I would be an insider with this seat, instead of an outsider waving a sign, making societal improvements through city government. I was reelected in 1990. When I ran to be the chair of the board of commissioners in 1993, I lost and took that pretty hard. This led to a crisis of purpose and to deep reflection.

I struggled with my place in the world and my outsize family name. I think most parents want their children to do better than they did. If Dad had been a physician and owned a medical clinic, I could have built on his work by opening a chain of clinics. But my dad's name is known throughout the world and honored with a national holiday. I can't better that, so I've recalibrated my expectations of myself. Instead of worrying I'd be saddled with the weight of his name, I've wondered how I can build on his legacy of love and forgiveness and creating community. I hope I can be known for my own body of work. Instead of "the son of," I hope to be known as Martin Luther King III, who happens to be the son of Martin Luther King Jr.

For five often rocky years, I led the Southern Christian Leadership Conference, a civil rights organization Dad founded. One of our goals was to redeem the soul of the nation and eradicate the triple evils of poverty, racism and violence. I'm particularly proud of our Gun Buyback Program. I've since focused on peace building, nonviolence and conflict resolution, traveling the world, teaching these tools to citizens and public officials. I know now that my ministry is human rights. I've come to feel this mission deeply in my soul. I've also continued to lead protests and marches. Sometimes, I still get hauled away in handcuffs, like in 2021, when Arndrea and I were both arrested for demonstrating for voters' rights outside the White House. During the pandemic, Arndrea and I reinvigorated a dormant organization, the Drum Major Institute, with the goal of furthering Dad's vision. I'm building on his work in my own way. This is my calling, my ministry, my mission, as I proudly carry his name.

Truth be told, I never really liked the name Marty.

Once we begin to view the crises we're facing through the lens of legacy, it's not hard to connect the dots. The collective legacy of the patriarchy, with its entrenched misogynist beliefs and systems, fuels persistent wage disparities between women and men and the underrepresentation of women in politics and corporate leadership. It also perpetuates threats to women's bodies, such as restrictions on reproductive and health care rights and the ongoing risk of sexual assault and gender violence. The fallout of patriarchy is vast, complicated and painful. For women of color or those who are gay or transgender, its impact is even more oppressive, as the patriarchy merges with other burdensome legacies such as racism and homophobia.

The legacy of colonialism led to the genocide and displacement of Indigenous people, leaving Native Americans separated from their rightful land ownership and struggling to reclaim and maintain their culture, language and traditional wisdom. Indigenous people still do not statistically have the same access to wealth, health care and resources as white Americans.

Our climate crisis is literally fueled by the legacies of materialism, industrialization and colonization, which continue to strip our land of resources. All these legacies pollute our air, soil and water—endangering plants, animals, and even human survival, in favor of consumerism and unchecked financial greed. We accept a cultural legacy narrative that we can dump massive amounts of pollution into waterways and landfills. We did not previously have science about plastics invading our bodies, appearing even in embryos, yet today's science cannot compete with the disposable lifestyle norms that we inherited from past generations. We've become so used to inheriting collective legacies that prioritize convenience and economic gain over planetary health and well-being that we accept them as "normal." If we hadn't inherited the normalcy of these priorities, would we adopt them now, knowing their consequences?

We see extremes in political leadership that make us shake our heads and demonize individual politicians. Yet, we rarely discuss these leaders as byproducts of the legacies that caused them to rise in popularity. Removing any of these extremist leaders won't change the fact that the legacies that gave them power will continue to produce similar leadership.

Pick any social or political crisis in the US or even the world today, and you'll find that when you follow the path upstream, you'll discover vast and surging collective legacies originating decades, centuries or even millennia in the past.

ONCE WE BEGIN TO VIEW THE CRISES WE'RE FACING THROUGH THE LENS OF LEGACY, IT'S NOT HARD TO CONNECT THE DOTS.

We also recognize the positive legacies that our forebearers handed to us. We are blessed to stand on the shoulders of giants. Abolitionists who fought to end the slave trade. Suffragists who secured the right for women to vote and have a say in how their lives and bodies were governed. Civil rights leaders who did so much for the advancement of humanity. There have been countless ancestors who've helped us confront, heal and transcend the harmful legacies we've inherited.

The Hidden Struggles for Civil Rights

Tommy Orange

In the late 1950s Martin Luther King Jr. collaborated with tribal elders from the Poarch Creek Indians to desegregate schools in southern Alabama, where darker-skinned Natives were not allowed to ride buses. This isn't a story we hear about the legacy of Dr. King. Similarly, people don't know a relatively large presence of Native people participated in the 1963 March on Washington. Or that without the work of Dr. King, and other leaders, the later Native American civil rights movements might never have happened.

In 2024, we are a nation as divided as we have ever been. This is in no small part because of a fight over the narrative control of this country, regarding its origins, its purpose then and now—its very soul. What does being an American mean? It depends on who you ask.

This is a relatively young country. A significant portion of its current population are the descendants of enslaved people brought here from Africa. But we have found a way to integrate this problematic part of this country's foundation. We frame the Civil War as being fought over slavery, led by a white savior figure in Abraham Lincoln, who—it is taught—freed/emancipated the enslaved people. But we haven't been able to come to terms with the genocidal aspect of this country's origin and foundation, because we don't have a way to talk about the genocide. No matter how you frame it, America comes off at worst as monstrous, and at best as armed robbers.

The colonial dream was and continues to be a nightmare for too many of us. We are just waking up to who we are, and just starting to look back at who we've been. I use the word "we" here, knowing we Native Americans were not always included in the "us" of the US. In 2024, we celebrated one hundred years of citizenship as Native people. Work is required to change the nightmare into a dream. And work can take so many different forms.

Service can be viewed as punishment, as in court-ordered community service. Or as doing something selfless for the public and for the community. But service also serves you as an individual, cultivating a sense of belonging and a purpose higher than yourself. We live in a world filled with different kinds of people, in a country with a complex and painful history no matter what part your ancestors played. It is not noble to have conquered, to have exploited, to have taken. The legacy of the oppressor lives on in the souls of Americans in the same way it does in the oppressed.

The stories we are just now telling ourselves in this, the new Native renaissance, are a kind of radical act to challenge yourself and what you actually know about Native people. Putting in time to watch or read or visit our art galleries and reflect on what we think about being part of this country, on what we think about the way things went down, this too is service, service to yourself and service to better understand a people too long misrepresented and misunderstood.

Dr. King's dream of togetherness and unity might be better served among Black and Native communities. We who know the cost of progress and democracy, freedom itself, and who first paid the price. But I'm not talking about making people pay for what they've done. Far from it. Doing the work that needs to be done to see clearly what constitutes your country and its people, and to give humanity back to them—this serves everyone involved, including you. Ask not what your country can do for you, or what you can do for your country, but what your country means and has meant, and how to make it a better place not just for people who look and think like you.

Tommy Orange is a novelist and writer, and a citizen of the Cheyenne and Arapaho Tribes of Oklahoma. His first book, There There (2018), won both the John Leonard Prize and PEN/Hemingway Award, which are recognitions for an author's first book, as well as the American Book Award. The novel was also a finalist for a 2019 Pulitzer Prize.

There is no question that life is better for many Americans today than for previous generations. Yet, for the first time, that fact does not appear to be a foregone conclusion for the next generation. Yolanda, as a sixteen-year-old girl, has fewer rights today than the day she was born, with voting rights being curtailed in her home state of Georgia and women's rights over their own bodies and health care being rolled back. We are seeing life expectancy decrease, driven by deaths of despair with drugs and suicide. The undertow of the past remains tenacious.

LEGACIES SPIRALING INTO CRISES

Collective legacies are not the only ones passed down through generations. Each of us also inherits familial legacies from our ancestors. These are legacies that are unique to you—personal inheritances that come down through your family line. It's important to note that when we talk about family lines, we include all forms of family, such as blood, adoption or other ways you may have been raised. The science of epigenetics confirms that familial legacies are not only passed on through genes, but they also shape adopted children, extended families and individuals in our wider circles. We'll explore these familial legacies and their burdens in more detail later. For now, it's important to recognize that not all familial legacies are burdensome. Many can be healthy, empowering and the backbone of our resilience. However, others, like substance abuse, physical and mental abuse and intergenerational trauma, contribute significantly to our inner struggles and crises.

In trying to make sense of what we've found upstream, we see how our collective and familial legacy burdens perpetuate each other, generation after generation. Though we separate them by naming their differences, these collective and familial legacies are tightly interwoven, feeding one another in a spiral of permacrises that we're all drowning in.

This is the cycle of outer crises fueling inner crises fueling outer crises and so on. The outer crises of global conflicts and social divisiveness add weight to the fear and anxiety that fuel our inner crises. The collective legacy of slavery and subsequent Jim Crow laws or the abuse of Native American children in residential schools in the United States and Canada fuels intergenerational trauma within those families, leading to harmful familial legacies such as substance abuse, addiction and depression.

Black Americans, for example, have higher rates of infant and maternal mortality,[11] a higher incidence of childhood asthma,[12] and higher rates of high blood pressure,[13] Alzheimer's disease,[14] and other illnesses. These are severe health problems that impact and shape familial legacies and are also attributable to the greater collective legacy of racism.

And the circle continues around. The more those collective legacies fuel our inner crises, breaking down our mental and physical health, the more we become susceptible to the harm of these legacies. In the US, this tyrannical cycle has caused heightened fear and anxiety and increased mental and physical health challenges, which are seriously worrying health professionals. Rates of depression have reached all-time highs.[15]

As we grapple with these intertwining legacy burdens, we are also experiencing an alarming rise in isolation and loneliness. The suffering of loneliness is reaching such proportions that the World Health Organization has identified it as a threat to global public health.[16] The amount of real-world face time people have with others, even within their friend groups, is plummeting.[17] A record-low number of people now say that community involvement is an important part of their lives.[18]

THE MORE THOSE COLLECTIVE LEGACIES FUEL OUR INNER CRISES... THE MORE WE BECOME SUSCEPTIBLE TO THE HARM OF THESE LEGACIES.

Loneliness can feel like your heart is an empty house or like you're standing on a cold street, looking through the window of a warm home where a dinner party is happening and you're not invited. Sometimes, it feels like you're withering away. Humans are social creatures, and without connections, primal alarm bells are triggered. Instead of hunger, thirst and physical pain, the feeling is an unbearable ache.

The inner crisis of loneliness is also taking a toll on our physical health. Living without meaningful human connection is like having a fifteen-cigarette-a-day habit, according to US surgeon general Dr. Vivek H. Murthy in his May 2023 special advisory on the crisis of loneliness.[19] The lonely—about half of us—are at risk of premature death, with a 29 percent increased risk of heart disease, a 32 percent increased risk of stroke, and a 50 percent increased risk of developing dementia in older adults.

So, even if we can see these legacies, why do we never seem any closer to overcoming them and reducing their impact on our lives and culture? Because we still need to get to the source.

TREKKING FURTHER UPSTREAM

When Marc and Craig first heard the "upstream" parable from

Desmond Tutu, they were in the midst of their humanitarian journey, trying to get at the source of one of Dr. King's evil triplets—global poverty. Their first charity, Free the Children, originally supported activists freeing enslaved children. But the brothers discovered that a few years later many of these children were right back in the factories, fields or worse. It was heartbreaking and humbling. As long as the children's families remained mired in extreme poverty, the children would have to work to help their families survive instead of going to school.

The brothers refocused Free the Children to empower communities in Africa, Asia and South America with the tools to lift themselves out of poverty—education, clean water, food, health care and economic opportunities. Their charity work impacted more and more lives every year, eventually reaching millions; yet, the brothers often felt they still weren't getting to the source of the problem.

So Marc and Craig went further upstream. Why is poverty so prevalent? Why is a child in Sierra Leone or India less worthy of basic health care, food security and freedom than a child born inside the borders of our own country? Why do we accept limits on compassion in a world of plenty? The brothers started service programs in thousands of schools, engaging young people, who naturally have a deep sense of right and wrong before they are inculcated to accept that the injustices of our world are normal and inevitable.

Yet, they always felt that they could travel further upstream, reshaping the cultural narratives and accepted beliefs that result in generations repeating such inhumane treatment of each other. This insight led to launching Legacy+ and to the realization that to truly reach the roots, we must answer the next logical question: Why did those harmful legacies form in the first place?

Women's Empowerment: A Legacy That Continues to Give Back

Melinda French Gates

Many years ago, I met a group of women in Malawi who were standing in a long line on a hot day to get their kids vaccinated. Many of them had traveled far to be there, and I was moved by their commitment to their children's health. When I noticed one young mother with small kids, I asked her, "Are you taking these children to get their shots?" She answered, "What about my shot?"

She wasn't talking about a vaccination. She was talking about Depo-Provera, a long-acting birth control injection. She knew that if she wanted to give her children a chance at a better life, she needed to be able to hold off on having any more. But she'd have to spend a day walking with her kids to a far-off clinic to get it, and there was a good chance the shot wouldn't be in stock anyway.

That conversation, and the countless like it that I had with other women in similar positions, ultimately inspired me to advocate for contraceptive access, which in turn opened my eyes to the countless barriers and obstacles that keep women from having their full power in society. It taught me something else, too: I'm not the expert. Women know what they need to lead the lives they want, and the most important thing I can do is to first stop and simply listen to what they have to say.

When women are empowered, their kids are healthier, their communities are safer, their countries are stronger economically.

I often think of the quote "To know that one life has breathed easier because you lived here. This is to have succeeded."

Everything I do is in the hopes that women and girls around the world will be able to breathe easier—to have access to the opportunities and support they deserve, the freedom to decide whether and when to have children, and the power to live life on their own terms.

One of the reasons I'm so passionate about this work is because I've seen the ripple effect of women's power. When women are empowered, their kids are healthier, their communities are safer, their countries are stronger economically. Some people see legacy as a static thing that never changes. But in my view, empowering women and girls creates a living legacy, one that continues to grow and give back.

Melinda French Gates is a philanthropist, businesswoman and global advocate for women and girls. Today, she heads Pivotal Ventures, an organization she formed in 2015 that works to accelerate the pace of progress and advance women's power and influence in the US and around the world. Previously, she founded and cochaired the Gates Foundation. French Gates is also the author of the bestselling book The Moment of Lift *and the creator of Moment of Lift Books, an imprint publishing original nonfiction by visionaries working to unlock a more equal world.*

Martin and Arndrea came to the same fundamental question on their journey upstream. They saw racism as a legacy burden, but why was it so constantly and easily passed on from generation to generation? Why were some Americans so willing to deny basic equality and rights to their fellow citizens? Why were people so willing to hate and oppress others because of their skin color or ethnicity? They could see that these cultural legacies were handed down from generation to generation—from slavery to Jim Crow to segregation and beyond.

But why did that legacy begin in the first place?

As the four of us came together and began to share our insights about legacy and its impact on our lives, we asked ourselves why we never seemed any closer to overcoming these burdensome legacies. How do we break this cycle of collective and familial legacies that keeps us swirling in crises? We believe these legacies are real and impactful but not the source. After all, these legacies don't just spring from the air fully formed. Something had to create the initial conditions allowing those legacies to start.

So further upstream we went.

Here is what we found as far upstream as we could see: All these collective and ensuing familial legacy burdens that keep us spiraling into crisis stem from a common source. They are all rooted in disconnection—disconnection from ourselves, from our values, from nature, from one another, from our basic humanity. This disconnection is the antithesis of the Beloved Community, which is anchored in the interconnectedness of all life.

This is not a hypothesis based on conjecture. It is a conclusion we have thoughtfully and jointly reached from our own lived experiences as we traveled up the river to find the source of the world's challenges that we each sought to fix. Every one of those legacies, every war that has ever been, boils down to people becoming so disconnected from their humanity that they believe killing is an acceptable path to settling differences and achieving greatness. Every child that has ever died of beatings and malnutrition in a carpet factory represents people so disconnected from their humanity that legacies of greed and wealth outweighed the life of a child. We have become so disconnected from one another and our values that people are willing to hurt, even kill, a neighbor because of which political party they support.

ALL THESE COLLECTIVE AND ENSUING FAMILIAL LEGACY BURDENS THAT KEEP US SPIRALING INTO CRISIS STEM FROM A COMMON SOURCE. THEY ARE ALL ROOTED IN DISCONNECTION.

We find disconnection in the great environmental challenge of our age: climate crisis. The deep connection to nature that our distant ancestors may have felt through gratitude or necessity is long forgotten. Because of this disconnection, the best efforts of all those who care about the environment struggle to make headway. You save a forest, but the forces behind it—the legacies of materialism and consumerism rooted in disconnection—will find another forest to destroy. We try to reduce our own carbon footprint and energy use, but the powerful legacies rooted in disconnection seem to override our best efforts. We can all start to feel powerless in our efforts to address the climate crisis because we keep trying to put patches on something without addressing the legacies of disconnection that lie at the source of it. Once again, we get the self-perpetuating feedback loop. The crises and the disconnection that lies at their source are complicit. They work together, reinforcing one another.

Here we are, like the children in Archbishop Tutu's parable, drowning in a river of legacy burdens—all stemming from a profound disconnection from ourselves, each other and the natural world. Let's return to the wisdom of Dr. King. He may not have used the exact language we are using now, and his journey upstream may have been different, but ultimately, he reached the same conclusion. The ultimate solution to the profound disconnection that has sourced these harmful and divisive legacies is to build the Beloved Community.

LET'S RETURN TO THE WISDOM OF DR. KING.

But how do we reach Dr. King's promised land? We believe that the best way to break the cycle, to change and heal the legacies that have led us into this mess, is to start creating new ones. This means living in a way that creates legacies that bring us together and connect us with ourselves and one another instead of disconnecting us. This is the essence of this book: healing the legacies of fear and disconnection by purposefully living new legacies of love and connection to heal ourselves and the world—now and for all generations to come.

Before we can explore what we mean by living new legacies of love and connection and how to do it, we need to examine the concept of legacy itself and understand how our culture has gotten it all wrong.

Hot Spots for Connection and Contribution

Dan Buettner

I've become known for discovering and popularizing blue zones, the places in the world where people live the longest, healthiest lives: Ikaria, Greece; Loma Linda, California; Sardinia, Italy; Okinawa, Japan; and Nicoya, Costa Rica. Part of my quest has been understanding why people in these places live to be one hundred years old at the highest rates in the world. I've looked for answers for more than two decades.

I went in thinking it was going to be a chemical or some sort of component that made people live longer. But the answer was right under my nose. These people in blue zones aren't doing anything to live a long time. They're not consciously on diets or exercise programs or taking supplements or stem cell therapies or any of the things that we spend billions on to live longer. They're living in the right environment, and the right community. And community, I would argue, is an offshoot of the right environment.

It's harder to be part of a community when you live in a suburb where everybody has a quarter of an acre and must drive for miles to bump into someone. Having three solid friends who care about when you're having a bad day is a litmus test for connection and community: Can I call this person when I'm down on my luck and borrow a few bucks? Can I call this person and cry because my partner just dumped me, and they'll sit and listen to me? Or are they just slap-on-the-back friends? About 30 percent of Americans don't have enough close friends; instead, they're lonely and isolated. And that's a problem for their happiness and longevity.

It's my goal to help people implement the blue zone findings so they can live longer, healthier, more connected lives. I want to set Americans up for success by making healthy choices easy or unavoidable. I would argue the microcommunity around you is probably the biggest predictor of whether you live an extra ten years—although eating a cup of beans every day also helps! So does moving every single day.

I've also applied these teachings to myself. In addition to consuming a 98 percent plant-based diet, I moved to the southern tip of Miami from Minnesota so I could live in a walkable and bikeable community. This was a big change. I didn't know anyone, so I set out to create a social circle of at least four people from scratch. I started volunteering and attending events to meet people. I found you don't have to try so hard; you end up working or sitting shoulder to shoulder with people who share your values. You bump into the same people over and over, and by the fourth or fifth time, you're having a conversation on your way to a friendship.

When I found someone I liked, I invited them to lunch.

It doesn't guarantee a friendship, but I would make that investment of time and money, and I'd buy lunch. I probably had two dozen lunches before I found four people I wanted to see a second time. I also host dinner parties around a defined topic of conversation, where I serve a blue zone–inspired meal of minestrone soup, sourdough bread and antioxidant-rich Sardinian wine. You either like people a lot more after this experience, or you dislike them a lot more, but it's the process of making friends and making connections. Creating a long and well-lived life.

Dan Buettner *is an explorer, National Geographic Fellow, award-winning journalist, author and producer. He discovered the five places in the world—dubbed blue zones—where people live the longest, healthiest lives. Buettner now works with governments, large employers and insurance companies to implement Blue Zones Projects nationally.*

CHAPTER 3

The Hazards of Old School Legacy

THEY WERE THE WORST MONTHS of Marc's life—the early days of the Covid pandemic and the summer of 2020. Everyone was scared, locked inside, hoarding toilet paper and hand sanitizer, becoming increasingly disconnected from their loved ones, their community and the world. Meanwhile, Marc was hunkered down in his basement, gripped by fear for different reasons. The charity he and his brother, Craig, had built into a global movement, helping millions of young people, was under attack, branded ignominiously as the "WE Charity Scandal." Twenty-five years of their life's work was being destroyed as they fielded calls from dozens of reporters, each determined to take their own swing at the brothers' good deeds. The media frenzy even fueled death threats from extremists on both sides of the political spectrum.

As the one managing the charity's day-to-day operations, Marc took it all especially hard. He took the vile things written about him online personally. He wasn't sleeping, as he was consumed by anger, which eventually turned to numbness. He began to wonder if there was a more permanent way to go numb. At his lowest point, he seriously contemplated ending his life, irrationally hoping his death would stop the destruction of the charity and protect its educational and development projects and remaining employees. Everyone who knew him was desperately worried.

In the end, it was revealed that the so-called scandal was nothing more than a public tempest created by misinformation, outright lies and political maneuvering. But it cost the brothers nearly everything.

We want to share what happened during that dark period because, in many ways, it led to this book and our partnership as authors. Marc came to understand what he truly wanted his legacy to be. It also made us rethink the meaning of legacy and why the definition of what we call "Old School Legacy" keeps us disconnected from others and contributes to our endless cycle of crises. Throughout our journey to writing this book, we realized we've gotten legacy all wrong.

Please indulge us as we share some of the intricacies of Canadian politics and the broad strokes of what happened in 2020 so you understand how unexpected and horrible it all was. At the height of the pandemic, the government of Canada decided to launch a national student-based service corps hiring one hundred thousand postsecondary students to help young Canadians affected by the pandemic and give students much-needed summer employment while school and many workplaces were closed.[20] Unlike the US, Canada does not have a large government service platform, such as AmeriCorps or the Peace Corps, so a senior government bureaucrat asked WE Charity to submit a proposal to build this emergency program within weeks to meet the urgent need. WE Charity already had established large-scale student service programs, engaging tens of thousands of schools and universities across North America, and had hundreds of staff with the capacity to run complex programs at that scale.

But during the pandemic, the charity planned to be laser focused on projects in the Global South, where early predictions suggested Covid would hit hardest. WE Charity in Africa and South America operated hospitals and mobile medical units and was turning pandemic-shuttered schools into medical facilities, bracing for the loss of life. So, initially, WE Charity declined the request from the Canadian government. But the charity eventually relented because the need was so great, and the senior team chose not to turn down a request for help during a global health crisis. Many of WE Charity's staff worked almost nonstop, pulling all-nighters to gather a coalition of more than eighty nonprofits to provide Covid assistance and sign up the first cohort of thirty thousand students ready for summer service.[21]

However, the nonprofits, students and people affected by Covid never benefited. The program shut within days of launch as politicians fought with each other, trying to score political points during a global pandemic.[22]

Prime Minister Justin Trudeau's family had been involved with WE Charity over the years. Most notably, his mother, Margaret Trudeau, a bestselling author and advocate for mental health, had been hired through a speaking bureau to speak at WE Charity fundraising events. In Canada, politicians must recuse themselves from votes where they have a personal interest. In this case, when the cabinet voted to award WE Charity the government contract, the prime minister failed to do so.[23] He voted along with his cabinet members. Without his vote, the motion would have easily passed anyway, but opposition politicians sensed blood in the water and pounced, claiming that the prime minister had violated the rules. The service program soon became a political football, with the prime minister quickly seeking to distance himself from the program to save his own skin, and opposition parties attacking the charity as a proxy to damage the prime minister.

The charity was stuck in the middle, and the losses piled up. The prime minister oversaw a minority parliament and was soon up for reelection, which further fueled the politics.

During the Covid lockdowns, certain media reached for anything to fill airways and print space. As time dragged on, the simple facts of the story were not sufficient. Canada is not immune
to social media conspiracy theories and underfunded newsrooms
circulating rumors and wild inaccuracies.

At the end of it all, Parliament's independent ethics commissioner cleared the prime minister, concluding that based on the
specific circumstances, he did not have to recuse himself from
the vote to award WE Charity the contract.[24] In the next election, the prime minister was reelected. Opposition politicians got
their fifteen minutes of fame, and certain media struggling with
declining ad revenue got some more clicks on their articles with
sensational headlines.

The charity was vindicated by multiple reports showing that it
operated with the highest integrity.[25] At the time of this book's pub-
lication, two defamation lawsuits still before the courts—one filed
by Marc and Craig's mother and another by WE Charity—had won
favorable rulings in milestone motions.[26] But once the harm was
done, it was hard to undo. The charity, and ultimately the children
it served, paid a heavy price for being used as a political football.

Marc seemed to have no choice in the matter except for his
own reaction. At first, he chose hate. The moral cowardice of certain politicians using a children's charity for a proxy war shocked
him. If we can't agree that children should be protected, what can
we agree on? These were elected officials who were, by tradition,
given the title "honorable" before their name, but instead they
acted in a partisan, dishonorable way. He was livid. More than
that, he'd considered the charity and its reputation a huge part
of his legacy, identity and, therefore, his self-worth. His despair
deepened until, with the support of his wife, Roxanne, and professional help, he found a way to cope.

This marked a dramatic turning point. Looking back, he's since realized that he was saved from the old version of himself. For a long time, even before the fabricated political scandal, he was disconnected from himself, others and the world. He didn't love himself, often putting too much weight behind what others thought of him. This is one of the main hazards of Old School Legacy. He came to realize that's a race no one can win.

"OLD SCHOOL LEGACY" KEEPS US DISCONNECTED FROM OTHERS AND CONTRIBUTES TO OUR ENDLESS CYCLE OF CRISES.

We all have unconscious legacies that define us and keep us entrenched in disconnection and permacrisis. That is what Marc realized. He was too focused on what he might be remembered for, instead of how he was living his legacy every day. Through deep reflection, working with a life coach, conversations with this book's other authors, and the loving support of Roxanne, he realized that we have been conditioned to think about legacy the wrong way. He realized the current version of legacy has kept us from healing and transcending the familial and collective legacy burdens we discussed in the previous chapter.

This realization has led us to reflect on the harm caused by the myths of Old School Legacy. If we seek connection and an end to permacrisis, we must challenge these long-held myths and show how the emphasis on what we leave behind fuels disconnection and permacrisis. How else will we reach the Beloved Community?

What Now

Billy Porter

I missed the whole thing. The actual civil rights movement. Dr. King was assassinated on April 4, 1968, a mere seventeen months before I was born. I grew up in a Christian household. Dr. King was anointed in our home to watch over us. Sainted. The power of his legacy based in nonviolent resistance, the bulk of which he learned from the queer leader Bayard Rustin, is what we all held on to. And I still do to this day.

And . . . What now . . . ?

For you see, the change came and the change went. We overcame and now we're back to domestic terrorism to silence anyone or anything that dares to speak truth to power. Of course, "when they go low, we go high." And it's time to put our activist heads together to figure out what "going high" looks like in this new world order. I love y'all, but it is not 1965.

> ***I still do believe in humanity and the resilience of the human spirit. I do believe that when we fight, we win!***

As an out, Black, gay, Christian man in the country—and in this world, quite frankly—the messaging I've received from all of the spaces, including "the movement," was that I was to shut up and sit my faggot ass down somewhere and wait for a more "convenient time." Women were also silenced in our original movement. And we took a back seat, and were silent . . . for the greater good.

What now, Dr. King?

Freedom and justice for all, right . . . ? The movement has evolved, and I'm grateful for that. But I always ruminate and dream—What if the women and the queers were all represented in the movement in the first place, how much further along would the world be? I don't know and I don't dwell. I simply hold on to hope. Albeit by an emotional thread at the moment. I still do believe in humanity and the resilience of the human spirit. I do believe that when we fight, we win!

I hope that my truth does not come across as negative. I don't mean it to be. *And . . .* the truth will set us all free. We must be in the moment we're in, not the moment we wish for. We ain't there yet. But we must be present for the urgency of this moment in order to move forward with grace, loving-kindness, compassion and nonviolence.

As Maya Angelou has taught, people know themselves best, so believe them when they show you who they are. We did this already. Our ancestors fought and died for every right and freedom we have. We cannot let them down. We will not abandon our history.

__Billy Porter__ is an award-winning actor, singer and fashion icon known for his groundbreaking role in the TV series Pose. *He has won numerous accolades, including an Emmy, a Tony and a Grammy. Porter's fearless style and advocacy for LGBTQ+ rights have made him a powerful voice in the entertainment industry, and he received the Isabelle Stevenson Tony Award at the* 77th Annual Tony Awards *for his humanitarian work with the Elizabeth Taylor AIDS Foundation and the Entertainment Community Fund.*

MYTH #1—LEGACY IS FOR THE DYING OR DEAD

Throughout history and across cultures, humans have acted out of a desire to carve their names into the history books or on the walls of buildings and towering monuments that will last long after they are gone. Think of the Valley of the Kings in Upper Egypt, where pharaohs, including King Tut, were buried in rock-cut tombs from 1539–1075 BCE, or older, wealthy people bequeathing a large sum of money or donating their collection of Picassos to a museum. In lay terms, legacy is defined as "something transmitted by or received from an ancestor or predecessor or from the past" (*Merriam-Webster,* online version) or "money or property that is given to you by somebody when they die" (*Oxford Learner's Dictionaries*). Most definitions conclude that legacy is often obtained, if at all, during the last handful of years on earth.

Humans can't help thinking about life after death. This is especially a symbolic form of legacy—how everyone, family, friends and even complete strangers, will remember us after we die. Why are we so intent on inscribing our names on walls, figuratively and literally?

WE OFTEN CRAFT POST-MORTEM LEGACIES THAT FOCUS ON ALL THE WRONG THINGS.

In "The Desire to Be Remembered," researchers from the University of Otago in New Zealand call the human drive for legacy "the most puzzling question of all." As they ask in their

2023 paper, Why do we care what others think of us after death? It turns out humans can't help but worry about our post-mortem reputation. In fact, "the desire and motivation to leave a legacy, even among those who do not believe in an afterlife, is ostensibly a powerful influence on our lives," they write.[27]

The problem is that we may put off thinking about our legacy until death is looming. And when we finally start thinking about our legacy, we often focus on it when we're nearing the end of our life, instead of living for now.

Brett Waggoner, one of the University of Otago researchers, extensively studied people's ideas and motivations around legacy. He writes, "For those who primarily fixate their efforts toward their post-mortem legacy, a potential conflict may arise between directing their attention and peace of mind to the present moment and lived experiences as opposed to the future when their legacy is successfully established."[28] In other words, if your definition of legacy is all about transcending death by trying to build something that outlives you, you're not really living. You're just fixating on the end. This sort of endgame thinking limits the potential of your legacy to have an impact now while you're alive to enjoy it, which is a huge missed opportunity. But it can also interfere with your capacity to be loved, valued and remembered post-mortem, as we often craft post-mortem legacies that focus on all the wrong things.

MYTH #2—LEGACY IS FOR SALE

Recently, Marc and Craig's elderly father has been undergoing treatments in a hospital, where every single room seems to have been named for a past donor. They joke that he expects to see a brass nameplate on the toilet whenever he goes into a washroom there. Even their dad is infected with the idea that legacy means putting your name on something. With his precarious health, he's considering donating money to have his name on a park bench at his alma mater.

Among the rich and the powerful, and even Marc and Craig's dad, it seems possible to buy a lasting legacy. To us, this desire to leave your name on something seems like people trying to purchase immortality or an exercise in post-mortem reputation management.

An extreme example of this way of thinking is the Sackler family of Purdue Pharma, who were behind the despicable legacy of pharmaceutical greed that led to one of the most devastating crises of our time: OxyContin opioid addiction. The family made a $13 billion fortune manufacturing and selling OxyContin. This highly addictive opioid fueled overdose and death, infectious disease and social issues such as poverty, homelessness and incarceration, while impacting the rural poor most. This crisis left a legacy of profound human disconnection. The family, in turn, donated tens of millions of dollars to ensure their name adorned dozens of buildings, wings and institutes, no doubt hoping their legacy of perpetuating opioid addiction would be made invisible by these imposing structures housing good works done by others.

There was, for example, the Sackler Institute at the Natural History Museum and the Sackler Center for Arts Education at the Guggenheim Museum. The Metropolitan Museum of Art in New York had the Sackler Wing, and Tufts University had the Sackler School of Graduate Biomedical Sciences. It did not stop there. Yale University, the University of Oxford, the University of Cambridge, King's College London, the University of Sussex, the Old Royal Naval College, and New York University had buildings,

Living a Legacy of Service

Russell and Ciara Wilson

For us, legacy is impact, and we strive to embody that through our commitment to family, faith and humanity.

We hope to leave a legacy rooted in service, one that helps improve lives and level the playing field for all individuals, especially the next generation. Martin Luther King Jr. dreamed of a world where kids would have an equal opportunity to dream, and that's why we founded the Why Not You Foundation.

All children deserve the opportunity to dream big and have the resources to reach those dreams, regardless of their background or circumstances. Together, we hope our family legacy is seen through the Why Not You Foundation and its work to positively impact the lives of others.

__Russell Wilson__ played quarterback for the Pittsburgh Steelers, Seattle Seahawks and Denver Broncos. In Seattle, he was named to the Pro Bowl nine times and helped the team win their first Super Bowl championship. __Ciara Wilson__ is a Grammy-nominated singer-songwriter and philanthropist who has worked with organizations such as Stand Up to Cancer, DoSomething.org, Why Not You, and others.

wings or institutes bearing the Sackler name. So did the Tate Modern, Shakespeare's Globe Theatre, the British Museum, and the National Gallery, London. Marc's alma mater, Harvard University, had no less than two buildings named after Arthur Sackler. None of this legacy building ended up lasting, and in the end, the Sackler name has been scrubbed from dozens of institutions, proving the perils and possible impermanence of purchasing a legacy.[29]

IN THE SPIRIT OF RETHINKING OLD SCHOOL LEGACY, THE TRUE INTENT OF THE GIFT IS WHAT REALLY MATTERS.

And if you're trying to purchase a legacy to bring end-of-life fulfillment, that will not work. Those on their deathbed seek connection with loved ones, not accolades. So, the desire to etch your name on a wall will likely leave you feeling empty and unsatisfied.

Marc and Craig's father has made a far more significant positive impact throughout his life than any bench ever could. Their parents were instrumental in supporting the brothers and the charity in its early days. They chauffeured youth volunteers to and from engagements and allowed their living room to be used as a hub for volunteers. As the charity grew, they made significant donations of time and resources.

Now, you may say that someone who has put their name on a hospital wing has also done a lot of good. This could likely be the case. Many professional fundraisers even ask donors to allow them to put the donors' names on walls, both inside and outside buildings, in the hope that by doing so, "it will inspire others to donate." Of course, those who have made generous donations have often positively impacted many lives. But, in the spirit of rethinking Old School Legacy, the true intent of the gift is what really matters. If it's a financial transaction to buff up a shoddy reputation, it doesn't matter how large your wallet is or the size of your gift. But if it comes from the heart, from a spirit of building connections with others, it might bring the fulfillment you seek at the end of your life.

MYTH # 3—LEGACY IS ONLY FOR THE FAMOUS

Legacy is frequently framed around the supersize accomplishments and contributions of the famous. Consider the sporting achievements of tennis great Serena Williams, who came back against the odds after a difficult childbirth to try to break the Grand Slam record, or even Evel Knievel, who broke hundreds of bones, making seventy-five ramp-to-ramp jumps to earn infamy and a place in the Motorcycle Hall of Fame. Beyond the record holders and great feats, there are also ample examples of famous thinkers, leaders and academics musing about the legacy they will leave behind.

We certainly revere the legacies of rare individuals whose outstanding accomplishments changed the world, such as Dr. King or Mahatma Gandhi—visionaries whose lasting impact earned them a permanent place in our history books. Or the legacy left through great sports achievements or creative works by many of the esteemed contributors to this book, including Dan Rather, Rev. Al Sharpton, Melinda French Gates, Rev. Michael Beckwith and Sr. Theresa Aletheia Noble.

But if the definition of legacy hangs on big fame and great accomplishments—what does that tell us? If you can't get celebrity recognition, enough zeros in your bank account or pages devoted to you in the history books, then legacy is likely out of reach for you. This kind of Old School Legacy thinking leaves all the folks who will never be A-listers or billionaires—the vast majority of people—out of the conversation. We end up feeling disempowered about our ability to have a lasting and meaningful impact on our friends, family, community and the world.

MYTH #4—LEGACY IS HOW WELL OTHERS PERCEIVE YOU

This perception that legacy is linked to how highly regarded or admired you are by others is the most widely accepted definition. It's also the most damaging.

When Marc was eighteen and in his first year of university, he worked as a page in the Canadian House of Commons. It was a small job of even smaller tasks, but just as in the US Congress, pages help keep the country running. Back then, Marc dreamed of a life in public service, perhaps in government itself, and felt he was on his way. Until one day, he delivered a note to the deputy speaker, who stopped Marc with an odd question: "What kind of legacy do you want to leave, son?" He'd previously said so little to Marc that he worried he must look lost on some existential level. Legacy was an impossibly distant concept. But the deputy speaker went on to tell Marc about his volunteer work in the poorest areas of Bangkok, work that he considered part of his legacy. He wanted to know if Marc was interested in doing the same.

So, at eighteen, Marc was forced to consider his legacy, which, back then, meant all the great and interesting things he was going to accomplish in his life. Going to Thailand would require him to forfeit his scholarship and his coveted job as a well-dressed water boy, but selfishly, Marc thought that service work overseas might look good on his résumé. His future wife, Roxanne—also a page— agreed to go with him.

What was initially supposed to be a three-week volunteer trip ended up being a nearly yearlong experience of self-discovery. They worked with AIDS patients at a time when little was understood about the disease, and stigma—especially in a religiously conservative country like Thailand—was rampant. Marc offered rudimentary medical care and held the hands of dying patients. He also spent time with unhoused children and lived in the community where he worked, getting to know the local people meaningfully.

When Marc returned to North America, he was a changed person. He enrolled in Harvard to study international relations and planned to join Craig in building big development projects around the world. Excited and motivated, he felt nothing could stop him. *Legacy, here I come,* he thought.

The brothers built WE Charity from nothing in their parents' home starting in 1995 and grew it into a global movement. Marc turned down job offers on Wall Street with expense accounts and wardrobe allowances for designer ties. No one believed two young people could start and run a successful global organization, especially reaching this scope and scale. But they did.

It was not to last as it was, and the events at the height of the pandemic forced Marc to confront the fragility of his definition of legacy. Marc was shattered. He felt the legacy he'd intentionally built from his early days in Thailand was destroyed.

The Symphony of Self: A Legacy of Balance and Connection

Tracy Anderson

My journey began with a vision, a belief in the potential for a greater good. I saw a world disconnected, people estranged from their own bodies, lost in discomfort and uncertainty. My mission became clear: to restore balance, to guide people back to themselves through the innate power of movement.

I imagine the body as an orchestra, each part a musician playing its note. Like a Mozart concerto, every note resonates through your being. In a world where quick fixes are peddled at every corner, I sought to remind people of the miracle within— their body's built-in symphony awaiting to be conducted.

My personal narrative is intertwined with movement; my mother, a professional ballerina, and my father, an entrepreneur and artist, instilled in me the rhythm of activity. A dance scholarship brought me to New York, where I faced my own struggle with weight and self-image. I gained forty pounds despite daily workouts. It was this challenge that shaped my resolve, my quest for natural harmony.

In my twenties, Dr. James Austin's *Zen and the Brain* opened my eyes to the profound mind-body connection, revealing the potential for transformation in our every movement.

This revelation led me to a research odyssey, beginning in 2003, where I trained 150 women to understand every part of their physical makeup so I could customize unique routines based on body type. I measured the women every ten days, totaling over twenty-seven thousand measurements in five years, and then tailored the workouts based on their progress. This led to Metamorphosis, which showed the deep link between movement and emotional experience, how reconnecting the brain, heart, soul and spirit during a workout can yield astonishing results.

When I began, fitness was uncharted territory—there was no extensive research on muscle design or balance. I envisioned a fitness journey that consistently fostered equilibrium in both body and mind. Before training celebrities like Madonna, Gwyneth Paltrow or Jennifer Lopez, or opening studios, I embarked on a five-year study, laying the foundation for a holistic approach to well-being. I showed that we possess an inherent resilience, an ability to connect with our bodies, to process, feel and restore. Yet, this connection has been forgotten, buried under the weight of life's traumas.

I went on to create the Tracy Anderson Method, which is more than exercise, more than dance; it's a subconscious nurturing of self-esteem, enhancing the brain's neuroplasticity and forging new neurological pathways. It's about connecting emotions to movement, addressing PTSD and participating more fully in the world.

I continue to develop thousands of new routines to ensure that no client ever plateaus. And I have developed MYMODE, a multifunctional apparatus that expands and mutates into diverse forms, offering thousands of movement algorithms. I've also launched HeartStone, a set of limited-edition weighted energy trainers beset with rose quartz.

These offerings are meant to create connection and inspiration with my community.

You are worth more than a fleeting moment. Your body deserves time to enact change, to enhance longevity. We are wondrous beings, and it's time we honor ourselves with the care we deserve. Harmony defines my life now, a harmony born from a place of self-advocacy and healing. My legacy is not just in the movements I've created but in the lives I've touched, the balance I've brought and the connections I've fostered.

Tracy Anderson is a global fitness and wellness pioneer, author, and the creator of the Tracy Anderson Method, MYMODE and HeartStone. Anderson's revolutionary and unique movement approach focuses on strategic muscle design, dynamic choreography and mindfulness, making her a sought-after expert. She owns several studios and has released over 170 fitness DVDs and TA Online Studio programs with clients in more than fifty-three different countries.

Standing amid the wreckage, Marc started reevaluating what legacy really means. It took months of self-reflection. And it was the hardest personal work he had ever done. In this process of self-discovery, Marc realized his definition of legacy was incomplete and primarily based on what people thought of him and his work. He'd been looking at how others saw him rather than how he'd impacted the world. He likes to say, "I had to lose my identity to find my identity."

This realization was a significant turning point in his life. Looking back, it was the greatest gift of perspective. His legacy had nothing to do with how well he was perceived by others. His legacy had never been destroyed. And his new understanding of legacy meant it never could be destroyed.

His legacy was alive in the millions of people, mostly children, who had benefited from Marc and Craig's charity work. Overseas, hundreds of thousands of kids had received a quality primary and secondary education, thousands of babies had been safely born at the hospital they built and operated in rural Kenya, and hundreds of girls had been the first person in their family to graduate from high school. Millions of students in North America have raised tens of millions of dollars for important social causes because of their domestic school programs and events. All these ways that Marc's life and day-by-day choices had helped others live healthier, more meaningful lives—none of that could be taken away. All of this had contributed to Marc's truest fulfillment. And all of those choices represented the truest power and meaning of legacy.

When Marc came to understand what legacy really means, he took that inspiration to build a new organization with Craig. Aptly, they named it Legacy+, and they gathered team members who had stuck it out—dozens of strategists, designers, creators, storytellers and more. Using everything they have learned over the past thirty years, Marc and Craig now help others bring their purpose to life and make a positive, large-scale difference in the world.

His true legacy was alive and well. And always will be.

IT'S TIME FOR A NEW MEANING OF LEGACY

The old traditional way of thinking about legacy doesn't work. It's death focused, often selfish and exclusive, and it leads to disconnection from yourself, others and the truth of what legacy really is. If your goal is to live a more connected and fulfilling life, Old School Legacy is an evolutionary dead end.

To counteract the flaws of the old myths of legacy, we need a framework that is accessible regardless of age, fame or financial status. A framework that integrates into our daily lives and connects us to ourselves and others.

That framework is a Living Legacy.

CHAPTER 4

Introducing Living Legacy: Healing Ourselves and Halting the Crises

OUTDATED NOTIONS OF LEGACY ARE strong but not unbreakable. Our world and our personal lives are formed by the legacies we inherit from history, culture and up-bringing. We grow up surrounded by these legacies—some burdensome, dividing us and perpetuating fear across decades and centuries. But we have the power to heal and transform the legacies that hold us back.

We know the King Dream is in a fragile state. Our trek upstream showed us that disconnection from ourselves, others and the world is the source of our permacrisis. Now that we know that disconnection, fueled by fear, is what got us into permacrisis, it's time to find our way out.

To create the Beloved Community, a society built on boundless love and respect for the interconnectedness of all of life, we need to first love ourselves. We also need to love others. As Arndrea says, the Beloved Community is achieved when we "be love." Be the love that overcomes our fear. Be the love that leads us out of the permacrisis. Be the love that heals the legacies of disconnection we inherited. Be the love that reconnects us. Connection and reconnection, fueled by love, is what will get us out of the permacrisis. In short, it is what will enable Dr. King's vision of the Beloved Community.

It's not like we are the first people to believe in the power of love. Every spiritual tradition recognizes it. Even the Beatles knew that all we need is love. But we also know it's not always easy to "be love." We know we need more love in the world. But tangibly how do we do this? How do we live new legacies of love and connection that help us become the Beloved Community?

The answer is simple but profound. We do it through the small daily actions of how we live our lives, through what we call Living Legacy.

Living Legacy acknowledges that everything we do, every decision we make and every interaction we have, creates a legacy. No matter how big or small—everything we do has an impact on the world and leaves a legacy of some kind in its wake. Just as we don't always see the legacies that have shaped us, we don't always see the power of our own actions to reshape our own lives and the world around us. We can heal the legacy burdens of fear and disconnection by consciously choosing to seed and live new Living Legacies that are rooted in love and connection.

LIVING LEGACY ACKNOWLEDGES THAT EVERYTHING WE DO, EVERY DECISION WE MAKE AND EVERY INTERACTION WE HAVE, CREATES A LEGACY.

We can make a conscious decision to make this way of life part of our very being. Building day by day, with the understanding that legacies are alive and being generated, reinforced or changed in ourselves and in the world, in every moment of every day. When we see that legacies aren't what happens when we die but are the consequences of how we live right now, we can shift into a whole new level of possibility. We can choose to stop perpetuating the old legacy burdens of the past by living in fear and disconnection. Instead, we can start the revolutionary process. In this way, our Living Legacies become the collective antidote to our permacrisis and the blueprint for building the Beloved Community.

WHEN INNER PURPOSE MEETS OUTER PURPOSE

As the four of us have developed new Living Legacies of love and connection, we came upon a framing that has helped us all in this process. It begins with aligning our "Inner Purpose" with our "Outer Purpose." These are two powerful expressions of purpose that help us in our ability to live new legacies of love and connection that the Beloved Community beckons from us.

Inner Purpose means becoming the best versions of ourselves. We discuss this concept in the coming chapters, but for now, the key component of Inner Purpose is living in alignment with your mental, physical, spiritual and emotional well-being. With these four areas of your life, you have the recipe for cultivating the self-love and self-connection that are the fundamentals of Living Legacy. You can connect with who you truly are and what you deeply care about.

We say it begins with Inner Purpose because the only way we can live new legacies of love and connection is to come from a place of health, wholeness and love for ourselves and what we truly care about. It's not a new concept, but it's hugely applicable to Living Legacy: You can't love others if you can't love yourself. You can't connect with others if you can't connect with yourself.

Outer Purpose means contributing to something greater than ourselves. It means fostering connection and contribution to others and the world—to your family, friends, community and the world itself. From a place of self-love and self-connection we move outward and live every day in every way in service to love and connection. With these four areas of your life, you can meaningfully connect with others and the world around you. The external connection derived from Outer Purpose, in turn, fosters greater internal connection through Inner Purpose, and the cycle of positive reinforcement continues.

In the pages to come, we will explore how to better define and live your Inner Purpose and Outer Purpose every day. You will notice, though, that throughout this book we will say Inner Purpose and Outer Purpose separately, rather than joining them as Inner and Outer Purpose. We carefully create this delineation because we see them as equally important and yet separate aspects of purpose to actualize for ourselves. However, aligning them—so they are not in conflict but rather support each other—is the scaffolding of Living Legacy.

LIVING LEGACY WITH THE KING FAMILY

One of the ways we can show you how Living Legacy works in alignment with Inner Purpose and Outer Purpose is by viewing it through the legendary lives of the King family.

For the Kings, Living Legacy is in the bloodline. When the four of us began our deep conversations about the concept, we all realized that Martin's parents each embodied the profound philosophy behind Living Legacy. Dr. Martin Luther King Jr. and Coretta Scott King lived with the Inner Purpose of boundless love, committed to nonviolence in the face of hate, working to build the Beloved Community despite inheriting hostile legacies. They each channeled their Inner Purpose into an Outer Purpose greater than themselves, making a profound impact through their work and faith. They lived this way not because they wanted to be in the history books but because they were living their core values. Ultimately, their alignment with Inner Purpose and Outer Purpose infused their lives with the greatest unconditional love of all—their love of God.

For Martin's father, an early incident shaped his understanding of racism and sowed the seeds of activism. When Dr. King was three years old, he had a white playmate whose dad owned the store across the street from the King home in Atlanta. The boys played together often until both turned six and entered different schools. Dr. King had to attend a school for Black children, while his friend went to a school for white children. Soon afterward, the parents of the white boy stopped allowing Dr. King to play with their son, telling him, "We are white, and you are colored."[30] For the first time, Dr. King's parents explained the history of slavery and racism in America, including discrimination they'd experienced personally. Dr. King would later state that he was determined to hate every white person, even though his parents told him it was his Christian duty to love everyone.

The legacies at work here are the collective legacy of racism, fear and disconnection that Dr. King inherited, as well as the familial legacy of values passed on from his father—the conviction to love in response to hate. Here we have the origins of Dr. King's Inner Purpose, commitment to love all of humanity, which he ultimately aligned with his Outer Purpose, profound activism. Let's be clear, that doesn't mean it was easy for Dr. King to love the enforcers of segregation. He said he could never get used to the separate waiting rooms, separate eating places and separate restrooms because "the very idea of separation did something to my sense of dignity and self-respect."[31]

Raising a Daughter and Guiding a Granddaughter

Arndrea Waters King

My daughter, Yolanda, and I landed in Boston after 1:00 a.m. on January 13, 2023, mere hours before *The Embrace* monument was to be unveiled in honor of her grandparents. Martin, who was already in the city, met us at the airport. It was foggy and damp. Christmas lights still twinkled throughout the city. We were all exhausted but so excited to celebrate Dr. Martin Luther King Jr. and Coretta Scott King's love and contributions, which changed all American lives for the better. On a whim, I asked our driver if we could pass by Boston Common to get a first glimpse.

As we passed 1965 Freedom Plaza, where the monument rests, I lowered the car window. Through an envelope of mist, I was struck by its immense size. It was one thing to see the conceptual drawings, another thing entirely to behold this country's largest public sculpture dedicated to Black love and racial equality.

While the world knows Yolanda's grandparents as iconic civil rights activists from the South, this monument resides in Boston, where they met and fell in love. Dr. King was a doctoral student in theology at Boston University. Coretta Scott was studying at the New England Conservatory of Music, paying for her room and board by working as a maid. The Boston monument represents the arms, shoulders and hands of the two hugging after Dr. King won the Nobel Peace Prize in 1964—a moment special to the monument's creator, Black conceptual artist Hank Willis Thomas.

"Wow, it's magnificent," I remember saying to Martin as we drove slowly past. By then, Yolanda was slumped beside me, asleep. I looked at her with deep love, and mild apprehension. She'd have to wait until morning to view this tribute to the grandparents she never knew, grandparents she is reminded of—and guided by—every day of her life. And in the morning, the press would be recording her first impressions. It's such a blessing for her, as a teenager, to have this ever-expanding platform to speak out about gun violence, voters' rights, racism, poverty and so many other issues. And it carries a lot of responsibility.

As her mom, my most important job is to keep her grandparents' memory alive for her, their only granddaughter, and guide her through the many expectations that fall on her shoulders. No matter what else I accomplish in my life, I am fulfilling my purpose and living my legacy for her.

We're still figuring out how to juggle the many speaking requests that compete with Yolanda's desires to be a normal teenager, whether participating in a school play, taking music lessons or going on a class field trip. We don't want her to take the stage too often, too early, if it means missing out on a normal childhood. We also understand her childhood isn't normal. Not just because of who her grandparents were but also because of the person she is.

All of us should be known for what we uniquely have to offer.

Yolanda first spoke publicly at March for Our Lives in Washington in 2019 to support the grieving youth of Parkland, Florida, after a mass shooting at a city high school.[103] That day, her speech demanded gun control, and she has since taken to public speaking with a passion. It's bred in the bone. Many who have heard her speak say she has a gift. She's also had the opportunity to see many young people speak out on causes they care about. I thank Craig and Marc for that.

When Yolanda was just five, she attended a youth empowerment event called WE Day, where twenty thousand students gathered to celebrate their year of volunteer service. These stadium-size live events were founded by Craig and Marc to teach and inspire young people to make an impact. She met incredible youths who'd volunteered for social justice and environmental protection and to stop homelessness. They spoke to thousands of their peers with boundless passion. Yolanda was mesmerized. And I remember her saying, "I want to do that." I should have realized that one day it would be Yolanda who was raising her voice.

When she was called on to speak in Boston in January 2023, Yolanda reminded those in attendance that *The Embrace* is about love. She suggested it be renamed *Love: 360* because when you step inside the embrace, you are surrounded by her grandparents' devotion and passion. Martin and I were proud of her interpretation. As Martin reflected recently to me, "Yolanda does a lot of analysis, asks a lot of questions, and often comes up with profound insights. She doesn't just accept anything at face value. She wants to know the full evolution of an idea or situation. Her conclusions are her own."

After Yolanda spoke, Congresswoman Ayanna Pressley (Massachusetts's Seventh District) took the podium and told Yolanda: "I was going to say if you lived in Boston, you might be coming for my seat, but I think you might skip Congress altogether and head straight for the White House."[104]

It's unnerving when people tout your teen daughter as destined for the White House. I don't want to be overly protective, but I also want to protect her. That's my instinct. No matter what Yolanda ends up doing, I want to make sure that she understands the many dimensions of the King legacy. I mean this as a Black woman, a mother and an activist, and having been close to Martin's mom. I put my heart and soul into making sure we raise her with loving-kindness and a sense of history. But I also decided early on not to let it overwhelm her life. Being the descendant of someone famous shouldn't be what makes her interesting or special, nor should she be impaired by it. All of us should be known for what we uniquely have to offer by answering the questions: What is my purpose? Who am I? Am I a good person? What is my Living Legacy?

I know Yolanda will answer with power and grace.

Dr. King attended seminary school, where he encountered Mahatma Gandhi's teachings and campaigns of nonviolent resistance for the first time. Before this, Dr. King had stated the only way to solve the problem of segregation was an armed revolt. But the concept of satyagraha, translated from Hindi as "love force," influenced him to see another way forward. This became a guiding principle of his life and a key part of his Inner Purpose. He found strength and moral clarity in his commitment to embody love.

Dr. King also embraced Gandhi's legacy of nonviolent resistance as a political and social tool. This became a key aspect of his Outer Purpose: he chose a path of activism to make things right while refusing to participate in the wrong. Dr. King aligned his Inner Purpose with his Outer Purpose in service to love, nonviolence and connection. And in doing so, Dr. King laid the foundation for his Living Legacy, which he lived and breathed every day until the day he was taken from us.

In the years that followed, Dr. King went on to lead numerous targeted, nonviolent resistance efforts against Jim Crow laws. Among them was the Montgomery Bus Boycott, a civil rights protest during which African Americans refused to ride city buses in Montgomery, Alabama, to protest segregated seating. Though the movement is often credited to Dr. King, he built upon organized political resistance already brewing in Montgomery. Black women founded the Women's Political Council (WPC) in 1946 and had been lobbying the city to improve conditions on city buses for decades. A local chapter of the NAACP was also active. Four days before the boycott, Rosa Parks was arrested and fined for refusing to yield her bus seat to a white man. And though she wasn't the first to stand her ground against the racist law, community activists, including the leaders of WPC and the local NAACP, saw an opportunity to galvanize folks around her arrest.[32]

Dr. King had recently moved to the city and was only twenty-six years old when he was asked to lead the Montgomery Improvement Association, which initiated the official boycott and legal challenge to segregated buses. It lasted more than a year—from December 5, 1955, to December 20, 1956—and is regarded as the first large-scale US demonstration against segregation. The bus boycott showed the potential for nonviolent mass protests to successfully challenge racial segregation. The US Supreme Court ultimately ordered Montgomery to integrate its transit system, while Dr. King emerged as a leading figure in the civil rights movement.

It was among the first public actions that defined his iconic legacy—but these actions were not for the sake of gaining fame or the dictionary definition of legacy. They were taken to fulfill his Inner Purpose of profound ethical, moral and spiritual beliefs in the hopes of healing the legacy burdens of racism. They were done by Dr. King aligning his Inner Purpose and Outer Purpose in service to love, nonviolence and connection. They were done in the spirit of living new legacies for America to find its way to the Beloved Community. Dr. King lived each day in defiance of racism and violence, legacies of disconnection. He took a different path forward, responding to the crisis he inherited by changing his relationship with himself (his mindset and instinct to hate his oppressors) and with others, as a mobilizer in the civil rights movement. He also upheld the legacies of Rosa Parks and local activist groups. Everyone involved played a part in changing the course of history through Living Legacy.

The civil rights movement recognized the importance of both Inner Purpose and Outer Purpose. We all know the Outer

Purpose aspects of the movement: marches, protests and grass-roots organizations. However, the movement recognized the need for a strong Inner Purpose, as manifested most evidently by the creation of Freedom Schools and training to prepare participants for nonviolent civil disobedience. For example, before participants could take part in lunch counter sit-ins or potentially volatile acts of civil disobedience, they were trained in the philosophy and mental mindset of nonviolence. Senior leaders in the movement would initiate the novices through role-playing by hurling insults at them, pouring water over their heads, even kicking and dragging them, to prepare them to maintain their steadfast mental commitment to nonviolence, no matter the provocation. Participants were taught to draw mental strength from their connections to each other, their faith or higher principles of the movement.

HE CHOSE A PATH OF ACTIVISM TO MAKE THINGS RIGHT WHILE REFUSING TO PARTICIPATE IN THE WRONG.

Coretta Scott King embodied her commitment to Inner Purpose and Outer Purpose through her family, her faith and the civil rights movement. She saw her husband become a symbol, not because he chose to be, but because he said "the zeitgeist" put him there.[33] He called it a divine dimension, stating, "Leaders do not ask for the task but are tracked down by the spirit of the times until it consumes them."[34]

Living a Legacy Beyond the Field

Pete Carroll

I've had the privilege of meeting many inspiring young people over the years, and I'd like to tell you about a few of them, starting with a young man named Damond Collier.

During the early 2000s, I spent significant time with local gang members, law enforcement and intervention workers in the inner-city areas of South Central Los Angeles. My goal was to bridge the divide, foster connections and promote understanding among disparate groups. I sought to understand the deep-rooted societal issues plaguing these neighborhoods and create a space for open dialogue, empathy and reconciliation.

I remember meeting Damond, a single father who had spent seven years in prison, at his house. After his release in 2007, he returned to his old gang life. It was clear to me that he just needed a chance and for someone to believe in him. I told him to meet me at the University of Southern California (USC) early the next morning, where I was coaching at the time, and promised him a job. Damond seized the opportunity and absorbed everything he could. Eventually, he founded his own organization, Pride in Unity, which uses the arts to reach people in his neighborhood. Damond's story is just one example of the transformative power of compassion, empathy and belief in the inherent goodness that resides within us all.

Similar to many parts of our country, South Central LA is a complex tapestry, and anyone seeking to help must start by listening, engaging in meaningful conversations with local gang members, building relationships with law enforcement officers and collaborating with dedicated intervention workers. Through these interactions, I gained invaluable insights into the systemic challenges faced by these communities and the factors contributing to gang involvement.

By facilitating dialogue and promoting mutual understanding, we were able to cultivate trust, promote peace and create opportunities for growth within the inner-city areas of South Central LA.

I have also had the opportunity to learn from inspiring young people from communities across Seattle through the A Better Seattle initiative, which focused on preventing youth and gang violence, as well as through my involvement with WE Day Seattle, an event that filled stadiums with young people who had earned their tickets through community service.

When it came to coaching, the talented athletes I have had the honor of working with over the years taught me so much about dedication and resilience, both on and off the field. It is impossible to separate the athlete from the human being, which is why a holistic approach to development is so important. A player's overall well-being has a direct impact on their on-field performance.

It took legendary University of California, Los Angeles, basketball coach John Wooden sixteen years to develop his personal philosophy. Wooden's book *Wooden: A Lifetime of Observations and Reflections On and Off the Court* significantly influenced the development of my coaching philosophy, "Always Compete." It's all about pushing oneself to the limits and fostering a culture of excellence within the team, both on the field and off.

If there's one message to take away from my experiences, it is to always strive to see the best in others, especially young people. You can become a mentor to youth in your community: a sports coach, a volunteer with service organizations such as Big Brothers Big Sisters, a youth pastor or simply a friend to youth in your neighborhood. You might be amazed at how much someone can achieve with your enthusiastic support and encouragement.

Pete Carroll spent fourteen years as head coach and executive vice president of the NFL's Seattle Seahawks, leading them to Super Bowl victory in 2014. Carroll also had a successful tenure as head coach at USC, winning two national championships. He is celebrated for his focus on competition, teamwork and developing players both on and off the field.

Coretta was a civil rights activist at Antioch College in Ohio before she met her future husband while attending the New England Conservatory of Music in Boston. Once she became Mrs. King, she devoted herself to his mission, even in the face of death threats and violence. During the Montgomery Bus Boycott, the King home was bombed while Coretta was inside with their ten-week-old first child, Yolanda, and a neighbor. Fortunately, no one was injured, but the dangers of Dr. King's calling were already clear. They contemplated a move, and it was Coretta's decision to stay, a challenge among many tests of their commitment to the cause and to nonviolence. She always knew she was married to a martyr, writing that her husband, like the biblical prophets, would most likely have a tragic end.[35] Why did she risk her life? She tells us in her autobiography: for the movement. She was driven by her unconditional love of God.

Though she didn't use the term, the civil rights movement was Coretta's Living Legacy, entwined with her husband's. When Coretta questioned how she would compartmentalize herself for her many roles and responsibilities, she seemed to be wrestling with the many aspects of her legacy's Outer Purpose as a mother, concert singer, public speaker and Dr. King's wife: "there was no map or guidebook . . . I had to live life and believe that God would define me and shape me for my purpose."[36] Thus, she relied on her Inner Purpose to guide her Outer Purpose.

Ultimately, Coretta gave up her career as a concert singer and made many more personal sacrifices. Coretta is an unsung hero of the civil rights movement. Like many Black women, she is a leader, often without recognition or reward, entangled in the twin legacy burdens of racism and the patriarchy. In her speeches, Coretta often quoted the Book of Esther in the Old Testament—"If I perish, I perish"—a passage about divine love over mortal will.[37] Still, she viewed her role as empowering, not subservient. No one would call her a cowering wife, particularly in the 1950s and '60s.

Coretta is proof that connecting with the highest forms of love can grow our sense of meaning beyond the self. When our Inner Purpose—for Coretta, this was the will of God—is aligned with our Outer Purpose, the greater world can be positively shaped by our connections to family, faith, community and the legacies of those who came before us. After Dr. King's assassination, Coretta understood that she was a symbol and her destiny was "a commitment even larger than Martin's." She knew she needed to "keep [her] husband's mission alive and institutionaliz[e] his legacy."[38] If it weren't for Coretta, who lobbied all one hundred US senators and many congressional representatives, we would not have the King holiday, signed into law by President Ronald Reagan in 1983 and first observed in January 1986. It took her twenty years to win this recognition for her late husband. She called it the most challenging thing she ever accomplished.

CONNECTING WITH THE HIGHEST FORMS OF LOVE CAN GROW OUR SENSE OF MEANING BEYOND THE SELF.

Coretta was among the first to instinctively understand how her own Living Legacy (as a mother, wife and activist) was entwined with the King family, as well as the collective legacy of racism and disconnection. She also dismissed the traditional dictionary definition of legacy, understanding that her legacy was bigger than herself. She did not want an "enduring post-mortem reputation," though she has one. She wanted to devote herself to something bigger. God and the civil rights movement called to her: "To discover what you're called to do with your life, I believe you have to be connected to God, to that divine force in your life, and that you have to continue to pray for direction. I did that. . . . I had a divine calling on my life, a charge, a challenge to serve not just black people, but all oppressed humankind."[39]

HOW THE KING LIVING LEGACY CONTINUES

Martin and Arndrea hold and honor the King family's Living Legacies and recognize they are inside of them and guide them each and every day. But even as they carry the King family's Living Legacies within them, Martin and Arndrea live their unique legacies in very personal ways that are relevant now. They don't live in the past or try to wedge the past into the present. They are inspired by what they inherited from the King family legacy, but they use it to support and live their own unique Inner Purposes and Outer Purposes.

For Martin and Arndrea, inclusion, equal rights and safety for all have been defining pillars of their Inner Purpose. To sit with them for even a few minutes, you will immediately sense their commitment to kindness and wanting everyone in their presence to feel at ease, accepted and respected—no matter your skin color, who you love, what political party you follow or your socioeconomic status. Marc and Craig spend time in their home in Atlanta and travel with them extensively, and they always marvel at how every person Martin and Arndrea encounter is treated to the same glow of warmth and acceptance.

So it is not surprising how much their Outer Purposes are aligned with their Inner Purposes. In this way, Martin's Living

Legacy has been as a human rights leader, motivational speaker and teacher of nonviolence and conflict resolution on all the continents except Antarctica. However, one specific example of Martin aligning his Inner Purpose of inclusion and safety for all with his Outer Purpose was in his home state of Georgia. While he was the elected leader of the Southern Christian Leadership Conference, Martin initiated a campaign to change the Georgia state flag, which then carried the emblem of the Confederate flag—literally covering half the state flag. His insistence that the Confederacy be removed from the state flag was not a popular stance, and Martin received death threats for his position. Even civil rights leaders gave him pushback, telling him it was just a symbol, but Martin remained firm and relentless in his campaign. He felt certain it was wrong for a state flag—a representation of the state's people and governing values—to uphold an emblem of the Confederacy: a symbol that was directly linked to the legacy of slavery and had hurt and continued to oppress so many Black Americans. It took years, but with the help of Governor Roy Barnes, the emblem was ultimately removed from the state flag of Georgia in 2001.

When Arndrea worked for the Center for Democratic Renewal (CDR), one of her main goals was to help the state of Georgia adopt legislation that protected people from hate crimes, aligning her Inner Purpose of love and nonviolence with her Outer Purpose of securing legal protections for all people. Initially, when she began lobbying legislators to adopt a hate crimes protection bill, she was told, "We don't have hate crimes here in Georgia." Arndrea saw the unfairness of this—the way people who suffer from legacy burdens, especially acts of hate and violence, often have the onus of proving the burden. But Arndrea did what she always does when there's work to do—she pushed up her sleeves and got it done.

Reflections on Reciprocal Altruism and Our Shared Humanity

Dr. Sanjay Gupta, as told to Shelley Page

In contemplating my Living Legacy, I find solace in the intricate interplay of my three identities—each intertwining to create the fabric of reciprocal altruism. As a doctor, my hands extend beyond healing; they cradle lives, nurturing individuals toward their best existence. As a journalist, I wield words as tools, asking, "How can I craft narratives that serve the collective good?" And as an individual—a husband and father to three remarkable daughters—I nurture our family's actions to create positive change.

Reciprocal altruism is the delicate balance between selflessness and self-preservation and is our best chance for humanity's survival. It defies the Darwinian dogma of "survival of the fittest." Instead, it suggests that our brains harbor a deeper impulse—a yearning to care for one another.

My first love and primary job is being a neuroscientist. From a scientific perspective, we would believe we are all programmed to live a life defined by looking out for number one, but that isn't the case. Societies that have thrived have been societies that cared about each other. The idea that our brains somehow predispose us toward wanting to care for other individuals is mysterious but hopeful. Perhaps it's rooted in our primal survival, transcending mere individualism.

As a journalist, I've covered almost every conflict and natural disaster in the world in recent decades, from wars in Afghanistan and Iraq to Hurricane Katrina, the 2010 earthquake in Haiti and the 2011 famine in Somalia to the ongoing humanitarian catastrophe in Gaza. People often ask me how I do it and how I keep showing up to these tragic moments in history. I have seen people profoundly suffering, and it has left me feeling deeply wounded and powerless. But through them, I've learned something about the untapped capacity of humans to help others. People rise up all the time. And frequently, these are the same people who, a week earlier, might have said they'd never help out if something terrible were to happen. Being in the presence of these everyday heroes is deeply inspiring.

It also feels good to do good. I know this to be true because I feel it in my bones. I feel good when I am in service to others. Some of the moments of greatest joy for me and my family are when we are in service to others. As a family, we look at the injustices in the world and where we can make a difference. Childhood hunger is important to us. It's unacceptable that 12 percent of American children go to bed hungry while 40 percent of the food in our country goes to waste. My family comes together to support charities that tackle hunger.

Through all this, I remember the importance of connection—the invisible thread binding us. During my grueling neurosurgery residency—110-hour weeks, head bowed at a microscope—I realized that contentment blooms in shared endeavors. Moments of true joy emerge when we collaborate.

Reciprocal altruism isn't a lofty ideal; it's a practical path toward a better future—one where compassion, cooperation and shared responsibility prevail. We can all be everyday heroes, shaping a legacy that transcends our individual lives and echoes through generations.

Dr. Sanjay Gupta is the multiple Emmy Award–winning chief medical correspondent for CNN, host of the CNN podcast Chasing Life, *associate chief of neurosurgery at Grady Memorial Hospital and an associate professor at Emory University Hospital in Atlanta. He has covered some of the most important health stories in the US and around the world.*

The work took almost two years, and it was grueling—she had to investigate and record crimes of hate all over the state. She was only in her twenties, documenting evidence of murders, cross burnings, horrible assaults, vandalism of gay bars, hate flyers being distributed and other atrocities. She had to gather witnesses to testify before the legislature. Ultimately, despite the evidence that showed a clear need for protection, the legislature did not adopt any hate crime legislation during her tenure at the CDR. But the documentation was there and the pressure on the legislature that began then did not end then. Sadly, it wasn't until Ahmaud Arbery was chased down and killed by white men while he was innocently jogging in Glynn County, Georgia, that the state legislature finally adopted a hate crimes protection bill in 2020.[40] By then the pressure to identify and prosecute hate crimes had been ongoing for decades, and the legislature was able to agree and act swiftly.

The King family had been pondering and living the philosophical concept now described as Living Legacy for some time, though they hadn't yet named it. This changed when we all came together to write this book. Martin and Arndrea both recognized they are stewards of a family legacy so entwined with world history that, at times, it can be overwhelming. But they've chosen to live that legacy in ways that are current but also led by a commitment to love and connection. In this light, they recognize that Living Legacies don't have to be iconic—they just have to represent the essence of who we are, what we choose to carry forward from our inheritances, and what we create in our own lives and the world.

Because of the ripple effects of her parents' Living Legacies, along with all the others who helped manifest these changes, their daughter, Yolanda, can grow up in a state with legislation to protect its people from hate crimes and without the Confederacy as its symbol. Martin and Arndrea are now teaching Yolanda to carve her own place within the outsize legacies she has inherited—to choose what she keeps and leaves behind, and to live that legacy for herself and others.

HELPING THE WORLD LIVE NEW LEGACIES

Craig didn't think much about legacy when he started a children's charity. He just wanted to end child labor and slavery, a knee-jerk reaction to injustice that proved naive (he was only twelve, after all). Still, both brothers grieved their old lives and careers when the charity they'd built over twenty-five years was attacked. Slowly, Marc and Craig came to a critical understanding. They hadn't lost a legacy—they were still living one. Their legacy was alive in the people they'd empowered and inspired and in the tens of thousands of Living Legacies they'd helped construct.

The singer Selena Gomez is one of those people. She traveled with Craig to Kenya's Maasai Mara in 2019, along with some of her closest friends, for a brief escape from the hustle and pressure of fame. Selena had been open about her mental health journey, revealing her anxiety, depression and bipolar diagnoses in press interviews.[41] Growing up in the bubble of child stardom, once the most-followed woman on Instagram and one of Justin Bieber's most famous ex-girlfriends, the things she was known for were largely outside her control. Fame is among the most obvious trappings of old legacy, a persona constructed publicly, by others. Selena visited the charity's projects one summer because she longed to do something else. She was actively looking for self-love, connection and purpose. She wanted to define herself on her own terms.

On campus at the local girls' high school in the Mara, Selena and the students swapped stories and she told them about her unconventional education—Selena was homeschooled on the set of a TV show. Off campus, Selena carried river water with the Maasai Mamas to their homes for cooking and cleaning, later sitting under the shade of acacia trees to rest. Then, one evening over dinner, cicadas chirping in the dark outside their gazebo, Selena shared her reflections with Craig.

She felt compelled to give back but didn't know where to start. Fans sent her messages almost daily, asking for help. She didn't know where to send them and felt powerless. She wanted kids like her to feel less alone. She wanted mental health support in schools. Children discuss their feelings openly, she said, but stop when they get older, just as those feelings become more complex. But what could she do about it? She was a singer, not a teacher.

Craig listened to one of the world's biggest pop stars, with massive wealth and endless resources at her disposal, talk about all the things she couldn't do. Fear seemed to stifle her profound abilities and her desire for fulfillment. Craig asked what he thought was a simple question: "What's holding you back?" Selena started to cry, listing more of her insecurities, saying she wasn't capable of such an undertaking. "The very thing that makes you feel that is why you can relate to others," Craig told her. "This is why you are the perfect person." Parts of the emotional exchange were caught on camera, in Selena's 2022 documentary, *My Mind & Me.*[42]

Essentially, Craig reminded Selena that everything she's endured is also part of her. She is more than a singer; she is a role model, equipped to help others by drawing on her own experience. Her authenticity and vulnerability are part of what her fans love about her, and part of what makes her who she is. Craig was coaching Selena in her Living Legacy. He helped her name and have confidence in her Inner Purpose—deepening the practices she used to care for her own mental well-being—and connect with a higher purpose in her daily actions. And similarly, she identified her Outer Purpose: wanting to help young people learn about mental health issues so they were less alone, like she had been, in their struggles. From there, he encouraged her to align her Inner Purpose with her Outer Purpose: A year after she visited the Mara, Selena launched her #MentalHealth101 education and advocacy initiative. Funded through her Rare Beauty social good program, Rare Impact, this school initiative and its lasting impact is part of her Living Legacy, something that has brought her fulfillment through connection.

CRAIG ASKED WHAT HE THOUGHT WAS A SIMPLE QUESTION: "WHAT'S HOLDING YOU BACK?"

Marc and Craig spent decades following their own philanthropic passion to realize that all of those experiences, successes, setbacks and learnings revealed their true life calling of helping others live their legacies of impact. They've helped people, from Selena Gomez to schoolteachers to parents, construct the scaffolding to support Living Legacies that have not only brought many the fulfillment they yearned for, but are also pulsating through the world right now as lasting emissaries of love and connection.

In a way, Marc and Craig have always been legacy architects. Before Marc and Craig talked about Living Legacy, they talked about making the biggest impact. The effect was similar, but Legacy+ is even bigger. Their blueprint for Living Legacy encourages people to think beyond what happens when they die and to shift their mindset and live every day in contribution to family, community and the world around them. Living Legacy is tied partly to service to others while at the same time connecting to yourself. Philanthropy and donations will always be welcome and necessary, but aligning the essence of yourself by devoting your time, effort and purpose to a cause that fosters love and connection—that is Living Legacy.

EMBRACING LIVING LEGACY

Celebrity pop stars and activist icons are humbling role models. You may not have millions at your disposal. You may not feel called by God, like Coretta, to put your life in danger. These extreme examples illustrate the most profound effects of Living Legacy. It's important to remember that when legacy manifests in daily actions and choices, those choices, by nature, are both big and small. Living Legacy is not about mighty deeds or impressive monuments; it's about daily actions that nurture greater connection.

When you live your legacy through a set of daily habits that align with your core values, your sense of self comes from within. This is so important, we are going to say this again because we want you to truly consider what we are sharing with you. *When you live your legacy through a set of daily habits that align with your core values, your sense of self comes from within.*

That's because Living Legacy is like a prism or filter, distilling what is most important to create fulfillment and achieve self-love. It cuts through the noise. Living Legacy is self-fulfilling, but it is not about any one individual; it's about our collective goal to build the Beloved Community.

Arndrea likes to say, "You don't have to wait for leaders." Do it alone. Person to person, as Mother Teresa encouraged us. Arndrea suggests we start by highlighting the love and beauty within and without.

The root of the word "legacy" is the Latin verb *legare*, which means "to appoint by a last will, send as an ambassador" or "envoy."[43] Throughout history, this meaning of the word morphed to mean bestowing gifts or leaving wealth, fueling the perception that legacy is reserved for the rich. Living Legacy returns to the root meaning of the word, making us envoys in our daily actions, traveling the path to connection and fulfillment—the very things old legacy tries in vain to establish. With the legacies you've inherited, you are an ambassador for those who came before you. You decide what to carry on and what to leave behind. You are not just an ambassador for future generations but someone who can bestow new legacies on those who will follow to help reach a state of profound love. You can be an ambassador for the Beloved Community. *You* are the antidote to the permacrisis.

CHAPTER 5

Yearning for Fulfillment, Connection and Love

AS LIVING LEGACY AMBASSADORS, OUR mission has a clear directive. We consciously connect with ourselves, others and the world. We do this by living our Inner Purpose (how we become our best version of ourselves) and applying that to our Outer Purpose (how we contribute to something larger than ourselves). The fuel that ignites our capacity to build this connection within us and all around us is love—love for self and love for the world. The outcome, we believe, creates the foundation for the Beloved Community.

Here we want to dive into another outcome of Living Legacy. Specifically, how it elevates your individual life as well as the health of the world. It turns out that Living Legacy is the pathway to finding one of the most sought-after and elusive states of being. A destination we all seek, but often find hard to reach.

Our dear friend Dr. David Baum tells a story of an important journey he took many years ago. He was in search of . . . more. Inspired by the Beatles' pilgrimage in the sixties, David traveled halfway around the world to India. This was before he earned his doctorates in both divinity and psychology and became a respected guide and mentor to many, including the four of us. Then, he was seeking the secret to the meaning of life and hoped he'd find a guru or uncover a profound insight that would help him achieve nirvana.

David stayed in an ashram for weeks, following a strict program of waking up before dawn, daily yoga and meditation, and a diet of vegetarian food, hoping to find a true state of happiness. It never came. In the end, David was a tad more flexible and a few pounds lighter.

Disappointed that he had not found the greater spiritual connection he sought, he checked out of the ashram and decided to become a tourist.

A taxi driver dropped David off near an old temple he wanted to visit. He dodged cows in the streets and their droppings—which looked like steaming landmines—tuk-tuks, hand-pulled carts and motorbikes. When he made it to the temple entrance, David looked up to see what was ahead of him. It was then his eyes locked with those of another man, whom David describes as "the poorest human" he had ever seen.

The man appeared to have leprosy. He walked on his hands. Parts of his feet and nose were missing. He wore a filthy red loincloth that barely covered his ravaged body. His only possession was a dirty wooden begging bowl. David looked away and then, after a few seconds, looked back again. Their eyes locked once more. The beggar gestured to David to bend down and, in a loud, upbeat voice, asked: "Are you happy?"

David muttered a confused response: "Sorry, excuse me?"

Smiling, the beggar again asked: "Are you happy?"

David thought about what was being asked of him. He looked the man straight in the eye and said, "Yes. Yes, I am happy."

The beggar looked up at David and replied, "Good. Me too!" He again smiled at David and dragged himself away.

For David, this simple interaction was one of the most profound of his life. On his worst days, he holds in his heart the perspective he gained that day. He believes this simple conversation was the reason he traveled to India. On the last day of his trip, he was given the gift he was seeking.

In relating the story of the beggar on the steps to us, David spoke about this interaction and the deeper meaning of this story. The question the beggar asked him was not whether David was happy at that particular moment but whether David was happy with his life. In other words, was David fulfilled? What he also understood was that fulfillment isn't reliant on external conditions or even on physical ease. It isn't something we find outside ourselves, though culture always tries to sell it to us. Fulfillment is possible for anyone—it comes from within us. And it radiates outward from there.

There is an innate human yearning for the glow of fulfillment David encountered in India. But often, we're just not sure how to find it within ourselves. We have come to believe that Living Legacy unlocks the key to fulfillment by showing us how to live every day in connection with ourselves, others and the world. While love helps drive connection, love is also reinforced by connection.

WHAT'S HAPPINESS GOT TO DO WITH IT? REALLY?

If we believe what we read, happiness is our highest goal; it's what we need to make life worth living. Social science researchers are constantly measuring our happiness levels and trying to help us find more of it. In 2011, the Organisation for Economic Co-operation and Development (OECD) released its first well-being report on member countries.[44] In 2012, the United Nations began releasing its annual World Happiness Report (which consistently ranks Finland at the top).[45]

A Life of Giving and Pursuing Passions

Julia Roberts

The friendship and generosity that Dr. Martin Luther King Jr. and Coretta Scott King extended to me when I was brand new to the world were profound. The King children attended my parents' theatre school, the Actors and Writers Workshop, and our families became friends. My parents could not afford the hospital bill when I was born, so Dr. Martin Luther King Jr. and Coretta Scott King helped us out of a jam. It's no wonder that I have a deep sense of joy and gratitude with a kickoff like that.

I was always raised to believe in giving. Whatever one has is to be openly shared. This could be time, money, cooking a meal or simply listening to someone in need. Growing up, these values were more than just taught; they were lived every day in our household.

> ## Life is a beautiful blend of giving and receiving, of supporting and being supported.

Looking back on my career, I sincerely appreciate that it was well established by the time we started our family. This afforded me the precious opportunity to nurture and luxuriate in the baby years, a luxury I was always aware my mother did not get to experience. She worked a full-time job with only a small window of time off for maternity leave. Watching her manage it all instilled in me a deep respect for the balance she maintained and a desire to prioritize family when my time came.

As our children have grown, maintaining this balance has presented its own set of challenges and rewards. I remember a profound moment of realization when I understood that while I have a responsibility to be at home with my family, I also have a duty to show them the importance of my creative life outside the home.

In 2021, emerging from the Covid lockdowns and returning to a semblance of normalcy, I found myself in a unique situation. Three roles I was interested in—Martha Mitchell in *Gaslit*, Georgia Cotton in *Ticket to Paradise* and Amanda Sandford in *Leave the World Behind*—were all coming together at the same time, presenting me with a workload that would last consistently for over a year. Times like these make you feel incredibly fortunate for the work opportunities and allow you to see the level of love and support your family provides.

Not only did my husband and children completely back me in these endeavors, but they were also there for me in ways we had never needed before. It was a beautiful experience, a true blessing to feel the strength of our love for one another. The bliss of working hard was deeply enriched by the love and support of my family, making the time together and the time apart meaningful.

In the end, I hope to pass on to my children the understanding that it is possible to pursue your passions while nurturing the ones you love. Life is a beautiful blend of giving and receiving, of supporting and being supported. And to me, these are true tenets to be guided by in life.

Julia Roberts is a wife, mother, activist, actor and curator of joy.

We got curious about the pursuit of happiness. Barnes & Noble lists more than eleven thousand book titles with the word "happiness"; Amazon boasts more than fifty thousand. In 2023, Arthur C. Brooks and Oprah Winfrey added to the impressive heap with *Build the Life You Want*, subtitled "The Art and Science of Getting Happier." And in *The Science of Happiness* (2024), psychologist and "happiness expert" Bruce Hood offers seven steps to breaking negative thought patterns and reconnecting with the things that really matter.

Yet, we're as depressed as ever. A third of American adults and more than half of British workers report symptoms of depression.[46] Even as a growing number of corporations employ "Chief Happiness Officers" in the hopes of turning workplace frowns upside down, almost eight in ten (77 percent) of employees sit somewhere between "disaffected and actively resentful," according to Gallup's latest study.[47] We're also lonelier than ever, as marked by the US surgeon general's campaign to tackle the epidemic of isolation.

EMOTIONS SUCH AS HAPPINESS AREN'T SUPPOSED TO LAST, AND THEY DON'T.

With more unhappiness and isolation than ever, Dr. Martin Luther King Jr. and Coretta Scott King's dream of creating the Beloved Community is more elusive. Sometimes, we collectively seem too far away from turning things around, but we believe that if we recalibrate our goals, we can reach the Beloved Community. Instead of searching for something fleeting like happiness, which often comes and goes depending on life's circumstances, we need to shape our Living Legacy toward the more lasting state of fulfillment.

Psychiatrist Dr. Gregory Scott Brown is the author of *The Self-Healing Mind*. Born to a Jamaican father and an African American mother, as a regular contributor to *Men's Health* magazine, he has written frequently about his mental health struggles and experience of racism. He has also spent a lot of time thinking about happiness and how to achieve it, because that's what his patients are often chasing. Dr. Brown says patients seek him out when they are unhappy with their work or personal lives, longing for a time they associate with happiness—the day they got married or graduated from college. "If I could just feel that way again, I would be happy," they tell him. But this hunt for happiness, he says, is a distraction from "what's really necessary for a better life—fulfillment."[48]

The problem, according to Dr. Brown, is that happiness is an emotion, not a state of being. Therefore, it's fleeting. Emotions such as happiness aren't supposed to last, and they don't. So seeking happiness is like "running after a moving target," he writes.[49]

Dr. Brown came to the realization that fulfillment was the most important state of being while he was working as a medical resident. He noticed some dying patients—despite age or diagnosis—"seemed to be more at peace than others." He found that some of them "could reflect fondly on their life and relationships" with a measure of gratitude and optimism.[50] They seemed fulfilled.

However, the question of whether someone is fulfilled and how to measure it is an area with limited research compared to happiness. We find this surprising considering that fulfillment is the state of being that so many of us seem to be seeking. However, when we were digging into this conversation, we discovered that

University of Zurich researchers Doris Baumann and professor Willibald Ruch in 2021 created a scale to measure people's fulfillment at different ages because "pursuing fulfillment is not a luxury, but essential for our mental health."[51] Writing for the World Economic Forum, Baumann asks, "Is the pursuit of a fulfilled life vanity, selfish, or a luxury? Quite the contrary, it is essential for humans not only to be free from mental illness but to thrive at all life stages." She also draws a distinction between happiness and fulfillment, as we do. "The latter is long-lasting and comes from deriving a sense of wholeness, from perceiving congruence, and from recognizing value regarding one's self, life, and impact," she writes, doubling down on the staying power of fulfillment.[52]

What we especially found noteworthy was her conclusion that fulfilled people are "able to develop and realize their full potential; become whole and complete, feel true to themselves, and lead authentic lives." So much of what we've come to understand about Living Legacy is how important it is to be anchored in connection with oneself, which we could also call being authentic.

NO ACTION IS TOO SMALL, AND WE CAN ALL MAKE A DIFFERENCE.

She also highlighted the exact reason why we believe Living Legacy can bring us the fulfillment we seek. "Fulfillment," she writes, "further involves the feeling that one's existence is significant and the ability to leave one's unique mark on this world and to contribute to others' well-being."[53]

Indeed, this belief that our lives matter is the foundation of our Living Legacy. Every decision, action and interaction we make leaves a legacy. We are certain that no action is too small, and we can all make a difference.

Like us, these researchers believe their scale to measure people's fulfillment could be used to spark reflections "on the kind of person they wish to become, the life they want to lead, and the legacy they hope to leave."[54] Which is exactly what we will be exploring in the coming pages.

We also discovered that this yearning for fulfillment is even shaking up staid investment houses that typically help clients build their nest eggs. For example, when Fidelity Investments studied the needs of their younger investors (meaning non-Boomers and non–Gen Xers), much to their surprise, the word "fulfillment" kept coming up. In fact, it was at the top of the heap of coveted goals. Millennial and Generation Z investors don't just want to grow their wealth, they want to make an impact and live a fulfilled life.[55] An impressive two-thirds of millennial and Generation Z investors want "planning, peace of mind, and fulfillment of their life goals" from their advisors.[56]

This was a surprise to many and prompted Fidelity to dramatically change how it serves its clients. Financial advisors must become life coaches to help their clients achieve fulfillment rather than simply focusing on money management and achieving financial goals. Fidelity defines fulfillment as "working toward the achievement of life's purpose and leaving a legacy."[57]

It seems to us that people who want fulfillment reflected in their investment accounts are really saying they want their lives to be aligned with their Inner Purpose and Outer Purpose—to live in connection with who they are and in congruence with what they truly value.

Marc has reflected on how his understanding of success has radically changed over the past few years as he realizes fulfillment is his goal. Before, success was the validation that came from external appreciation, which he had in abundance. But now it's about living in alignment with what is important to him: his values, work, family, community, spirituality and consciousness. He has come to finally understand what "success" is *really* all about.

All four of us have personally experienced the power of fulfillment in our lives. But it's also difficult to explain unless you have it. Once discovered, you feel this state deeply within you. It is an inner state that you never want to go away. It is a way of being—a perspective and a mindset all at once. It cannot be bought and must be nurtured over time.

So, how do you find fulfillment? We believe Living Legacy is the means—building on the connection and love we're so vigorously emphasizing. While the formula may sound straightforward, we recognize the mission isn't always easy to accomplish.

A LIFE OF LENGTH, BREADTH AND HEIGHT: THREE DIMENSIONS OF FULFILLMENT

The monument to Martin's father on the Washington Mall portrays a determined and purposeful Dr. King emerging from the stone. Like the stories told of his life, it suggests a man who entered public life fully formed and steadfast in his goals to live a life of deep meaning, purpose and fulfillment. The truth is that, just like any of us, Dr. King had to work hard to forge his path.

As a boy, he learned about the injustices facing Black Americans from his father, and he experienced them every time he was forced to walk past the empty seats at the front of a bus. Nevertheless, he did not set out from childhood with the purpose of fighting segregation or other social injustices. Nor was there a formal moment of revelation that called Dr. King into the unbending faith he would become known for. He was the son of a minister in a family strong in its religion, but as a college student, he questioned the fundamentalist doctrines he had been taught in Sunday school. He often questioned how "the facts of science could be squared with religion."[58]

He found his faith gradually after intense study of the Bible and voracious consumption of the ideas of many philosophers. Even then, after Martin's father left the seminary to earn his doctor of philosophy in systematic theology at Boston University, he was deeply torn between the quiet life of academia versus taking on an active pastoral role. After much consideration, he accepted a job as the minister for Dexter Avenue Baptist Church in Montgomery. That simple choice changed the course of his life and those of many others. As we recounted, the following year, in December 1955, civil rights activist Rosa Parks was arrested in Montgomery for refusing to give up her seat for a white man on the bus. Local leaders asked Dr. King to help organize the Montgomery Bus Boycott and then, to King's surprise, elected him leader of their new local civil rights organization.

The bus boycott was a defining moment for the US civil rights movement *and* in helping Dr. King figure out how to live his Inner Purpose aligned with his Outer Purpose. Throughout his short time on earth, he frequently explored in his sermons what an impactful life could and should look like, and he determined that the highest goal was to live a life of fulfillment.

At New Covenant Missionary Baptist Church in Chicago in April 1967, a year before his murder, he told parishioners that a life of fulfillment must have three dimensions: "length, breadth, and height."

Building a Legacy of Love and Acceptance Through Design

Bobby Berk

My journey with *Queer Eye* has been an incredible testament to my vision of creating a future where acceptance, love and inclusivity are at the forefront. When I joined the show, I already believed in the profound impact of design on mental health. But being a part of *Queer Eye* for eight seasons showed me just how impactful design could be for so many different people from so many varied walks of life. I realized the power I had been given and how I could use design to make someone feel good, bring them joy, and help them deal with loss, connect with their family, physically move around their space, or even make their daily life much easier.

One project that particularly stands out to me is Wesley Hamilton's home. Making his space wheelchair accessible was more than a renovation; it was about restoring his sense of independence and dignity. The relief and joy on his face when he saw his newly designed home were unforgettable. It brought tears to my eyes to realize I had a part in that and to know I was able to use my talents to improve lives and build a legacy of giving back to those who have given so much.

But my story starts long before *Queer Eye.* Growing up in a deeply religious community, I quickly learned that the church I belonged to was not a welcoming place for someone like me. It made me feel ashamed, and I wondered, *Why did God make me this way?* I was confused and felt like I had nowhere to turn, so I decided to leave the church and ultimately leave home.

That legacy and the pain associated with the church stuck with me for a very long time, but I never let it define me. Instead, I transformed my pain into a powerful motivator.

I'm dedicated to bringing the legacy that began on *Queer Eye* with me by carrying the mindset of acceptance, love and inclusivity to every project I work on. It's about using my platform to support organizations and individuals making a positive impact, making the world a more equitable and accepting place and truly showing up for the LQBTQIA+ community.

As an individual, the easiest way to build on that work is by showing empathy, acceptance and kindness to others. Think about how a small act can make someone's life a little easier or bring them happiness or hope. Treat people who are different from you with respect and take a stand when you see anyone being mistreated. Volunteer your time or be an advocate for others.

These actions can have a ripple effect in your family, your neighborhood and your community and contribute to building a legacy of leaving the world a better place.

Bobby Berk is an Emmy-winning design expert, TV host and author. He rose to prominence in 2018 for his work transforming lives and living spaces on Netflix's Queer Eye. *He has since established himself as a preeminent leader in the design industry. Berk leads his eponymous multifaceted brand with a design firm that has become one of the most sought-after in the homebuilding industry.*

To Dr. King, the length of life is "the inward concern for one's own welfare" that "causes one to push forward, to achieve his own goals and ambitions." He found fulfillment through this connection to himself. He defined the breadth of life as the "outward concern for the welfare of others," which brought him fulfillment by connecting him to his fellow man. And the height of life is "the upward reach for God," which expresses the profound interconnectedness he felt with humanity. He believed you had to "have all three of these to have a complete life."[59]

THE QUEST FOR FULFILLMENT IS THE ENGINE THAT GETS US OUT OF BED IN THE MORNING.

The way we interpret this is that a "complete life" is a fulfilled life with these three dimensions: inner connection (supported by our Inner Purpose), outer connection (supported by our Outer Purpose) and a reverence for the interconnectedness of all of life. The vehicle to find all three is love.

We hold his vision about living a fulfilled life in our hearts and invite you to do the same. The quest for fulfillment is the engine that gets us out of bed in the morning. It is the hand that lifts us up and pulls us along when the sky is black and the path rock strewn. Like Dr. King, we believe it is our higher calling, our guiding star on our path through life.

We've seen the quest to answer this higher calling in secular terms: "Why am I here?" Or religious terms: "Why did God put me on this earth?" As the popular saying goes, "The two most important days in your life are the day you are born and the day you find out why." We believe the answer to these questions is that we are here to love, we are here to reconnect, we are here to heal the legacies of disconnection and we are here to build the Beloved Community.

Dr. King's ultimate goal was reaching the Beloved Community. Ours too. What's standing in the way of building the Beloved Community is disconnection, largely stoked by fear and unfortunately aided by a lack of fulfillment in the lives of so many. If each of us understood what we're really searching for—fulfillment—and that a possible path to get there is Living Legacy, we would likely live our lives differently, focusing on a state of connection and love instead of being in a cycle of disconnection and fear.

BRIEF BUT MEANINGFUL JOURNEYS

Dr. Jessika Boles's work is important but also impossibly sad. She is an expert in how to honor the legacies of dying children. She shows up where grief lives and hope has been lost, and then tries to make meaning out of the shared moments of a family's daily life. This could be simple things like throwing a baseball around, reading Harry Potter books together, devouring stashes of Halloween candy or scouring the house for a lost stuffed animal. What she has learned about the importance of connection is vital for readers of this book who want to know how to live a fulfilled life.

We met Dr. Boles at a conference, and we were astonished by her groundbreaking research.

When Dr. Boles was twenty-four, she began working as a child life specialist with dying teenagers and with parents who were facing heartbreaking end-of-life decisions. She told us she didn't have much life experience to be working in a "very emotionally charged space of literal life and death for kids and families." She had to prepare a so-called legacy intervention, which meant she would cast the child's hand or foot in plaster or maybe help them paint a handprint on canvas, so their parents had something to remember them by. It was a typical practice in most children's hospitals.

"I didn't know any better, so I bought into that, at first," recalls Dr. Boles, now a professor at Vanderbilt University in Nashville. Then one day, a colleague was "bawling her eyes out" because a child didn't want to make a plaster mold or painted handprint. Dr. Boles heard her say out loud: "If he doesn't do these things, how will we build his legacy?"

What are we doing? she remembers thinking. Legacy isn't what's left of someone after they have died, no matter how long one lives. "Legacy is all these, like, wonderful, infinite, beautiful, large and minute little things that this child has lived through his years of life, even if short. It's not the painted handprint or the cast of their foot." She went on to earn her PhD and devote herself to answering the question, What is legacy and how do we honor the legacies of dying children? She knew it must be more than casts and canvases.

No matter where she looked, she saw that legacy was about all the connections people make throughout their lives, regardless of age.

Parents losing a child get a reluctant crash course in exploring how to measure a fleeting life and considering what a well-lived life means, even for a four-, eight- or sixteen-year-old. Moms and dads always talk about the moments and connections their children have shared as being most meaningful. Dr. Boles points to a better legacy-making activity as doing a series of interviews with the dying child and their loved ones and making a video that captures shared moments. The family of one teen she worked with treasured the CD their son made so much that they have created a foundation to pay it forward and give kids with terminal illnesses the same opportunity to share their legacies in a way that makes sense for them and to build lasting connections.

Through her research and experience, Dr. Boles shows us that moments of true love and connection are what we treasure and value about life, especially under the most difficult circumstances imaginable. They are what people will most remember about us and what we will most remember about others.

Living Legacy is a pathway to this kind of connection and re-connection. As a reminder, putting the word "living" in front of "legacy" sets an intention to create daily habits that foster connection. Through Living Legacy, we make daily choices when living our legacy to connect with ourselves, our friends and family, our communities, our faith and spirituality, our work and wealth. And love is the vehicle for this connection.

MOMENTS OF TRUE LOVE AND CONNECTION ARE WHAT WE TREASURE AND VALUE ABOUT LIFE, ESPECIALLY UNDER THE MOST DIFFICULT CIRCUMSTANCES IMAGINABLE.

When we speak of the importance of love being the vehicle of connection, many people might think we are talking about finding love through a romantic partner or with your family or friends. And yes, these kinds of personal love do facilitate connection with our partners, family and friends. But there is another kind of love that also fuels connection with oneself and others. It's called *agape* love. And this is where the Beloved Community comes in.

Creating a Legacy of Connection

Dr. Vivek H. Murthy

There is an epidemic of loneliness and isolation in America. Roughly one out of every two Americans is experiencing measurable levels of loneliness—and the struggle is even more common among young people. Nearly everyone experiences loneliness at some point. But the shame that too often comes with it makes it particularly painful.

Loneliness is more than just a bad feeling. It has profound consequences for our health and well-being. When people are socially disconnected, their risk of anxiety and depression increases. So does their risk of heart disease (29 percent), dementia (50 percent), and stroke (32 percent). The increased risk of premature death associated with social disconnection is comparable to smoking daily—and may be even greater than the risk associated with obesity.

Loneliness and isolation harm communities as well. Social disconnection is associated with reduced workplace productivity, worse school performance, and diminished civic engagement. When we are less invested in one another, we are more susceptible to polarization and less able to pull together to face the challenges that we cannot solve alone—from climate change and gun violence to economic inequality and future pandemics.

Rebuilding social connection is not only a top public health priority, it is also a societal imperative. It will require reorienting ourselves, our communities and our institutions to prioritize human connection and healthy relationships. That is a legacy worth building, and the good news is that we know how to do so.

First, we must strengthen social infrastructure—the programs, policies and structures that aid the development of healthy relationships. That means supporting school-based programs that teach children about building social connection, workplaces that foster relationships and community programs that bring people together.

Second, we have to renegotiate our relationship with technology, creating space in our lives without our devices so we can be more present with one another. That also means choosing not to take part in online dialogues that amplify judgment and hate instead of understanding.

Finally, we have to take steps in our personal lives to rebuild our connection to one another. Here small steps can make a big difference. Our relationships with one another are medicine hiding in plain sight. Evidence shows that social connection is linked to better heart health, brain health and immunity. This could take the form of spending fifteen minutes each day to reach out to people we care about, introducing ourselves to our neighbors, sitting down with people with different views to get to know and understand them, or seeking opportunities to serve others.

I have struggled at many points with loneliness. One of my deepest bouts came about after my first term as US surgeon general. It took more than a year of struggling with the pain and shame of loneliness, but I eventually found my footing. I didn't do it on my own. My parents, sister, wife and closest friends were instrumental—they patched me up with their acts of love and connection. And I am a better father, husband, friend and surgeon general as a result.

Every generation is called to take on challenges that threaten the underpinnings of society. Addressing the crisis of loneliness and isolation is one of our generation's greatest challenges, and we can only do so together. By building more connected lives and more connected communities, we can strengthen the foundation of our individual and collective well-being and be better poised to respond to the threats we face as a nation.

This essay was adapted from an opinion piece published in the New York Times *in April 2023.*

Dr. Vivek H. Murthy is the twenty-first, and was the nineteenth, surgeon general of the United States. In that role he serves as vice admiral of the US Public Health Service Commissioned Corps. Dr. Murthy has worked to address a number of critical public health issues, including our nation's mental health crisis and the epidemic of loneliness and isolation.

The term comes from the ancient Greek names for different kinds of love, such as *eros* (the kind of love associated with romance and passion), *storge* (familial love, particularly parent-child love), and *philia* (the love we find in friendship or brotherly love, which Philadelphia is named after). Agape love is the universal or divine love we feel for all of life, based on the understanding that *all of life is interconnected*. It is the love and connection we feel for humanity. It's also the love we can feel for the natural world, such as the profound appreciation and nourishment we get when we are connected to our surroundings—a sunrise, a walk in the woods, swimming in open water, a sunset, the stars.

Agape love is how we see beyond skin color, or how we understand—and feel in our heart and soul—that poverty and the suffering of others are not separate from us. Agape love enables us to see and honor the beauty of our shared humanity in everyone, including the dust-covered beggar on the temple steps in India or the seeker chasing nirvana. Agape love means we can love the human but stand up against their evil act—a hugely important tenant of the King legacy and something you will hear Martin and Arndrea quote often.

Martin's father understood the role of agape love in engaging individuals and communities in building the Beloved Community. For Dr. King, love was not sentimental or an easily dismissed emotion. In his final book, *Where Do We Go from Here: Chaos or Community?*, published the year before his assassination, he laid out his vision of an inclusive and equitable society built on love for our shared humanity.[60]

When Dr. King spoke about agape love, he described it this way: It "does not begin by discriminating between worthy and unworthy people. . . . It begins by loving others for their sakes" and "makes no distinction between a friend and enemy." He described it as "understanding, redeeming goodwill for all," an "overflowing love which is purely spontaneous, unmotivated, groundless and creative . . . the love of God operating in the human heart."[61]

MARTIN AND THE REDEMPTION OF AGAPE LOVE

Martin knows all too well the central role agape love plays in building the Beloved Community. He often speaks to the power of agape love when he travels the world, offering his teachings on nonviolence and his vision for the revitalized Drum Major Institute. Throughout his life, Martin has drawn inspiration from others who've shown incredible acts of agape love and forgiveness, like his granddaddy Rev. Martin Luther King Sr.

When Martin was sixteen, having just finished his junior year of high school, he courageously headed to Washington, DC, to work as a page for Senator Edward Kennedy, the brother of the late John F. Kennedy. Martin felt he was ready to step outside the close-knit world he lived in with his mother and siblings and, despite having lost so much, venture out into the world alone—or at least somewhat alone.

The King and the Kennedy families had been friendly since Martin's father first wrote to President Kennedy in 1961, congratulating him on his election and requesting a conference with him to talk about civil rights issues. Caroline Kennedy also worked in her uncle Ted's office, and like Martin, her dad had also been assassinated in the prime of life. The two became fast friends and confidants. Martin was so grateful for the chance to work with the Kennedys and play on the office softball team. He felt safe there, knowing he was surrounded by people who understood profound loss, public grief and constant fear—people who understood he was tentatively making his way in his upside-down world.

But on June 30, 1974, another special news bulletin shattered the veneer of safety to which Martin clung. His dear grandmother, Alberta, had been shot in Atlanta.

Mama King, as everyone called her, was playing "The Lord's Prayer" on the organ during Sunday service at Ebenezer Baptist Church when twenty-three-year-old Marcus Wayne Chenault Jr. opened fire with two revolvers.

She was shot in the very church where her father, her husband and her son (Martin's dad) had each served as pastors. As the four hundred–some worshippers bowed their heads, Chenault had entered the church, determined to kill Mama King's husband, Daddy King. When Chenault found out Daddy King wasn't there that day, he turned his guns on Mama King. She died later that day at age sixty-nine.

Martin immediately rushed home to Atlanta without even saying goodbye to Senator Kennedy. He felt like he couldn't face the senator's condolences. Again, Martin's family had been ripped apart. And again, the precious life of a thoroughly nonviolent person ended with violence. Mama King's life embodied love and demonstrated unselfish service to humankind. Again, the indomitable faith of the King family was tested. But again, love would prevail.

There is so much to say about Mama King, who was the choir director who led Ebenezer Baptist in spiritual and musical life. Like so many powerful Black women, her contributions have largely been forgotten by many, erased from modern history. She attended high school at Spelman Seminary in Atlanta and went on to enroll in Hampton Normal and Agricultural Institute, where she obtained her teaching certificate. She was an active member of the NAACP, the Young Women's Christian Association, and the Women's International League for Peace. She was fierce, passionate and committed to change. She also raised two esteemed preachers and civil rights activists, Martin's dad and his uncle A. D. (who was also deceased by then). Her daughter, Dr. King's sister, Christine, became an esteemed educator, author and activist.

Martin reflects that after Mama King's assassination, his own festering bitterness could have surfaced and overcome him. It would have been easy to hate everybody, Black or white. His dad was killed by a white man, and Mama King was killed by a Black man. That hatred would have made for an awful existence. But his grandfather Daddy King showed him a different path. He refused to allow any man to reduce him to hatred—not the man who killed his wife, not even the man who killed his son. He transformed his pain into agape love. "I love everyone," he preached. "I'm every man's brother."

HE REFUSED TO ALLOW ANY MAN TO REDUCE HIM TO HATRED.

Martin often thinks about the story his granddaddy told him about going to the jail where the gunman was held, staring him down and asking, "Son, why did you kill my wife?" His granddaddy recalled how Chenault's eyes were wild. Chenault told Martin's granddaddy that when he got out of jail, he was going to come find him and finish the job. His granddaddy could have smacked the gunman on the head with his cane, and no doubt the sheriff and deputies would have looked the other way. Instead, he said, "Son, I'm going to pray for you because I know prayer changes things." He offered the killer forgiveness.

Martin's granddaddy said: "I won't let the person that killed my son and the person that killed my wife turn my heart to hate. I still believe in love." He used agape love to counter those negative forces, but he also used it to protect the humanity within himself. Martin saw his grandfather do exactly what Dr. King also asked us to do—separate the evil act from the person—and he was able to hate the act of violence but love the person. For Martin, it was a lifelong lesson to refuse to let hatred poison one's heart and, instead, let the healing power of agape love shine within.

Chenault claimed insanity during his trial but was convicted and sentenced to death in the electric chair. His sentence was later changed to life in prison due in part to the wishes of Martin's family, who opposed the death penalty.

We recognize that is an extreme example of agape love, forgiveness and perspective. We know many of us will, thankfully, never be in that position to make the choice Daddy King made. However, we can all draw inspiration from this path that helped Martin and his grandfather live a legacy of fulfillment rather than a legacy of bitterness and hate. And we can once again ask ourselves the question that Dr. David Baum was asked by that beggar, with a small but essential edit—"Are you fulfilled?"

We encourage you to look deeply into your heart when you ask that question. If your answer involves words such as "somewhat" or "most of the time" or "almost never," we equally encourage you to pursue a greater path of fulfillment through connection and agape love. If you choose this path, the soul-stirring and life-changing rewards of Living Legacy will only multiply as you help us build the Beloved Community.

AGAPE LOVE IS THE UNIVERSAL OR DIVINE LOVE WE FEEL FOR ALL OF LIFE, BASED ON THE UNDERSTANDING THAT *ALL OF LIFE IS INTERCONNECTED.* IT IS THE LOVE AND CONNECTION WE FEEL FOR HUMANITY. IT'S ALSO THE LOVE WE CAN FEEL FOR THE NATURAL WORLD, SUCH AS THE PROFOUND APPRECIATION AND NOURISHMENT WE GET WHEN WE ARE CONNECTED TO OUR SURROUNDINGS—A SUNRISE, A WALK IN THE WOODS, SWIMMING IN OPEN WATER, A SUNSET, THE STARS.

CHAPTER 6

How Do You Measure a Life?: Finding Our Legacy Thus Far

JUST BEFORE DR. KING WAS murdered, he wrote his own obituary. It still haunts and inspires the world. "The Drum Major Instinct" is one of his finest sermons and certainly his most prophetic, tragically so. It was delivered on February 4, 1968, at Atlanta's Ebenezer Baptist Church, where he was co-pastor with Martin's grandfather. At the pulpit, Dr. King imagined his own death and concluded with instructions for the eulogy, words to be spoken at his funeral if he were to die.

Exactly two months later, on April 4, Dr. King was assassinated.

Much has been written since about the masterful construction and heightened emotion of that prophetic sermon.[62] It wasn't an iconic address like his "I Have a Dream" speech during the 1963 March on Washington. Rather, it was part of a Sabbath service delivered to his home flock. In it, Dr. King speaks to his congregation about the destructive forces of "the drum major instinct," which is the desire to lead the parade, be first, be recognized and receive distinction. Instead, he told his flock that greatness comes from humbly serving others.

And this path to distinction, Martin's dad insisted, is available to all. It's a path he hoped he embodied and would be remembered for, realizing as he did that his time on earth was limited. At the close of the iconic sermon, Dr. King said: "Every now and then I think about my own death, and I think about my own funeral.

And I don't think of it in a morbid sense. And every now and then I ask myself, 'What is it that I would want said?'"

He wanted to keep the funeral short, leave his résumé and accolades out of the eulogy and instead remember how he lived—pursuing justice:

> I'd like somebody to mention that day that Martin Luther King Jr. tried to give his life serving others. I'd like for somebody to say that day that Martin Luther King Jr. tried to love somebody. I want you to say that day that I tried to be right on the war question. I want you to be able to say that day that I did try to feed the hungry. And I want you to be able to say that day that I did try in my life to clothe those who were naked. I want you to say on that day that I did try in my life to visit those who were in prison. I want you to say that I tried to love and serve humanity.

He concluded with an emotional, grief-driven summation of his personal drum major instinct:

> Yes, if you want to say that I was a drum major, say that I was a drum major for justice. Say that I was a drum major for peace. I was a drum major for righteousness. . . . Yes, Jesus, I want to be on your right or your left side, not for any selfish reason. I want to be on your right or your left side, not in terms of some political kingdom or ambition. But I just want to be there in love and in justice and in truth and in commitment to others, so that we can make of this old world a new world.[63]

Martin's mother, Coretta Scott King, was a trained and joyful pianist and singer. Left to right: Martin (6), Coretta (38), Bernice (11 months), Yolanda (8) and Dexter (3) in February 1964.

Martin likes to remember happier days in the King family household, before the devastating loss of his father. Left to right: Yolanda (8), Bernice (11 months), Coretta Scott King (38), Dexter (3) and Martin (6) in February 1964.

Martin was two years old when a cross was burned on the front lawn of the King family's Atlanta home. Threats like this remained constant in the King family's household, even after his father was killed.

The world remembers Dr. Martin Luther King Jr. as a civil rights icon, but Martin remembers him as a loving dad. Left to right: Yolanda (7), Dexter (18 months), Coretta Scott King (35), Dr. King (33) and Martin (4) at their home in Atlanta in July 1962.

Above: Music was a part of family life in the King household. Front to back: Martin (3), Yolanda (5), Dr. King (31) and Coretta Scott King (33) in Atlanta in 1960.

Left: The King family's Atlanta home in 1960.

Martin with his sister Yolanda and dad in Atlanta.

Martin and Dr. King walking up the front steps of their Atlanta home. There was a time when Martin was called Marty. His mother feared Martin would be too burdensome of a name to live up to. Martin says, "I wish I could hug that younger version of me and assure him that one day, he would proudly grow into his father's name."

Above: Martin and Yolanda outside a trailer, listening to their father address a group about the importance of voting. To this day, Martin remains a passionate activist on behalf of voting rights.

Left: Martin and his father greeting parishioners at Ebenezer Baptist Church after Sunday services. The King family's unwavering faith sustained them and their community through the darkest days to come.

Dr. King serves chicken to Martin and Dexter at Sunday supper.

Coretta Scott King and civil rights activist Rev. Ralph Abernathy led a massive march on April 8, 1968, in Memphis, Tennessee, only days after Dr. King's assassination. With them are Yolanda (in a white coat at left), singer Harry Belafonte, Martin, Dexter and Dr. King's top lieutenant, Andrew Young (to the right of Rev. Abernathy).

At the funeral of his father, Martin recalls taking his cues from his stoic mother: Be strong and do not break, because the world is watching. Left to right: Bernice (5); Dr. King's brother, Rev. Alfred Daniel King (37); Martin (10); Dexter (7); and Coretta (40) in April 1968.

Dr. King's funeral service was held in Ebenezer Baptist Church, where he was the co-pastor with his father, Rev. Martin Luther King Sr. ("Daddy King"). Martin (10) is sitting between his uncle Rev. Alfred Daniel King (37) and his sister Yolanda (12).

Coretta (56) and Martin (25) at a rally in Washington, DC, for the twentieth anniversary of the "I Have a Dream" speech and March on Washington in August 1983.

Coretta (58) and Martin (27) carried the torch of nonviolent activism for human rights. Mother and son getting arrested together as they protested apartheid at the South African embassy in Washington, DC, in 1985.

Yolanda speaking at the 2022 National Action Network Breakfast—hosted on the King family holiday by Rev. Al Sharpton. Martin and Arndrea believe Yolanda inherited her innately charismatic gift of oration from her grandfather.

The King family visiting the Martin Luther King Jr. Memorial in Washington, DC.

Craig and Marc organized WE Day events to celebrate youth who volunteered community service hours on issues such as homelessness, the environment, racism and inequality. It wasn't unusual for crowds of over twenty thousand youths to attend. Events featured world leaders, such as the Dalai Lama, Malala Yousafzai, Mikhail Gorbachev, Elie Wiesel, Jane Goodall, Magic Johnson and countless entertainers.

Above: In 1995, young Craig traveled to Asia to see first-hand the conditions of child laborers. Here he is dutifully interviewing a brickmaker.

Left: Craig (upper, center) with friends in 1995, organizing petitions to "Free the Children."

Early "Free the Children" fundraiser, selling soda in a park. Craig and Marc began as child activists, never dreaming of the global impact their charity work would achieve.

When Marc was eighteen years old, he embarked on a yearlong journey to Thailand, volunteering with AIDS patients and AIDS orphans. The experience set the course for his Living Legacy.

Craig's first meeting with the Dalai Lama at a 1997 gathering in Stockholm, Sweden. At the gathering, the Dalai Lama suggested "the greatest challenge facing our time" was that "we are raising a generation of passive bystanders." Those words helped ignite Marc and Craig's youth empowerment work—helping youth become active participants in building a more just, safe and equitable world.

The first time Craig was on *Oprah*, she offered to build one hundred schools. Eventually, Oprah asked Marc and Craig to help her build her O Ambassadors program, to provide service-learning programs to over two thousand American schools.

The Baraka hospital staff unloading supplies at the beginning of the pandemic. In 2020, the Legacy+ Kenya-based Baraka Hospital as well as the Legacy College in Kenya were suddenly turned into emergency centers for local Covid-patient care.

Marc and Craig's parents, Fred and Theresa Kielburger, who generously supported their sons in becoming renowned charity leaders. Through writing and researching this book, the brothers better understood how they were shaped by the rich and complex ancestral legacies they inherited from their parents.

Craig embracing Selena Gomez at a WE Day event she hosted in 2015. Craig would eventually help Selena define and launch her #MentalHealth101 education and advocacy initiative—helping young people learn about mental health issues so they didn't experience the loneliness and isolation in their struggles that Selena once had.

Twelve years after their fateful meeting in Stockholm, the Dalai Lama agreed to attend one of Marc and Craig's WE Day events in Vancouver to address more than fifteen thousand middle and high school leaders. He was set to speak for ten minutes and went for thirty—his obvious joy in speaking to the enthusiastic crowd of young people lit up the entire stadium.

When Yolanda was five, she attended her first WE Day event with Martin. Martin remembers her seeing all the young people speaking about their volunteer work and activism and Yolanda saying, "I want to do that." Martin was so impressed with Marc and Craig's commitment to raising compassionate and engaged young people, he became a frequent guest speaker at WE Day events and ultimately a close friend of the brothers.

Marc with Archbishop Desmond Tutu. The brothers were fortunate to meet and receive guidance from the archbishop early in their lives. He taught them the parable of "going upstream" (told in chapter 2), which had a huge impact on their life's work.

Marc and Craig speaking at WE Day to an arena of twenty thousand young people who earned their way through service.

Battled child labor, boy, 12, murdered

Defied members of 'carpet mafia'

ISLAMABAD, Pakistan (AP) — When Iqbal Masih was 4 years old, his parents sold him into slavery for less than $16.

For the next six years, he remained shackled to a carpet-weaving loom most of the time, tying tiny knots hour after hour.

By age 12, he was free and travelling the world in his crusade against the horrors of child labor.

On Sunday, Iqbal was shot dead while he and two friends were riding their bikes in their village of Muritke, 35 kilometres outside the eastern city of Lahore. Some believe his murder was carried out by angry members of the carpet industry who had made repeated threats to si-

lence the young activist.

"We know his death was a conspiracy by the carpet mafia," said Ehsan Ullah Khan of the Bonded Labor Liberation Front (BLLF), a private group in Pakistan.

Iqbal, a Christian, was home from school in Lahore for the Easter holiday.

A man known only as Ashraf, a laborer in Muritke, was arrested in connection with the shooting, but has been released, Khan said.

Rana Iqbal, deputy superintendent of police for the district, said yesterday he was investigating the shooting but had no details.

The killing came only months

IQBAL MASIH: Shown getting an award in Boston last year for youth work.

☞ Please see Child-labor, A24

Child-labor 'activist slain

The original newspaper article that inspired twelve-year-old Craig to learn about and visit children forced into labor in Asia. The tragic story of Iqbal Masih's enslavement and murder eventually led the brothers to build the hugely successful charity Free the Children.

His words remain a gift to the world, and to those of us who had to go on after he was gone. Martin says his mom, Coretta, believed that his dad was trying to prepare his family, friends and congregation for his death. For his homegoing service, five days after he was killed, Coretta asked that the final words of Dr. King's sermon be broadcast to the assembled at Ebenezer Baptist in Atlanta.

We can't think of a more tragic, poignant and chilling example of a heroic but hunted man imagining how his life might be summed up, only to have his deeply reflective words used a few months later at his funeral. Such was Dr. King's journey of faith. But it is also instructive, a guide for those of us who are fortunate to be alive and still able to build our Living Legacies to help create the Beloved Community envisioned by Dr. King.

We know Martin's father was an unflinching auditor of his own actions.[64] He frequently paused to take stock of his life. He was constantly asking himself, "Am I doing the right thing? Am I achieving what I set out to achieve in a way that is aligned with my beliefs and values? Have I built a life of connection: to myself, my family and others? Have I lived a life of love?"

He knew that when one is charged with a divine mission and purpose greater than oneself, one must keep looking back to make sure one hasn't strayed from the path. A philosopher himself, Dr. King well understood what ancient Greek philosopher Socrates meant when he said, "The unexamined life is not worth living."

If our goal is to live lives of deep connection, love and fulfillment, we must take stock of where we are and where we're heading. For the four of us, this is an essential practice. If not daily, at least a few times a year, we stop and consciously assess how we are living our legacies as we move toward creating the Beloved Community.

In these times of reflection, we ask ourselves whether we are nurturing our Inner Purpose (living your best self) and our Outer Purpose (living for something greater than yourself). Are we nurturing and growing our self-love and love for others? Remember, love is the fuel for connection. When we have this deep connection with our true selves and our well-being and we live our Inner Purpose and Outer Purpose, we generate even more self-love and love for others. Ultimately, agape love will thrive in this generative ecosystem—leading to the highest form of love and fulfillment. And, yes, we do know this represents a lifelong journey to get there.

When we each ask ourselves "Am I there yet?" the answer is always "Not yet."

If you're reading this book, it may be because you too have arrived at that "not yet" stage in your life. You may have found that the spectacular CV or impressive investment portfolio that you've focused your life on building has not yet brought you to a place where you are truly fulfilled. You may be an artist of some kind who has disconnected from your creativity and hasn't prioritized finding your way back. Or you may simply be walking through your days not feeling deeply connected to your inner self, the soul of who you are—unable to feel much love for yourself or connection with others. Maybe you haven't identified your Inner Purpose or Outer Purpose yet. These are big arenas of "not yet" to confront. The "not yet" gap between where we are and where we want to be isn't insurmountable or a failure. It is more like an ongoing pursuit. Arrival isn't the goal; it's living a legacy that takes us toward where we want to be that we are concerned with here.

You may have decided now is the time to figure out what direction you want your Living Legacy to be taking you. The four of us found that the first step in this process is to pause and take stock. In this chapter, we will encourage and hopefully inspire you to take measure of your own life. This means assessing the connections you've built to your authentic self and others, evaluating whether you are nurturing your Inner Purpose and Outer Purpose, and whether you're living a legacy of deep love, for yourself and others.

WHEN WE EACH ASK OURSELVES "AM I THERE YET?" THE ANSWER IS ALWAYS "NOT YET."

To "take stock" effectively, we invite you to look at the course of your life up until now to figure out what needs to genuinely change. In doing so, we strongly encourage you to not criticize or shame yourself for past failings or for not accomplishing everything you'd hoped. Don't get down on yourself because you haven't yet lived up to your own expectations. The key word here is *"yet."*

IF I DIED TOMORROW . . .

It's such an interesting and perplexing question: How do you take stock of a life lived thus far? Unless one is only interested in shallow material calculations, like net monetary worth, there's no purely objective yardstick for quantifying a life. However, we've read numerous books during our research where authors suggest asking yourself: "If I died tomorrow, would I be truly proud of the life I've lived?"

Wins, Glories and Gratitudes: Write, Pray, Repeat

Arndrea Waters King

I love new beginnings. New jobs, stories, babies, shoes, adventures—and a fresh tube of red lipstick! I especially get a thrill from opening a brand-new journal and writing down my intentions for the day, week, year. There is a fullness of hope in the new, a reconnection with possibility. The chance to get it right or keep it right.

And after what feels like a long season of discontent, chaos, division, polarization and sorrow, we truly have before us a glorious opportunity to commence a personal rite of passage—initiating a new phase for ourselves, our families, our communities, indeed for humanity. We all have untapped power that resides with and within each of us, and we must set our intention to embrace this power to fuel the vision that a better world is possible. To find and fulfill our purpose, we must first know ourselves. We can dare to hope. And we can unleash our passion to be part of the solution. We can craft the world that we dare to believe in by becoming the person we are meant to be.

Part of embracing our purpose and our power within is to shape our Living Legacy. To do this, we must set goals and intentions that build toward the Beloved Community that my father-in-law, Dr. King, envisioned. I wholeheartedly take this practice seriously. I manifest it in my "Wins, Glories and Gratitudes" journal. If you were to bump into me during my travels, perhaps at a speaking event, you might catch me sitting in a corner, deep in thought as I write. When I'm not on the road, you'll find me at my kitchen table, facing the trees in my backyard, putting pen to paper to express my gratitude and set my intentions for that day and beyond.

With gratitude, appreciation blooms in our hearts and urges us to pay attention, to look around at the community of love and kindness that surrounds us. The late Bob Proctor, a mentor of mine and master in personal growth, explained that expressing gratitude shifts our energy instantly. He practiced gratitude every morning, as I do. He also believed in the power of setting intentions.

In my journal, I include affirmations, visualizations, even notes for important upcoming interviews and conversations. Holding my goals in mind, putting them on the page, I'm fueling my intentions. My journal is a written record of what I want to attract. I believe energy flows where attention goes. If we build intentionality into our lives, we can attain the incredible success that had previously seemed beyond our grasp. At day's end, you'll find me propped up in bed, journal on my lap. I'm dipping back in to acknowledge the small and large victories, like a special moment with my daughter, a celebration, a win for social justice and equality, or reflections on life's blessings.

We are so much more powerful than we know, than anything we've been taught. How can any of us build a Living Legacy until we understand how much power we have to shape our world?

Anyone who has built a lasting legacy, whether it's Dr. King's vision of a Beloved Community or the founding fathers' vision of "a more perfect union," has undoubtedly tapped into their power and pursued something greater than themselves, putting positive energy into the world to create positive change.

At the start of each year, I ask Martin, Yolanda and my wonderful sisters, Glynnis and Katha, (who run a bakery in Atlanta), to plot their goals for the coming year. This practice helps us define and refine our purpose. Sometimes we find inspiration outside our little group. One year, we followed a program called Lifebook,[105] determining our goals for improving twelve dimensions of our lives, including career, wealth, health and relationships, among others. In 2023, we followed comedian and TV host Steve Harvey's #300wishlist challenge. He encouraged people to write down three hundred things they want from God. From our pens to God's ears.

These lists can include dreams, hopes, homes, cars, friends or family you want to support. I was specific. The sixtieth anniversary of Dr. King's "I Have a Dream" speech was approaching, and I asked myself what my prayer for that event would be. I wanted people to join in working toward the Beloved Community.

It's often called the "obituary test"—or sometimes the "eulogy test" or the "headstone test" (a lot of references to death and tests!)—and it's one way of measuring our lives thus far. The test taker is supposed to imagine what people would say about you in an obituary if you died tomorrow. How would the obit writer explain your life? What stories would they tell? What would they say your impact was?

Now, it may not surprise you, but we take issue with this "obit test" because we worry that people end up using the wrong measurements—achievements, awards, wealth—since tallying those things when taking the obit test is a common approach. We now know these kinds of old school measurements of our life's worth and legacy are what led to Marc's crisis. But we also know there's a reason why this is our default setting. Obituaries reflect what society values, for better or worse.

WE CAN SEE CULTURAL EXPECTATIONS AND BIASES REINFORCED IN HOW PEOPLE ARE WRITTEN ABOUT WHEN THEY ARE GONE.

Several years ago, a trio of philosophy professors opened the newspaper to the obituaries to better understand what values our society holds in high esteem.[65] "Speaking well of the dead enables us to tell the story both of individuals who have passed away and of the cultures that shaped them and to which they contributed," they reasoned, and "in so doing, we weave those we held dear into the fabric of human nature, human achievement, and human possibility." The qualities the deceased were praised for in their obituaries would naturally reflect the qualities the writer assumed everyone else would praise as well. Using data-mining techniques, they gathered and performed text analyses on over thirteen thousand obituaries of ordinary Americans to extract patterns of evaluative judgments.[66] They saw people—especially men—lauded for their accomplishments, but also for what society valued. Women's obituaries tended to focus more on domestic and care-related affairs, whereas men's obituaries tended to focus more on public and political matters.

We saw this tendency to stereotype up close in June 2023 when we said goodbye to Martin's aunt, Willie Christine King Farris, the last of his father's siblings to pass away. In obituaries marking her passing, from the *New York Times* to the UK's *Guardian*, the ninety-five-year-old educator, who was called Christine, was praised for her public service and for being a quiet torchbearer for her brother's legacy—one who didn't seek the limelight, a tireless advocate for justice and equality.[67] She was lauded for having "worked behind the scenes, organizing marches and speeches for her brother," taking a back seat as women were expected to do during the civil rights movement.[68] Some obits also noted her resiliency and how she carried on through the loss of so many family members over the years. Obit writers reminded readers how she sought to humanize the memory of her famous brother, to demystify him and make him relatable to anyone who might follow in his footsteps. Her career achievements were often downplayed or mentioned only briefly at the end of articles—Farris was the longest-serving tenured professor at her alma mater, Spelman College, from 1958 to 2014, and the backbone of the Ebenezer Baptist Church in Atlanta.

We can't help but note how her obits inadequately captured

the lives she touched outside the prescribed roles society expected her to play.

What does the obituary of Martin's aunt Christine have to do with a study by three philosophy professors? We can see cultural expectations and biases reinforced in how people are written about when they are gone. The lives we've touched and the people we've loved are what truly matter.

Behavioral scientist Victor Strecher has another form of assessing whether we're living in alignment with the things that truly bring fulfillment, only he calls it the "headstone test." In his case, it was the tragic death of his daughter that also forced him to rethink his path and reevaluate what matters.

When Strecher's daughter Julia was born, she contracted chicken pox, which caused a rare complication that almost destroyed her heart. Baby Julia successfully underwent a heart transplant, but her family knew she would always be vulnerable, and that death could be waiting around the next corner. They gained a clear purpose—to give Julia her best possible life for as long as they had her.

Strecher says it made the whole family rethink their own lives and what was important. "We stopped expecting a certain life to happen to us and instead started creating our own lives," Strecher writes in his book *Life on Purpose*.[69] "When this happened, our lives turned from black and white into Technicolor."[70] And as an assistant professor at the University of Michigan, he started caring less about getting tenure and more about making a difference in the world. He also reports caring less about what people thought of him and more about what he thought of himself.

When Julia died in her sleep of a heart attack in 2010 at the age of nineteen, the grief and loss of purpose once again had Strecher examining his life, focusing on what's important and questioning what's not. For example, as a frequent flyer, he had become obsessed with the miles he was amassing—until he realized the epitaph on his headstone might one day read: Vic Strecher, "Three Trillion Frequent Flyer Miles."[71]

After Julia's passing, Strecher devoted himself to helping others create purpose in their lives. By our way of thinking, he discovered his Inner Purpose and aligned it with his Outer Purpose. When you find yourself conflicted between competing purposes, we encourage you to ask yourself, "Do I want [*insert current obsession here*] to be on my headstone?" Strecher did not want his obituary to celebrate his academic achievements, or his whopping air miles balance, but the good he had done. Many people reach middle age or a life setback and feel similarly.

When you do your own obit or headstone test, we invite you to ask some of the questions Dr. King asked himself in his "Drum Major Instinct" sermon: Do you live your life serving others? Do you prioritize love? Do you try to love humanity? Do your actions align with your authentic self and your deepest values? These are big questions, but we guarantee they will help you set your path right if you've gone astray or forgotten what's most important to you.

BEWARE THE BUCKET LIST TRAP

A final word of caution as you ponder who you want to be and how you want to live in this next phase of your life: beware of what bestselling author and Harvard professor Arthur C. Brooks calls "the bucket list trap." We all know about the bucket list; many of you may have one. This is the list of all the stuff you want to see, do and acquire before you die. We have known many people who have followed this strategy to plan what they want for the rest of their lives.

Embracing Death to Live Fuller Lives

Sr. Theresa Aletheia Noble

Leaving a legacy, or better, living a legacy, requires dying before you die. No one knew this better than Dr. Martin Luther King Jr. The day before his death, Dr. King proclaimed, "Like anybody, I would like to live a long life—longevity has its place. But I'm not concerned about that now. I just want to do God's will."[106] For Dr. King, living a legacy was not about reaching old age but about accepting that death—whether literal or figurative—is inevitable for anyone willing to risk everything to follow in the way of beauty, truth and goodness.

Memento mori, or "remember you will die," is a phrase long associated with reminders of death and the spiritual practice of remembering the end of one's life—which can come at any time. Taking up the spiritual practice of memento mori can be as simple as reminding ourselves every day of our impending death. Reminding ourselves regularly of the inevitability of death might sound morbid to modern ears. But centuries-old wisdom tells us that putting our lives in the perspective of our inevitable death can help us to live fuller lives.

Dr. King knew firsthand that reminders of our death contextualize and give meaning to our everyday actions, thus empowering us to make difficult decisions in order to do what is right. For Dr. King, the threat of death was around every corner precisely because of the risks he took for the sake of justice, peace and righteousness. His life teaches us that death, in some form, often comes with taking the risks necessary to live in radical solidarity with the marginalized and oppressed.

As a Catholic "nun," or religious sister, I began meditating regularly on my death almost a decade ago. I took up and helped popularize this practice mostly by happenstance. One day, I stumbled upon a passage in an old book that described the ancient tradition of meditation on death. Fascinated by the idea, I then began to read about and research the practice throughout the ages, particularly in the Catholic tradition. Incorporating meditation on death into my life completely changed the way I made daily decisions. The practice helped me to contextualize my decisions in the reality of death and eternal life, thus impelling me to take the risks necessary to follow Jesus radically, even if it led me to the cross.

As I shared online about the benefits of memento mori, people of all backgrounds began to share with me that the practice was also changing their lives. Then, several years after beginning my daily habit of meditating on my death, I heard a call from God to leave my community to begin with Sr. Danielle Victoria Lussier a new group of religious sisters. We feel called to a mission of reaching out to those on the fringes of society and the church, especially those who have been wounded or abused by fellow Christians. Of course, all this might sound strange to those unfamiliar with the Catholic faith, but suffice it to say we have risked everything to follow God's will into an uncertain future. And we almost certainly would not have had the courage to take this risk without the practice of reminding ourselves daily of our inevitable death. Memento mori helped us to step into terrifying uncertainty so that we might live for eternity.

Years after his death—with a national holiday and numerous books and school lessons about his life—Dr. King's legacy might look neat and tidy. But as Dr. King knew far too well, in the midst of living a legacy, we are apt to feel lost, bewildered and unsure. Because living a legacy involves death, if not literally, then certainly to our comfort, to our ease and to our desires to avoid suffering and sacrifice. Amid the uncertainty of living our own legacies, Dr. King's life shows us how God's power can be made evident in small daily choices to step forward in faith for the cause of justice and truth.

Sr. Theresa Aletheia Noble, *along with Sr. Danielle Victoria Lussier, began the Sisters of the Little Way of Beauty, Truth, and Goodness. Their mission is one of solidarity with people on the fringes or outside the church, especially those people who have been wounded, scandalized or abused by other Christians.*

For a time, when Craig was a younger man without a wife or children (he now has three children and a very patient wife), he maintained a bucket list filled with goals and challenges like sky-diving, climbing Mount Kilimanjaro and visiting as many of the world's 195 countries as possible (he's visited 81 at last count). No one would accuse Craig of forgoing a life of impact for a life of list making. Yet, as he crossed items off his bucket list, each item seemed to be less meaningful. He yearned to share his experiences with a life partner. At specific locations, he made a mental note of wanting to return with his future children. The bucket list clichés from movies and magazine articles became less and less important to Craig than what he was truly seeking—partnership, family and true fulfillment.

As Brooks writes in *From Strength to Strength: Finding Success, Happiness and Deep Purpose in the Second Half of Life*, there is a risk that the sense of purpose and meaning can fall by the wayside as you chase the items on your list for the sake of saying you did it, not for the fulfillment they'll bring you or the impact they'll create in the world. Worse, it becomes a competition as you try to make your bucket list cooler than everyone else's. The more privileged you are, the more likely you are to win the bucket list competition. And at the end of your life, what do you have to show for it? A list. We aren't totally negating the pleasure that comes from chasing a bucket list. If you dream of climbing Mount Kilimanjaro or riding Route 66 on a vintage Harley, go for it. You do you. Just don't do it for the sake of ticking boxes.

The goal we are hoping you attain is finding fulfillment through Living Legacy, which centers around the love and connection we are all seeking. The typical obit test or the bucket list mentality so often leads us to superficial measurements of legacy and a life well lived. Rather, we suggest starting this inner assessment with evaluating how well you are living your Inner Purpose and Outer Purpose.

HOW INNER PURPOSE AND OUTER PURPOSE SUPPORT LIVING LEGACY

To remind you: Living in alignment with our Inner Purpose and Outer Purpose is how we reconnect with ourselves, others and the world. It is how we live our legacy. However, we do not see one's Inner Purpose or Outer Purpose as having to be set in stone. Both can change and evolve over a lifetime. We find that the connection we experience when living in alignment with Inner Purpose and Outer Purpose isn't dependent on the specific ways you personally define them. What's more important is that you live in alignment with them.

For example, in many ways, Martin and Arndrea's Living Legacy evolved over time, but their Inner Purposes have remained consistent—inclusion, equal rights and safety for all.

Nowadays Arndrea and Martin have again joined their Outer Purposes to rededicate themselves to realizing Dr. King's dream of building the Beloved Community with their work with the Drum Major Institute (DMI). DMI was founded in New York during the civil rights era to raise bail for jailed activists, but during the pandemic, Martin and Arndrea resuscitated it to help fund programs and create initiatives so people can take actions that promote peace, justice and equity to build the Beloved Community. As we were writing this book, increasing opportunities appeared for Arndrea to refine her Outer Purpose once again and take on a broader leadership role in the face of the erosion of many rights, including women's rights. So Arndrea is making meaningful connections with people across North

America, speaking at numerous public gatherings and sharing her writings as she continues to hone and tend to her Inner Purpose and find ways to share it with the world.

THERE IS NO TIME LIKE THE PRESENT TO TAKE STOCK OF WHERE YOU ARE AND WHERE YOU ARE HEADED.

As shared earlier, Craig was fortunate that, when he was twelve, he found his Outer Purpose in a newspaper headline about a Pakistani boy his own age who was murdered after standing up against child labor. He went on to devote his life to empowering people to make a positive change in the world. In this case, the work involves constant travel. Craig has always been a spiritual person with a strong connection to God, but he's had to work hard to nurture other aspects of his Inner Purpose. When he became a husband and a father, he reduced his overseas travel to visit development projects and worked hard to focus on deep and meaningful connections with his family.

Both Martin and Craig navigate this conflict of fulfilling their Outer Purposes, which involve extensive global travel, while staying in alignment with their Inner Purposes of being attentive, engaged parents and spouses. Craig reads stories to his three boys over videoconference, brings them on trips when possible and never lets his children go to sleep without hearing his voice and telling them how much he loves them.

When taking stock of this alignment, begin with Inner

Purpose. Are you living your best self physically, mentally, spiritually and emotionally? If yes, what evidence shows you this? If no, what gets in the way? What steps can you take to move closer to living your best self so that you can also live for something larger than yourself? Are you too burned out or exhausted to live your best life, unable to align your physical, mental, spiritual and emotional well-being? If you're not yet able to live your best life, how can you move closer to focusing on these areas? It's also possible that your Inner Purpose got mistakenly attached to something external rather than an internal barometer.

When you consider your Outer Purpose, are you living for something greater than yourself? Are you able to foster your sense of connection and contribution to your family, friends, community or the greater world? If you don't feel this connection and belonging, what do you think is stopping you? How might you enhance it?

Finally, ask yourself whether your Inner Purpose and your Outer Purpose are in alignment, working in harmony to support your Living Legacy. If not, what changes might you make to better align them?

EXAMINING CONNECTION WITH YOURSELF AND OTHERS

An important inquiry of your Living Legacy "taking stock" assessment is questioning how you can deepen your connections with others and the world around you. Do you feel connected to others? If not, what is holding you back? On the flip side, where do you feel limited in your connection with others? What holds you back when connecting with others? What are the relationships you need to heal to meaningfully connect with others? What relationships are most important to you, that you need to create a deeper connection with? What do you feel the strongest sense of connection to? There is no time like the present to take stock of where you are and where you are headed.

We want to share the story of our friend Walter Green, who took stock in this way and reshaped his Inner Purpose and Outer Purpose in doing so.

Walter learned early that life is short and the time we have with the ones we love can be especially fleeting and precious. When he was nine, Walter's mother suffered the first of two bouts with breast cancer. Then his father had a heart attack; another a few years later proved fatal. Amid this foreboding and loss, Walter moved eight times before he was sixteen. Due to all these circumstances, Walter didn't develop the close relationships he longed for until he was much older.

Let's leap ahead many decades. Walter is now a successful CEO. He's blessed with a wonderful family and a wide circle of friends. Those friends are also getting old. He's attended many memorial services, struck by the beauty of the tributes, but even more so by their timing: the guest of honor was in a casket and never heard a word of it.

Walter did not want that fate for himself or his loved ones. So, he made a plan and sprang into action, drawing up a list of the forty-four people closest to him. For his seventieth birthday, he gave a gift to himself and, unbeknownst to him, many others. He traveled the world to meaningfully connect with each person on that list. Over cups of tea, long lunches and amazing dinners, one by one, he explained to each family member or friend the impact they had on his life. He sought to thank them, give them a hug, and open his heart in the process. It was the best year of his life. It was the best birthday gift he had ever received. The year was one of many tears, much laughter and incredible moments of love and inspiration.

Shortly after his yearlong journey, Walter's dear friend Denny mentioned that he wanted his funeral to be more like a party. "Wouldn't you rather be there?" Walter asked. With Denny's permission, Walter began planning a huge seventy-fifth birthday bash, where all of Denny's friends turned out to express their love. Denny reveled in the tributes, feeling the deep connection and fulfillment that friendship brings. When Denny passed away unexpectedly eighteen months later, Walter saw the potential to start a movement.

Walter came to Marc and Craig, asking for their help to launch *Say It Now*, a movement encouraging small expressions of gratitude for people who have made an impact in our lives. These could be private, one-on-one moments, or loved ones gathering to honor one person . . . before they are gone. Through the support of Legacy+, Walter has shaped a curriculum, built the *Say It Now* guide, written an illustrated book, delivered a TED Talk, and inspired over five million acts of gratitude (and counting!). Most importantly, he has lived this movement through his own actions of constantly expressing to his family and friends how much they mean to him. Walter has aligned his Inner Purpose with his Outer Purpose and is working to help us tell our loved ones how we feel about them before it's too late.

This is Walter's Living Legacy. He is the perfect illustration of this bold new idea. His Living Legacy is a vehicle for connecting with himself, others and the world. He created more meaning, happiness and fulfillment for himself, those close to him and everyone else he reached out to. And crucially, Walter literally brought legacy back from the dead, giving back to others in small but meaningful ways that, at scale, could help heal the world.

The Transformative Power of Purpose and Service

Jay Shetty

In my journey of understanding purpose, I've come to realize that many of us approach it as if it's finite, certain, end position, that we find, almost like a treasure chest or a lost item. And once you've found it, you can never lose it. This static view of purpose, however, can limit us and hinder our growth. Instead, I've learned that purpose is a dynamic, ever-evolving aspect of our lives, shaped by how we choose to live, act and perceive the world.

When I was a monk, I believed my purpose was tied to that role. Leaving the monastery left me feeling conflicted, as if I had lost my purpose. I'd externalized my purpose; it meant being a monk, dressing as a monk and living as a monk. That felt purposeful. But all of a sudden, when I was back in the "real world," it almost felt like I couldn't be purposeful here. But I was wrong. There was a way to still care about people. There was a way to carry myself mindfully. There was a method to focus on the things that were important to me and significant to me.

I had to reframe my understanding: being a monk was an occupation, not the essence of my purpose. My true purpose lay in the values and practices I embodied—meditation, service and mindfulness. I could still choose to embody the best parts of that lifestyle without having to live that way externally. This shift taught me that purpose is an internal pursuit, not dependent on external labels or roles.

Two people can perform the same act—such as donating to charity—but their underlying motivations make the difference. One person does it because it makes them look good in society, and the other does it because they deeply care about the people it affects. And the latter is the one who's going to experience purpose.

A powerful quote by Charles Horton Cooley resonates with me: "I am not what I think I am, and I am not what you think I am.

I am what I think you think I am."[107] This highlights how we often perceive ourselves through others' eyes, leading to incomplete and inaccurate comparisons. Instead of avoiding comparison, I encourage deeper understanding. By fully understanding others' lives, we realize that everyone faces challenges, and this understanding can diminish envy and foster empathy.

People often ask me, Jay, how do I find my purpose? And the answer is through service. Serve with your time. Serve with your money. Serve with your energy.

Become successful. So that you can serve. Become great. So that you can serve. Achieve more. So that you can serve. Make service the guiding principle of your life, the underlying intention, and recognize it as the epitome of all experiences. When you feel lost, serve. When you feel happy, serve. When you feel sad, serve.

Find a way to improve the lives of others, and you will always find your way.

Jay Shetty is a global bestselling author, an award-winning podcast host of On Purpose and a purpose-driven entrepreneur. Shetty possesses a talent for making purpose and ancient wisdom not only relatable but also practical and easily accessible to millions across the globe.

EXAMINING HOW WE GIVE AND RECEIVE LOVE

There are many ways you can take stock of where you are on your journey to self-love and agape love of humanity. How we come to this love—just like how we come to fulfillment and connection—is a very individual path. It's not automatic. And not every day will we easily love ourselves and others. We assembled questions to ask yourself that have helped us in this inquiry:

1. Are you showing yourself forgiveness?
2. Are you showing others forgiveness?
3. Are you showing yourself gratitude?
4. Are you showing others gratitude?
5. Are you prioritizing agape love for yourself and others? Remember, this doesn't mean unconditionally loving your own and everyone else's behaviors and actions. It means loving the fundamental beauty and humanity that reside in yourself and everyone else.

You might need to retreat into therapy, nature or meditation, or realign with your Inner Purpose to better support love and connection with yourself and others. You might need to let go of the things that are holding you back. You may need to become more creative.

One of the creative ways Arndrea fosters self-love is by keeping a picture of herself as a little girl by her bed. Every night she looks at her younger self and lovingly thinks, *Gosh, she was fearless. With her shiny black shoes on, she thought anything was possible.* Recently, though, she found another way to nurture even more self-love. Instead of looking back at the picture of the little girl and thinking what she'd like to say to her younger self, she asks a different question. What would my younger self say to me that would help me love myself more?

We encourage you to be patient with yourself, particularly as you cultivate more self-love—which sadly seems like one of the most challenging asks of this book.

Arndrea reminds us that we tend to think of self-love as a destination, but it's something we need to continually practice. It's an ever-expanding quest. In taking stock she realized that she'd always been a seeker. She always knew there was something more. But now she knows the "something more" she's always been seeking is self-love.

Each of us has a unique path to tending our Inner Purpose and Outer Purpose while generating greater love and connection as we shape our Living Legacy. In the next chapter, when we talk about beliefs and values, we continue to help you carve your distinct path of self-love, contribution and connection. We do know that this is the pathway to fulfillment and reaching our goal of the Beloved Community.

CHAPTER 7

A Legacy with Integrity: Establishing Core Values and Beliefs

THE WAR IN VIETNAM WAS escalating. It was 1965, and the draft was sending tens of thousands more young Americans to fight while a campaign of aerial bombing rained daily destruction on the Asian nation. American public opinion was starting to swing against the war, with protesters taking to the streets. For Martin's father, it was a major test of his values and beliefs. Before 1965, Dr. King had expressed only reserved concern about the war. His focus was the civil rights campaign. His advisors thought it unwise to offend the very people whose minds and laws they were trying to change. Then, in June of that year, Dr. King received a letter that would rock his perspective.

Thich Nhat Hanh, a Buddhist monk, wrote to Dr. King, describing the human suffering the war had brought to his country. Nhat Hanh identified parallel philosophies in the campaign of nonviolent resistance waged by the monks of Vietnam against the war, and Dr. King's own nonviolent creed for civil rights. Two months later, at the Southern Christian Leadership Conference, Dr. King took a stand, calling for a diplomatic end to the war, echoing words Nhat Hanh had written to him: "Neither the American people nor the people of North Viet Nam is the enemy. The true enemy is war itself."[72]

Dr. King's intervention on the side of peace would not prove popular. He was condemned by newspapers across America. Even some of his allies in the civil rights movement urged him to stay in his lane and remain silent about the war. But after much reflection, Dr. King had come to believe that if he truly held the value of nonviolence, he could not honorably demand that Black communities eschew violence in their fight for civil rights while ignoring his country's use of violence around the world. He observed the brutal fighting for rights and freedoms elsewhere—the same freedoms denied to Black people in America. He questioned military defense spending in the face of poverty and oppression at home, criticizing the deep war chest and lack of social safety net in a nation that struggled to feed and house its citizens.[73] Dr. King couldn't reckon with the morality or the economics of war, and once he took a stand publicly, he spoke out fiercely against it until his death. "There comes a time when one must take a position that is neither safe, nor politic, nor popular, but he must do it because Conscience tells him it is right," King wrote in his autobiography.[74]

VALUES AND BELIEFS FORM THE NAVIGATION SYSTEM FOR OUR LIVING LEGACY.

Dr. King's values and beliefs around nonviolence, poverty and racism are essential parts of the Living Legacy he passed on to his children.

Not a day goes by when we don't hear some mention of values. American values. Religious values. Family values. Cultural values.

In the West, it's common to value democracy, independence and individualism. We hear a lot about beliefs, too. Belief in a God. Belief in a particular political ideology. The belief that Pepsi is better than Coke (or vice versa). We hear these words so often about so many things, from world views to fountain drinks, it's easy to take the whole idea for granted. But what we value and believe is vitally important.

Values and beliefs form the navigation system for our Living Legacy. They guide daily habits and actions, aligning us with our Inner Purpose and Outer Purpose. When we act in ways that uphold those values, we remain true to ourselves and, therefore, forge our path to greater love, connection and fulfillment.

To use this navigation system, you must first properly define it—input the default settings, so to speak, and decide where you want to go. Or, in this case, how you want to live. Values and beliefs are not the same thing, but they are intrinsically linked. Knowing your values and beliefs enables you to live in alignment with your Inner Purpose and Outer Purpose so you can reconnect to yourself, others and the world. Through reconnection, you can live your legacy every day. Together, we'll pose some questions that will help you identify the values and beliefs you hold, then observe whether or not they are empowering, propelling you forward, or disempowering, holding you back from your Living Legacy.

VALUES AND BELIEFS: DEFINITIONS AND DISTINCTIONS

The concept of values is one of the oldest ideas in the history of philosophy. Once humans evolved beyond asking "Where is my next meal coming from?" we moved on to deeper questions, like

"Why am I here?" and "Is it bad to punch my neighbor in the nose and steal his food?" The *Cambridge Academic Content Dictionary* defines values as "the principles that help you to decide what is right and wrong, and how to act in various situations." We all prefer the simplified definition offered by author and researcher Brené Brown: "A value is a way of being or believing that we hold most important."[75]

A way of being. That is the essence of values. Values direct your life. Every decision, every action, every interaction is—or, in a perfect world, ought to be—set by the navigation system of your values. Think of values like an internal compass or the original version of Google Maps. They carve out a path, guide you and give you bearings. When you are deeply committed to your values, their direction becomes so ingrained it can be subconscious, like an instinct. A gut feeling might not tell you to turn left or right in an unfamiliar place, but it will help you intuit what to do and how to do it. How to treat others. How to make major life choices. How to show up for yourself, others and the world.

Values are often aspirational, reflecting how you want to exist in the world. But what is most important is whether we live our values. Are you really infusing your values into your daily actions? Are you really living in alignment with these values? Do your daily choices and how you spend your time and money really reflect these values? Craig often says, "Don't tell me your values. Tell me what you do, and I'll tell you your values."

When you live by your values, you are more balanced, connected and confident about choosing the right path for you. Similarly, when you stray from those values, you wind up lost, directionless and prone to self-doubt. Living according to your values is how your Living Legacy stays connected with your Inner Purpose and Outer Purpose. In other words, your values help you both live your best life and live a life larger than yourself. And this alignment helps you know you've made the right choice because your actions reflect who you are inside.

We could all use a bit of help making choices. It's been estimated that the average American adult makes thirty-five thousand decisions each day.[76] With Living Legacy as our mindset and values as a navigation system to guide our actions, choices become easier. Now, this isn't a panacea. Clear values don't prevent all negative consequences. But even when things don't go according to plan, values ensure your moral compass remains intact, which is crucial for positive well-being. Accepting life's disappointments and setbacks is easier when you know your choices and actions reflect your core values and you won't compromise yourself even if you make a mistake. Once we've established values, we can let go of some of the anxiety that comes with each individual decision, safe in the knowledge that our actions reflect our Living Legacy.

A WAY OF BEING. THAT IS THE ESSENCE OF VALUES.

"Our values should be so crystallized in our minds, so infallible, so precise and clear and unassailable, that they don't feel like a choice—they are simply a definition of who we are in our lives," writes Brené Brown.[77] Living Legacy, then, is the totality of these values-based actions and their effects. Living Legacy is a mindset; it is how you live your values, every day. It is also the sum of your daily actions lived, throughout your lifetime, in accordance with your core values.

What We Want Our Children to Be, We Should Also Be

Martin Luther King III

Inheriting my father's legacy didn't protect me from life's many challenges. Even with his looming presence and strong moral compass, I didn't always know what to do. Numerous times, I've ended up in a pickle. For example, in 1965, when I was sent in to desegregate an Atlanta public school. I was eight. That was an adventure and more. I had to practice what my daddy preached or end up an ongoing target of my first bully, a tall white boy who didn't want me in his class.

First, a bit of a scene setter. In 1963, as public school desegregation battles raged across the American South, my dad and other prominent Black people quietly enrolled their own children in several of Atlanta's most prestigious private schools—which had, unsurprisingly, managed to remain all white. Dad claimed he wasn't looking for a test case but instead wanted me and my sister, Yolanda, to get the best possible education, including the experience of integrated schooling.

At that point, I'd only attended all-Black schools. Lovett, an integrated school, denied my application in 1963.[108] Then, in 1965, my dad enrolled us in Spring Street Elementary School, a modest brick building off the corner of Eighteenth Street, then considered Atlanta's outskirts.[109] Without much fanfare, I became the only African American student in my newly desegregated third-grade class. Being the child of Dr. Martin Luther King Jr. and Coretta Scott King in racially divided Atlanta made me an object of interest. And a target for bullies.

I didn't know many whites, but my daddy preached that I should not hate them, just as his father before him had. In the early days at school, one boy began calling me the N-word, among other slurs. "I don't know why you're here at our school," he said, accusingly. I was a bit fearful of him. He had a temper. When our class played dodgeball during recess, he'd fly into a rage for no apparent reason. I was a shy kid and needed to figure out how to survive this, or I would have a rotten school year. I also wanted my dad to be proud of me for how I handled the situation.

My parents had always taught me to show understanding and empathy to others. I figured my bully had emotional problems. Maybe he was missing something at home. Instinctively, I drew on the lessons of nonviolence my father preached. I noticed my bully was also a talented artist. He could draw a detailed military battleship with guns and everything. One day, he was drawing a ship. I decided to compliment him. "Hey, man, what is that? A battleship?" I asked. "That is really good." He looked up, surprised, and said, "You think so?" It was so small and simple. When I noticed something he was good at and offered a compliment, he forgot I was his punching bag. Our relationship began to change. There wasn't exactly a warm embrace between us, but it was an improvement.

What we want our children to be, we should also be. Our kids are reflections of us.

Dad had a way of disarming his enemies because he never attacked them. He might attack a principle, but never a person. Looking back, that's what I subliminally picked up on. This boy had a deficit, and I still believed in his ability to have a good character. It became a lifelong lesson for me, a tactic I have turned to many times since. That said, responding with kindness is obviously not a panacea for bullying—especially in the tragically extreme cases where teens are driven to suicide. But it will help fight the problem in many cases. If our children see us treat others with kindness and respect, they follow our example. Sometimes kindness is the best way. Just like Dad said, "Darkness cannot drive out darkness; only light can do that. Hate cannot drive out hate; only love can do that."[110] Nonviolence and forgiveness are powerful tools.

Inheriting my father's legacy didn't protect me from life's many challenges.

I inherited numerous values, beliefs and ways of being from my parents and grandparents. I learned stoicism from my mom. After my dad was killed, I saw my mom remain powerful and dignified in her sadness and refuse to show weakness as the world watched. I learned forgiveness from my grandfather, who forgave my grandmother's killer, which I discussed in chapter 5. And I learned from my dad to defuse any situation with loving-kindness and nonviolence. I'm trying to instill these values in my daughter, Yolanda. I want to raise her the way I was raised—to care for others and resolve conflicts nonviolently. To do that, I need to teach by example. What we want our children to be, we should also be. Our kids are reflections of us.

Because the term "values" can be overused, we'd like to rename these guiding principles. We prefer to say "core values" to reflect a deeper understanding that makes up who you are, part of your very core. We call these values "core" because they are your highest, most essential, uncompromising values.

In some contexts, core values can be dismissed. In corporate settings especially, core values evoke marketing exercises or meaningless HR initiatives. Lists of core values are printed on posters peeling off walls in break rooms. We gloss over them, especially when they hang next to signage about where to congregate in case of a fire and how to properly wash dishes in the communal sink. In these places, we have lost the true spirit of core values, along with the original meaning.

Let's look at the word's origin, like we did with "legacy." The word "value" comes from the Latin *valere*, meaning "to be worth." The word "core" is derived from the Latin *cor*, which means "heart." When we examine core values this way, as essential to our self-worth, we can reclaim the concept from the HR department. Core values, by definition, make us worthy. They define us. They are personal, cherished and held in our hearts as part of who we are and how we behave.

Core values are always in the back of our minds, shaping thoughts. Those thoughts inform emotions and actions: how we perceive and treat ourselves and interact with others and the world. For us authors, some core values on our respective lists do indeed prioritize love, but they also include other values that nurture and maintain connection, such as honesty, loyalty and compassion.

Like his father, the core value of nonviolence is a vital part of Martin's identity and Living Legacy. He has been arrested numerous times for peaceful civil disobedience—including in 2021 while protesting at the White House for voting rights.[78] If he started hurling bricks and shoving police, he simply wouldn't be Martin anymore. Core values aren't just about what you do. They enable better choices, it's true, but they also enable actions that lead to deeper self-love and love for others. Because core values come from the heart and foster authentic relationships, they are the conduits for love, connection and the Beloved Community.

CORE VALUES ARE ALWAYS IN THE BACK OF OUR MINDS, SHAPING THOUGHTS.

What about beliefs? Beliefs may well be even older than values in the history of higher cognitive reasoning.

We often speak of values and beliefs in the same breath, but while they are intimately related, they are very different. Yes, dictionary definitions of "values" often include the word "believe." For instance, the Britannica Dictionary says values are "a strongly held belief about what is valuable, important, or acceptable."[79] But we hold that they are distinct concepts—closely linked but separate. Core values develop, but once they do, they remain constant and immutable. They're not contextual—you don't (or ideally shouldn't) have one set of core values at home and another at work, for instance. If one of your core values is honesty in personal relationships but not professional dealings, honesty is not your core value. In the above case, it's more like a tactic.

A person's beliefs, on the other hand, are contextual, arising from learned experience and cultural surroundings. Your beliefs will constantly shift throughout your life, along with your experiences, causing you to develop new beliefs and amend or leave behind old ones. You stop believing in the tooth fairy, for instance, and start believing in the importance of quality dental care.

Beliefs may develop from core values, and core values may result from beliefs. It's a bit chicken-and-egg. Many of our own beliefs arise from core values. For example, learning and equality are two core values that we authors share in common, and based on this, we all hold the belief that every child has the right to an education. Other times, belief comes first. You may believe in God, the creator. From that belief, one of your core values might be living in service to divine love.

GETTING AT THE CORE

No one can agree on a universal list of core values, nor should they. In ancient China, Kong Qiu—known in the West as Confucius— taught a system of five thought-based core values: benevolence, righteousness, propriety, wisdom and trustworthiness.[80] The Greek philosopher Aristotle proposed a list of eleven core values: courage, temperance, generosity, magnificence, justice, ambition, good temper, truthfulness, wittiness, friendliness and modesty.[81] We appreciate that Aristotle considered wittiness—which to him meant joking around at leisure—an important value. We like to imagine him wisecracking with his friends at the Lyceum, a serious academic institution in Athens. You can see what we're getting at—these are entirely different catalogs.

It wouldn't be possible—or at least, it wouldn't be true to yourself—to simply pick values from anyone else's list. You must decide whether these concepts hold meaning for you. It is essential to go through your core values and beliefs systematically because, as we said, they are part of who you are, an enabler of connection and reconnection. These are the pillars of your Living Legacy.

Here is another approach, better than choosing values from other lists. First, think about what is most important to you. Go with your gut. What is fundamental to your being? If nothing immediately comes to mind, complete the prompts below.

- I was raised with these core values . . .
- The core values that matter most to me are . . .
- The core values I want to pass on to the next generation are . . .
- The core values that define who I really am inside are . . .

Once you have filled in these statements on instinct, contemplate them. What emotions arise when you imagine each thing you hold most valuable? Do you feel happy, sad, angry, resentful, grateful? Do these emotions match the core values you arrived at in the above statements? Which core values make you feel most like yourself? Put another way: Which core values make you feel most connected to yourself, others and the world? Which breed love and connection? Which will spur actions that align with your Inner Purpose and your Outer Purpose? For instance, if you listed education as a core value you were raised with, ask yourself: Does lifelong learning inspire me? Will my relationship with myself be improved if I live each day seeking wisdom? For us, the answer to these questions is a resounding yes. Therefore, we hold education as a core value.

When reflecting on the prompt "I was raised with these core

values," it's important to remember that the values or beliefs you unwittingly inherited from your family or surrounding culture do not need to define you or your actions. They may be based on past harmful legacies, and it's okay to let them go. In fact, it may be necessary for your personal growth and fostering connections and love with others. Some of us are unwilling to change the values we were raised with because we think they are immutable, but once we understand we have the power to create our own Living Legacy, we can define our core value system. You can start to discern what core values resonate most with you, regardless of the influences that surround you.

Defining and reminding yourself of your core values are among the most important exercises you will ever do. This is your map to life, the core of your being reflected in words. Once you have identified your core values based on your first list—keeping the ones that most invigorate you—feel again the emotions brought by each one. Let them wash over you. Unlike a corporate mandate, there is emotional and spiritual power in writing down your real core values. Consider putting them on a beautiful card and placing it somewhere you often look (a mirror, a nightstand).

Make your core values into a physical object, your personal reminder of who you are and why you are here. Craig and his wife, Leysa, sought to create a set of family core values. They engaged in a process of personal self-reflection and discussion as a couple and involved their children in dialogue. They have three boys, and only the eldest was starting to read, so everyone created a collage of images using old magazines, akin to a vision board, that represents their family's core values. The children can point to the pictures when discussing whether an action or choice aligns with their family's core values.

Answering the Call of Activism

Martin Sheen

It was 1965, and Dr. Martin Luther King Jr. was on Broadway. Backstage at the Majestic Theatre, standing just a few feet from me, was my hero.

Sammy Davis Jr. had organized a benefit concert. Weeks prior, more than six hundred activists marched over the Edmund Pettus Bridge in Selma, Alabama, for their right to vote in the Jim Crow South. Nonviolent protesters were met by state troopers with billy clubs, tear gas and white spectators waving Confederate flags. When I heard about the riots that Bloody Sunday, I was doing a play called *The Subject Was Roses*. I was so disturbed by the violence, I went to my theatre manager and suggested a benefit for the Southern Christian Leadership Conference, one of the protest's organizing groups, which Dr. King had been elected to lead. "It's a small theatre," my manager said. "We wouldn't make very much money." That's when Sammy got involved, and it became Broadway Answers Selma, with a bigger venue and a bigger guest list. Everyone showed up: Barbra Streisand, Maurice Chevalier—and Dr. King.

At intermission, I stood backstage arguing with myself, two adversaries in my ears. One voice said, "Just go over and get the reverend's blessing. Tell him what an inspiration he is." The other voice said, "Leave him alone. Wait for a time when he's receiving." Before I could make up my mind, he'd left.

That moment remains one of the biggest regrets of my life. I would never get another chance to meet Dr. King. Writing this, I think about what I would have said to him, and two words come to mind: Thank you.

To be honest, I don't think in terms of my own legacy, per se. I am a product of the legacies of others, and of America's volatile 1960s. It was the middle of the Vietnam War and the civil rights movement, a devastating and equally inspiring decade that nourished me for the rest of my life. Coming out of the '60s, we learned the only causes worth fighting for are the seemingly lost causes, and the only weapon to use is nonviolence. If what we believe is not costly, we are left to question its value. Often, we win with this approach; the Selma Marches led to the passing of the Voting Rights Act in 1965. This peaceful view of activism is true no matter what we are fighting for, whether the cause is civil rights, environmental protection or nuclear disarmament.

The first time I was arrested for civil disobedience, in 1986, I was protesting President Reagan's Strategic Defense Initiative, which would have stationed weapons in outer space. My wrists were in plastic cuffs; I was terrified but mostly delighted. Looking back, it was one of the happiest days of my life because I'd done everything possible to object to the idea.

I stand on the shoulders of giants who showed up for the causes that seemed lost, giants including Rev. Dr. Martin Luther King Jr. and Coretta Scott King, Bobby and John Kennedy, Harry Belafonte, Medgar Evers and so many more. With my own contribution, I just hope to continue the legacy that I and my generation were so generously given.

Martin Sheen is an actor best known for his performances in films such as Apocalypse Now *and television series like* The West Wing*. A multi-award winner, his acknowledgments include a Golden Globe, two Screen Actors Guild awards and an Emmy. Sheen earned a star on the Hollywood Walk of Fame in 1989.*

It is equally significant to examine your core beliefs. We all believe a lot of things. Most of them aren't relevant to our goal in this book—helping you find fulfillment through your Living Legacy. For example, your belief that the Buffalo Bills will someday win the Super Bowl may bring you a small dose of hope. But it probably won't make a difference to your growth and contribution or positively impact your life, others and the world.

We suggest a similar exercise to help identify your core beliefs, the ones that really do matter. Start by writing three to five responses to these prompts:

- I believe I am . . .
- I believe people are . . .
- I believe the world is . . .
- I believe one of the most important things in life is . . .

Repeat the exercise, sitting with the thoughts and feelings arising from each response and distilling the list down to what resonates most with you and represents who you are.

We realize this is a big undertaking. It's not always easy to identify which core values and beliefs make up who you are and how they will guide your Living Legacy going forward. The thoughts and feelings arising from some of the concepts on your initial list might be complicated, even conflicting. We often hang on to core values or beliefs out of habit, not because they serve us. So, let's drill down a bit further to separate what empowers you from what is holding you back.

EMPOWERING CORE VALUES AND BELIEFS

Not all core values and beliefs are created equal. Only *empowering* core values and beliefs make us feel connected and fulfilled. To understand this, let's first examine core values and how they foster the kinds of connection we need and yearn for.

As we've already discussed, when we live by core values, we are more connected to ourselves because a powerful inner GPS guides our actions, which reflect our most authentic selves, bolstering self-love. This logic is clear, but it's just as important to remember how much our core values and beliefs connect us to others. When we love ourselves, it's easier to give love.

This is especially profound. If we don't love ourselves, we might admire or even worship someone else. We might respect or glorify them, but how can we know true love for another person without first truly loving ourselves? We can't. Self-love is essential for building strong connections, and strong core values are essential for building and sustaining self-love. They are interrelated and inseparable.

Core values also enable deeper relationships with others because we can more easily identify people who share our values. Connections based on common core values are deeper than those based on mutual goals, interests or geography—the typical foundations for friendship. These kinds of interactions can be rewarding, too, but we often remain guarded when we are unsure of a person's true heart. Shared core values are a catalyst for richer conversations and learnings from one another. You can be more vulnerable with someone who shares your values because, even if you disagree, you understand who they are, where they are coming from and why they may have acted a certain way. Shared core values establish clarity between one's actions and intentions. All of this is a foundation for richer relationships, bringing more love and connection into the world.

Martin and Arndrea saw the connective power of shared core

values early on in their courtship. Arndrea was a psychology student at Emory University in Atlanta when she first met Martin,
then thirty-eight and still living at home with his mom, Coretta.
With his father gone, Martin had taken on the role of protector.
Given his childhood, Martin didn't trust easily, so much so that
the couple's first date almost didn't happen. A friend of a friend
had given Martin Arndrea's number. But when Martin called, his
best friend and wingman, Phil, was also on the line. Because of
all he'd been through, Arndrea thought it made sense he would
come with an entourage, some insulation from strangers. She gave
him a pass. Then, on the day of their planned meeting, Arndrea
was left waiting in the skin care spa where she worked part time.
Naturally, she was furious. When Phil finally called with an excuse, he explained Martin had rushed out of town on an urgent
matter. (Martin still swears this is true.)

Reluctantly, Arndrea agreed to meet again, still curious about
this man she'd heard so much about, the son of a civil rights hero.
She waited at the Crab House on Atlanta's outskirts—book in
hand, with low expectations. Phil walked in first, checking her
out. He turned on his heel to reappear with Martin, who'd been
"parking the car." By then, Arndrea was really looking forward to
telling him off. But as Martin strode into the restaurant, she was
immediately drawn to his energy. After just a few minutes of conversation, she realized how much they had in common. Martin
escaped her scolding.

Once the two got talking, Arndrea recognized that she and
Martin both wanted to spend their adult lives empowering people
and fighting against the violence of hate. They both believed in the
principles of the Beloved Community and deeply valued and honored the King family legacy. Each of them had inherited the core
value of service from their parents. Dr. Martin Luther King Jr. and

Coretta Scott King's service was more renowned, but Arndrea carried and cherished her mother's core value of helping people in need. Everyone who knew Arndrea's mother, "Mrs. Gladys," knew she was the person to go to if you were going through a hard time and needed some loving care and wise counsel. She immediately saw how Martin's parents instilled in him that same legacy of care and compassion for others. Arndrea always says her mother had the biggest heart she's ever known—her only competition being Martin's. Because of their shared core values, she saw the bigness of his heart within minutes of meeting him. Martin more than made up for his dating mishaps with a deeper connection.

Empowering core values—a commitment to nonviolence and service—and belief in the Beloved Community can enable multifaceted and life-changing connections. Empowering core values are both inward and outward focused, enabling you to be the best possible version of yourself, while at the same time connecting you to the world in a way that makes a positive contribution.

Another example: forgiveness, love and compassion. Some social psychologists call a trio like this "intrinsic values"—core values that we uphold for their own sake, not for the reward they will bring us. Studies have found a link between a strong commitment to intrinsic values and greater well-being and life satisfaction.[82] "People with a strong set of intrinsic values are inclined towards empathy, intimacy and self-acceptance. They tend to be open to challenge and change, interested in universal rights and equality, and protective of other people and the living world," observes British journalist and author George Monbiot, a columnist for the *Guardian* who writes about the intersection of values, psychology and politics.[83] In other words, empowering values and beliefs help to uphold you and propel you forward. They open doors to positive action.

Serving Through Sharing Knowledge

Radhi Devlukia

The process of creating a cookbook was a significant challenge for me. I grappled with the idea of monetizing something closely tied to my heart and heritage. None of this is mine. Yet, I realized that sharing these recipes was a form of honoring my family. It was about making their knowledge accessible to a wider audience, ensuring that their legacy of love and service reached beyond our family.

Sharing knowledge is one of the simplest yet most profound acts of service. I've been blessed with so many teachers in my life. So, part of service for me, and my way of showing gratitude to them, is sharing the knowledge they've given me with other people.

In my mind, I was not enough of an expert to share. But I started seeing myself as a bridge between my teachers and people.

I started from a place of being very scared of sharing anything online, not feeling like I had anything to offer, or not even knowing what my purpose was or how I contributed to the world. And then I remembered something one of my spiritual teachers, Radhanath Swami, once told me: "Knowledge is useless unless it's shared."

That, to me, was this sudden turning point of realizing that I was actually being selfish. It was my ego holding me back. In my mind, I was not enough of an expert to share. But I started seeing myself as a bridge between my teachers and people.

Through the transmission of culture, heritage and the ancient practices of Ayurveda—a five-thousand-year-old holistic health science—this knowledge has the power to transform health, minds and hearts. And I serve others by making this information accessible and practical, giving people a chance to benefit from wisdom they might never have otherwise. How can I take that information, package it in a way where people can understand it and use it practically in their lives? How can I turn a simple experience of eating food into something that is teaching you something, something that is infusing you with gratitude and love?

I don't have to be perfect in every way to share what I'm sharing, but I can at least translate it and be the bridge between you and that person or that information.

Radhi Devlukia is a social media influencer and foodie who brings new flair to traditional recipes, infusing them with the ancient health science of Ayurveda to guide followers to better health in both body and mind. She and her spouse, Jay Shetty, founded Juni, a sparkling tea company.

Let's look at some examples of empowering beliefs using our guiding statements from above:

- "I believe I am very fortunate in the circumstances of my life. I, therefore, have an obligation to share my good fortune with others."
- "I believe people are essentially good."
- "I believe the world is facing challenges that can be solved."
- "I believe one of the most important things in life is, through my actions, to leave the world just a little bit better than I found it."

These statements focus on hope. They see the best in other people and in the world, which not only keeps the door open to taking positive action but actively calls upon us to do it. Empowering core beliefs come from a mindset of abundance. There is enough for everyone, and therefore I believe my contributions will lift everyone up, not just me. These kinds of beliefs propel us on our Living Legacy journey rather than holding us back.

DISEMPOWERING CORE VALUES AND BELIEFS

Sometimes core values and beliefs cause further disconnection, leaving you empty and unfulfilled. They tend to be inward focused. Disempowering core values and beliefs are all about getting the most for "me." For example, core values that say wealth and power are an end game. Core values like this make little to no positive impact on the world because they don't connect you to others in a constructive way (and can also disconnect you from yourself). Where they do connect you to others, it is not to uplift people but to rise above them. These are "extrinsic values," the opposite of intrinsic values.

To be clear, many people use considerable power and wealth to give back and pursue positive impact. These qualities can be tools for real social change—in fact, money and influence are necessary to move the needle. However, as stand-alone core values, power and wealth can be hollow and unfulfilling. They are often treated as extrinsic values, which are all about reward—what will these values bring for me? This kind of selfish mindset can even harm us. "People with a strong set of extrinsic values are more likely to suffer from frustration, dissatisfaction, stress, anxiety, anger and compulsive behaviour," writes Monbiot, who has observed in his writings how values impact our psychology.

Remember what we discussed earlier: Success does not bring fulfillment. Rather, fulfillment creates success.

Ron Carucci is an author and change management consultant for renowned CEOs and thought leaders. After noticing a pattern in the mindsets of his clients, he wrote in *Harvard Business Review* about redefining your relationship to achievement, or, as he put it, "recalibrating your enoughness gauges."[84] Essentially, Carucci found his wealthy, successful clients often came to him unhappy and unfulfilled, always focused on things they hadn't done, money they'd left on the table. These are examples of disempowering core values. When he encounters values that leave people feeling disempowered, Carucci encourages clients to explore deeper questions, including "What meaning have I attached to having more money?"

Operating from a place of scarcity, we might seek instant rewards and dopamine hits in the form of external achievements, never feeling we're good enough because we're always afraid of losing that status, which is a finite resource. There isn't enough for everyone, so I must take what's mine before it's too late. It's also fleeting.

Disempowering beliefs can also tear us down or move us in a difficult and dangerous direction. For example, to use our belief prompts again: "I believe I am not good enough," "I believe that everyone is just out for themselves," "I believe the world is doomed," and "I believe the most important thing in life is to look out for number one." It's obvious how every one of those things is based on a negative outlook that is demotivating, preventing you from making a positive impact or living an inspiring and fulfilling legacy.

Finally, some core values can be a two-sided coin—heads for empowering, tails for disempowering, depending on how you look at them. Humility is one example. Humility helps us keep our role in the world in perspective and prevents us from straying into negative behaviors like arrogance and entitlement. Taken too far, however, humility can easily become self-deprecation and inertia. Humility is a core value you might not want to leave behind entirely, but instead, realize when it has reached a point that inhibits your potential.

Ultimately, there's no singular method for defining our empowering core values and beliefs, but we hope these prompts will inspire you to set your navigation system on your own terms. Whatever the method, examining core values and beliefs is vital, a process that clarifies our Inner Purpose and informs how we live our Outer Purpose, bringing more love and connection into our lives. Remember, the totality of your daily actions makes up your Living Legacy, and those actions become easier, more effective and more meaningful with guiding principles.

Sometimes you may find that the core values that you hold dear contradict with how you are living. This may mean your Inner

Purpose and your Outer Purpose are not aligned with each other or your core values. If something feels off, or untrue to yourself, scrutinize whether your core values are truly aligned with your mental, physical, spiritual and emotional well-being: your Inner Purpose. And also examine whether these values show up in your daily actions—how you are living your Outer Purpose in your contributions to your family, friends, community and the world. Alignment here is the key. You may have to adjust your actions to make sure that your Inner Purpose and Outer Purpose are in sync and you are living a legacy that's true to yourself.

The Beloved Community will be the result of collective action rooted in deep connection and agape love. To reach that state, as individuals, we must live in alignment with our true selves and make more meaningful connections with ourselves, others and the world. Empowering core values and beliefs ensure that we do, that our inside matches our outside. They guide the daily actions that will become your Living Legacy. In the next chapter, we'll explore the legacies that shape us with the same level of scrutiny.

CHAPTER 8

The Legacies We've Inherited

MAYA ANGELOU, THE LATE AUTHOR, civil rights activist and friend of Martin's parents, once said: "You can't really know where you are going until you know where you have been."[85]

Facing who we are and what made us that way is the essence of our next inquiry. In our quest to experience the full potential of our Living Legacies from this day onward, we need to first look at the legacies that shaped us. From family to community to nation to socioeconomic class, each inherited legacy that we were born into has contributed something material or spiritual to our makeup.

This is where we ask ourselves: What are the legacies I've inherited? What are the legacies that influenced my upbringing? And how have they shaped how I've lived until now?

We need to ask these questions explicitly. If we don't consciously recognize the legacies we carry, especially the burdensome ones, they will continue to work through us unconsciously. Unrecognized legacy burdens can get in the way of crafting and living new legacies that offer the healing and connection the world needs. Ultimately, the purpose of this assessment is to help us decide which legacies we want to carry forward on our journey and which ones need to change because they're holding us back. And remember, identifying and making choices about the legacies we've inherited isn't just about you. Legacy burdens are often responsible for the inner crises we experience as individuals, as well as the outer crises that harm our world. By confronting these legacies directly, we take control over how they live in us and how they live in the world.

WE ARE FAMILY

Everyone inherits something from their parents, grandparents and all the generations who came before. We're not just talking about material things like wealth, property and great-grandma's silver cutlery. Nor the curls you got from your mother's family or dad's smile dimples. There is so much more that gets passed on generation after generation that isn't stored in a bank or a dining room drawer or encoded in our physical appearance. We all inherit intangible familial legacies that significantly impact who we are and who we become as people.

We want to stress that there are many ways to make a family and just as many ways to transmit a legacy. You may never have known your biological family, perhaps being raised as an adoptee or refugee. Nevertheless, the ancestors you have never met have had a real impact on you, and more than you likely realize.

Whether we have biological or adopted families, the life experiences of the ancestors of the family we were raised in provide us with a buffet of traits, attitudes, beliefs and perspectives. These inherited legacies greatly impact how we view and connect with ourselves, others and the world. Learning the history of our forebearers helps us gain a greater understanding of the hardships and often the traumas they faced. We might even draw greater strength, recognizing how our ancestors once struggled with similar challenges and traumatic experiences and survived them.

Sometimes, the survival skills that our ancestors cultivated get passed on to us, helping us face adversity with courage, creativity and a belief in our resilience. Sometimes, though, the legacies of familial and collective traumas our ancestors endured have painful aftereffects that we inherit, such as tendencies toward substance abuse, depression, anxiety and hoarding. Understanding family members, past and present, through the lens of legacy can inspire greater love and compassion for their flaws and missteps. This can easily translate into greater self-love and compassion for our own perceived flaws and past mistakes as we begin to see the influences that shaped us.

WE ALL INHERIT INTANGIBLE FAMILIAL LEGACIES THAT SIGNIFICANTLY IMPACT WHO WE ARE AND WHO WE BECOME AS PEOPLE.

All four of us have undertaken—and continue—this personal inquiry, assessing the impact of our different family legacies, sometimes together and sometimes individually. We've all found the process beneficial as we've tried to step into Living Legacies that are guided by connection, love and Inner Purpose and Outer Purpose. We encourage you to see this as an ongoing investigation, leading with curiosity and compassion for yourself and your ancestry.

For Martin, his assessment includes inheriting a family

legacy that is an internationally known piece of American history. As we shared, Martin's grandfather Martin Luther King Sr. was a Baptist pastor with an abiding sense of social justice. King Sr., known as "Daddy" King, served as the head of the NAACP in Atlanta during the late 1930s, and fought for equal pay for Black teachers and the elimination of segregated elevators in the local courthouse. Once, when stopped by a police officer who referred to him as "boy," King Sr. glared at the officer and threatened to ignore him until he was treated with respect.[86] It's easy to see where his son—who marched in Montgomery and stood before a quarter of a million people to declare "I have a dream!"—got his courage and convictions. Dr. King also followed the legacy of Daddy King's religious footsteps, becoming a Baptist minister and sharing the pulpit with him at Atlanta's Ebenezer Baptist Church.

Like Dr. King's family, Coretta Scott King's family emerged from the legacy of the Jim Crow South. Coretta's father, Obie Scott, once started a sawmill business, only to have it burned down by a white man when Scott wouldn't sell it to him. Because he was the first Black man in the region to own a sawmill, no one would sell him insurance. So Obie lost his entire business in the fire. It was a huge setback, but he picked himself up and carried on for his family, giving his daughter a lesson in resiliency.[87] Even before she met and married Dr. King, Coretta was a powerful activist for justice and equality in her own right. As a college student at Antioch College in Ohio, she joined the NAACP and served on the college's Race Relations and Civil Liberties Committees.[88] Though Coretta gave up her promising career in music to care for the family and support her husband's work, she continued to use her beautiful singing voice to give Freedom Concerts across the US.[89] Her familial legacy of picking yourself up and carrying on was seen in Coretta after the assassination of Dr. King. Coretta determinedly picked up her husband's torch, fighting for human rights in the US and worldwide until her passing in 2006.

Martin and Arndrea both inherited profound familial legacies of public service and breaking through the barriers of racism, paving the way for others to follow. Arndrea's father, Arnold, became one of the first African American Allstate insurance agents in Tallahassee, Florida, where Arndrea grew up. Her mother, Gladys, continues to be Arndrea's most admired role model—a woman with a famously generous heart and a legacy of compassion and courage. Soon after Gladys was born, her father left the family, leaving her mother with three young children to raise on her own. Gladys began working at an early age, cleaning houses on weekends, to help her mother make ends meet. While she was still in high school, one of Gladys's employers saw her intelligence and impressive work ethic and offered to help Gladys secure a scholarship to nursing school. From there, Gladys became the first Black nurse to work at the local hospital in her hometown of Live Oak, Florida.

Both of Arndrea's parents had the fortitude and vision to pursue dreams that often seemed out of grasp for Black Americans at that time, especially in the small town they grew up in. Arndrea likes to say she inherited a tough head and a tender heart from her parents—who both had to rely on hard work and willpower to live their Outer Purpose while letting the tenderness and kindness of their Inner Purpose guide the way.

All to say the King and Waters families saw themselves as part of a wider world with a purpose to reach out to others and impact their lives in positive ways. For Martin and Arndrea, they inherited the most treasured legacies of love and connection.

On Being a Child of Trauma: My Reflection on Resiliency

Martin Luther King III

In the days after my dad's assassination, Nina Simone sang what has been called the saddest song ever written, capturing the rage and desperation of America in April of 1968. "Why? (The King of Love Is Dead)," she sorrowfully asked, as she prayed for the hatred to end. In my teen years, her song would become a sad anthem and a refuge for me. Alone in my Atlanta bedroom, I must have listened to it hundreds of times as tears poured down my face. "We can't afford any more losses," Simone sang. Her words could be spoken today. "They're killing us one by one . . ."

There were many lines in that haunting song I found profoundly moving. But the ending question of the song was so deeply personal to me. "What will happen now that the King of love is dead?"

How could a man who was on a mission of love be a recipient of so much hate?

What will happen now that my dad is gone? The world grieved the loss of a hero, "the King of Love." His purpose was bigger than he was, and so his death was shocking for those who mistook his calling from God for the same thing as being an immortal man. Certainly, the assassination of my father defined my life, but even before then, my body and brain absorbed small traumas as I was exposed to his work and those who opposed him. Subconsciously, I grew up in fear that, at any moment, my dad might be killed. A subconscious fear, too, that our whole family was in danger. Even now, I wonder at the cost of being a witness to all this history.

A little more than a year after my dad died, his younger brother, A. D., also a Baptist minister and civil rights activist, died under suspicious circumstances. He drowned in his swimming pool, even though he was an excellent swimmer. And six years later, my grandmother Alberta Williams King was assassinated in Ebenezer Baptist Church.

I am a child of assassination, a child of loss, a child of trauma. There was no road map for how I'm supposed to *be* in this world. I wonder what lessons are in my experience that I can share with those of you who are searching for your Inner Purpose and Outer Purpose and crafting your Living Legacy and dealing with setbacks and challenges that require you to muster resiliency or draw on your courage. I realize my story is unique, but I do hope writing about my experience can be helpful, maybe even inspirational.

Certainly, the assassination of my father defined my life, but even before then, my body and brain absorbed small traumas as I was exposed to his work and those who opposed him.

As a little boy, I eavesdropped on hateful phone calls in the middle of the night. And I stood beside my dad, watching a cross burning on our front lawn. Sometimes when he took his undershirt off, I'd glimpse the cross-shaped scar on his chest, caused by a woman who stabbed him with a letter opener at a book signing. When I was just five, my mom took me to visit Dad in Albany, Georgia, where he'd been jailed after another protest. I saw Dad in prison clothes, confined to a small, dank cell. Mom explained that Dad hadn't done anything wrong but was trying to make things right for other people. Going to jail, she said, was a "badge of honor."

Still, I didn't understand the logic of it. How could a man who was on a mission of love be a recipient of so much hate? The same question Nina Simone asked later.

> *I came to understand that he possessed a spiritual quality that God endowed him with. It meant my father feared nothing, but also instilled that feeling of safety in others.*

My first real memory of being a witness to the civil rights movement was when Dad took me to St. Augustine, Florida, in June 1964, where he and others were trying to desegregate schools, swimming pools and motels while pressuring US president Lyndon Johnson to pass the Civil Rights Act. He did, a month later. My memories are blurred. I remember marching in a nonviolent protest and a policeman passing us with his snarling dog. Out of fear, I grabbed my father's pant leg. I also remember the Klan, deputized as police officers, roaming the streets on horses, trying to suppress the Freedom Movement with fists, clubs, whips and guns. I saw a lady who had marched with us and had been beaten badly by the Klan—her nose was broken, she had bandages all over her face, and she reminded me of a mummy.

In those moments, Dad was my dad, not the civil rights leader. He showed me the love and concern that made me feel safe. I saw him as a preacher on Sundays, but I didn't understand as well the work that took him away from home—his dangerous fight for civil rights. I came to understand that he possessed a spiritual quality that God endowed him with. It meant my father feared nothing, but also instilled that feeling of safety in others. My parents were intent on exposing me to my dad's work, which

I am so grateful for. But now, as a parent, I ask myself: Would I send my child to a place where confrontation was likely? I can only say that my parents were on a deeply spiritual journey and believed God would keep me and my other siblings safe. For now, He has.

I'm also aware that Dad shielded us from the worst of the indignities of Jim Crow. He hinted at this in his famous 1963 "Letter from a Birmingham Jail," which he wrote in solitary confinement in an Alabama jail after being arrested for violating the anti-protest injunction. A group of moderate white clergy had been urging him to be patient and let the new Birmingham mayor slowly bring about the changes for which he was advocating.[111] This was Dad's response:

> Perhaps it is easy for those who have never felt the stinging darts of segregation to say, "Wait." But . . . when you suddenly find your tongue twisted and your speech stammering as you seek to explain to your six year old daughter why she can't go to the public amusement park that has just been advertised on television, and see tears welling up in her eyes when she is told that FunTown is closed to colored children, and see ominous clouds of inferiority beginning to form in her little mental sky, and see her beginning to distort her personality by developing an unconscious bitterness toward white people; when you have to concoct an answer for a five year old son who is asking: "Daddy, why do white people treat colored people so mean?"[112]

We eventually did go to FunTown with Dad. He rode all the rides as if he were a carefree child. That is a memory I cherish. In 1967, Dexter and I joined Dad as he crisscrossed Georgia on his Poor People's Campaign, where he was fighting to improve conditions for all, not just Black people. Mom told me later it was Dad's hope that we could freeze the memory of his commitment to fairness, equality and justice for the rest of our lives. Mom wrote something very poignant about that trip: "It was like a snapshot of his character. After all, Martin had no money to leave behind. All he could implant in their consciousness was an outline of his character."[113]

My mom, sisters and brother were home the night we heard the bulletin on TV that Dad had been shot. We ran to our mother's room, looking for an explanation, for comfort. She was already preparing to go to Memphis to be by his bedside. At the airport, she learned the heartbreaking news that Dad had died. She immediately returned home to be with us. She told us his spirit had gone home to live with God. "One day, you will see him again," she told us.

I could have become bitter, but I chose another path, looking to my faith, my family's love and my father and mother's lessons of nonviolence.

I wanted to cry until I couldn't cry anymore, but I took my cues from Mom, who was stoic. Just a few days later, she went to Memphis to lead a march Dad was supposed to have led. Few men would have that strength, whereas she didn't flinch. She demonstrated such courage, making it harder to understand how to grieve, to move past the mounting trauma, whether in public or private. I could have become bitter, but I chose another path, looking to my faith, my family's love and my father and mother's lessons of nonviolence. As I grew older, I also came to understand the forces that killed my dad were complex, not just rooted in hatred but in the partisan politics of the time, influenced by the actions of the FBI.

For many years after, we lived a very strange life filled with security people and safety precautions. Dad's absence was omnipresent. So were the threats. There were so many phone calls at odd hours that we gave up answering the phone. Somehow, I learned to just deal with the fear. I didn't know what else to do but navigate through and step up to be my mother's protector. Except for my time as a student at Morehouse College and my internships in Washington, I remained at home with her for the next thirty-seven years, trying to live up to my assignment, tragically earned in boyhood, to be "the man of the house." I closed curtains, locked doors and created a place of safety for us. I even attempted to tell my siblings what to do—and that didn't go over well, especially with my older sister. While I held public office and traveled the world, I was never far from home. I often wonder if I would have taken more risks or carved out a more daring path if I hadn't been a child of trauma.

> *I am a child of assassination, a child of loss, a child of trauma. There was no road map for how I'm supposed to be in this world.*

What I can tell you is that I made a choice not to be bitter and to believe that love and a nonviolent approach can conquer all. That doesn't mean I'm not sometimes knocked sideways by grief that makes me question our world and my place in it. On January 15, 2023, on what would have been my dad's ninety-fourth birthday, I sat in a Washington hotel room listening to Nina Simone's sorrowful voice, which enveloped me in feelings of fresh loss. I took a few moments to myself, then I straightened my tie, put on my jacket and headed to the next speaking event to share my message of love and hope.

At the same time, however, Martin and Arndrea inherited the fallout of the legacy of the racism their families endured as Black Americans. They recognize they both inherited the trauma from the violence that was inflicted upon their families. We talk more about trauma later, but we can say here that fear and trauma are disconnecting forces. They create fractures and disconnections within our psyches and can interfere with our capacity to connect with others. While Martin and Arndrea live purpose-driven legacies devoted to love and connection—the opposites of fear and disconnection—they can do so because they have consciously reckoned with the many aspects of the complex legacies they inherited.

FEAR AND TRAUMA ARE DISCONNECTING FORCES. THEY CREATE FRACTURES AND DISCONNECTIONS WITHIN OUR PSYCHES AND CAN INTERFERE WITH OUR CAPACITY TO CONNECT WITH OTHERS.

Marc and Craig also assessed how they were shaped by the familial legacies of their parents and grandparents, which are typical of the immigrant stories of many Canadians. Poverty. Homelessness. Hard luck and hard work. Their mother, Theresa, the second youngest of four children, was born in Windsor, Ontario, across the border from Detroit, Michigan. She was only nine when her father passed away. At ten, she was working weekends in a neighborhood store. One summer, her family's only shelter was a tent. There were years of hardship and sacrifice. Marc and Craig's maternal grandmother was dedicated to creating a better life for her children. With only an eighth-grade education, she taught herself how to type at night while cleaning people's houses during the day. She then got her first office job, becoming a secretary at the Chrysler Corporation (she eventually worked her way up and headed her department).

In this light, it is easy to see why Theresa spent years working as an advocate for people experiencing homelessness in downtown Toronto before becoming a teacher for disabled children. Theresa would never walk past an unhoused person without stopping to talk with them. People often wondered how a twelve-year-old and his teenage brother could start and lead such a successful children's charity. Their mother made a huge impression on them, passing on a lifelong dedication to helping those who were dealt a tough hand in life. Through her stoic example, she also instilled in her children the belief that they could achieve anything they wanted in life with enough hard work and determination.

Marc and Craig's paternal grandfather arrived in Canada from Săcălaz, Romania, just before the Great Depression, when he was only eighteen. He gave up a promising musical career to earn "suicide pay" fighting in Toronto boxing rings. It was dangerous work, but every bruised rib or black eye was, in his mind, a small price to pay for achieving a not-so-humble Depression-era dream. He went on to run a small corner store, working every day to earn the money to send his son Fred, Marc and Craig's father, to university. Fred also became a teacher.

Like Martin and Arndrea's families, there is a legacy of public service in the Kielburgers—a feeling of connection to and duty toward the wider world. Fred and Theresa Kielburger became teachers to positively impact the lives of younger generations. From their family history, they knew what it meant to be in need, so giving back to the community was an integral part of their family culture. The responsibility to give back is a familial legacy Marc and Craig greatly appreciate and go to great lengths to continue to live and model for their children.

The flip side of that legacy is an inherited fear of failure, of not wanting to return to those desperate circumstances the family once endured. Marc and Craig see how this translates into a powerful work ethic. Obviously, this isn't a negative inheritance in and of itself. Craig admits he likes the spirit of a strong work ethic and hopes his children inherit it. But they also recognize the inherited fear of failure behind that work ethic that sometimes drives the brothers to overwork and push themselves too hard, risking connection with themselves and their loved ones. It's an ongoing issue both Marc and Craig struggle with—phone calls and sharing photos from the road are never adequate replacements for being present and spending live time with a family.

RECODING OUR LEGACIES

Before we began writing this book, Marc and Craig hadn't thoroughly researched their ancestors' histories. In learning more about their families' immigration stories and their hardships, as well as their successes, the brothers could better see the legacies that molded them from birth. But because they know legacies can be transformed, their research also helped them identify the legacies they wanted to keep and the ones that needed to be lived differently.

We encourage you to research and consider the legacies of

your family. Where did your ancestors come from? Do they have a migration story? What challenges did they face? Why? How did they respond to those challenges? Do any of those long-ago responses still live in you as tendencies or unquestioned beliefs and values? How have those experiences shaped who you are and influenced your outlook on life? This is not a one-time-and-done inquiry. We see this as an ongoing investigation that forges a greater connection with our ancestors and forges a greater connection with ourselves as we consciously set out to heal our legacy burdens. Once you commit to living a new legacy for yourself and the world, you will be surprised by all the familial and collective legacies of the past you find within yourself that are asking to be seen and transformed.

Recent scientific research is even confirming how much our familial and collective legacies are alive within us. For a long time, scientists thought our DNA (our genetic blueprint) determined everything about us from the moment we were conceived. But as they dug deeper into genetics, they discovered something fascinating. They found out that our genes don't always act the same way. It's like having a recipe book where the same genetic ingredients can make many different dishes depending on how you cook them. In our bodies, special proteins called messenger RNA and other helpers decide how genes are used. They can turn genes on or off or tell them which hormones to produce.

This area of science is fascinating, fast emerging, and it is called epigenetics. Though the science of epigenetics is new and still being explored, the research suggests our life experiences can actually affect how our genes work. So, even though our genes are fixed, they can express themselves in lots of different ways. It's like adding extra layers of instructions on top of our genetic blueprint, shaping who we are and how we grow.[90]

Understanding Where We Have Come From and the Trauma That Shapes Us

Ken Burns

My passion for history and my approach to trying to engage audiences with historical events is rooted in a personal tragedy that has deeply influenced both my life and my work.

I was a young boy when my mother was diagnosed with cancer in the late 1950s. The shadow of her illness loomed over our family, a constant, silent presence. It was a time of great fear and anxiety for me. As a child, I was acutely aware of the "guillotine" hanging over us, poised to fall at any moment. When it finally did, on April 28, 1965, the impact was profound.

Afterward, my father, who never cried—not when my mother was sick, not when she died nor during her funeral—cried while showing me the movie *Odd Man Out*. At that moment, I realized the emotional safe harbor that film had given him. It was then, at age twelve, that I committed to becoming a filmmaker.

My journey to documentary filmmaking was not straightforward. I initially envisioned a career in Hollywood, but my time at Hampshire College, surrounded by social documentarists and filmmakers, steered me toward a different path. There, I was reminded that tragedy and loss exist in both the past and the present. My interest in history was ignited not by textbooks but by the lived experiences and personal stories of those who came before us.

Growing up, I was a terrified child, plagued by anxieties and stomachaches. I vividly remember the night I awoke, sick with worry not just for my mother but for the injustices I saw on television—the dogs and fire hoses unleashed on peaceful protesters in Selma. This was my first realization that the "cancer" of racism was just as insidious as the disease ravaging my mother. From that moment on, I became deeply invested in the civil rights movement.

Martin Luther King Jr.'s speeches, with their lyrical cadence and urgent messages, resonated deeply within me. He was the first person I ever saw as a "holy man," someone whose words could move mountains. His influence has been a guiding light, constantly reminding me of our shared humanity and interconnectedness.

It wasn't until I was nearly forty that I began to confront the grief of my mother's death. My late father-in-law, an eminent psychologist, helped me understand that my work was, in essence, an attempt to "wake the dead." "You make Jackie Robinson and Abraham Lincoln and Martin Luther King come alive," he said. "Who do you think you're really trying to wake up?" And I began to realize that this work, which I had assumed and seemed to be coming from the outside, was, in fact, an inward expression. Through my films, I was able to explore and lean into that grief.

I call myself an emotional archaeologist. I am interested in the facts and dates and events of the past, but they're just dry unless there's some larger emotional glue. I am not talking about sentimentality or nostalgia, but there are higher emotions that we are often afraid of. That's what I'm interested in.

Tolstoy once said that art is the transfer of emotion from one person to another. Dr. King was an artist of words and of meaning, and the art he gave us is the possibility of communicating with each other, of cementing that human bond which is broken by our own fragility and our own inattention.

I'm always drawn to something Dr. King wrote. "All I'm saying is simply this: that all mankind is tied together; all life is interrelated, and we are all caught in an inescapable network of mutuality, tied in a single garment of destiny. Whatever affects one directly, affects all indirectly. For some strange reason I can never be what I ought to be until you are what you ought to be. And you can never be what you ought to be until I am what I ought to be—this is the interrelated structure of reality."[114] I keep this up on my wall. It's right in front of me at every moment.

Ken Burns *is an acclaimed documentary filmmaker known for his in-depth exploration of American history. Over four decades, his notable works, including* The Civil War, Jazz, *and* The Vietnam War, *have won sixteen Emmys, two Oscars and two Grammys.*

Imagine your DNA as a library full of books (your genes), and epigenetics as the librarian deciding which books are available for reading and which ones are tucked away on the shelves. Your behaviors and environment act like notes to the librarian, telling them which books to bring out and which to keep hidden. These instructions don't change the actual content of the books (your DNA sequence), but they do affect how often certain books are read and used.

What's fascinating is that these instructions can be reversed, meaning the librarian can pull out or stow away the books based on new notes. This happens a lot during your life, especially during your early years. As you grow and experience new things, your epigenetic instructions can change, influencing how your body responds to the world around you.

BELIEFS, PHILOSOPHIES, ATTITUDES, SOCIAL ROLES, TABOOS— ALL THESE THINGS AND MORE ARE INHERITED LEGACIES.

When a life-altering event like trauma occurs, the librarian starts grabbing new books off the shelves to give your body instructions on how to manage the crisis. This will, in turn, affect how your body will manage other crises throughout the rest of your life.

This has big implications for psychology, too. Changes in your genes, guided by your experiences, can affect things like your behavior, personality and even your mental health. So, not only does epigenetics play a role in physical traits like height, but it can also shape who you are as a person.[91]

Here is where intergenerational legacies come in. Scientific research suggests that genetically coded instructions, which are based entirely on your life experiences, can be passed on to future generations.[92] This is incredibly profound and important to consider. It means the library that your personal epigenetic librarian has curated—the specific books that they selected for instructing your body how to manage situations—can then be passed down to your children and even their children. Their bodies are more likely to use the same books to figure out how to function. So, if your ancestors experienced collective legacy burdens and traumas like slavery, Jim Crow or the Holocaust, it could have likely left a mark on their genes that are passed down to you. Near the end of World War II, the Nazis punished the Dutch for their resistance by cutting off food supplies to a large part of the country. Some 4.5 million people were affected by the ensuing famine and an estimated 22,000 died of starvation. Years later after the war, scientists studied individuals who had been in their mothers' wombs during the "Dutch Hunger." They found that these children of the Hunger, and even *their* children, had disrupted metabolic processes that contributed to higher rates of health problems, like diabetes, and also appeared more vulnerable to mental health issues.[93] We don't just inherit physical traits but also the afterlife of our ancestors' experiences.

Beliefs, philosophies, attitudes, social roles, taboos—all these things and more are inherited legacies that the world around us starts to program us with from the moment we're born. Each generation inherits them from the one that came before. And these legacies have an enormous impact on us individually, as well as collectively.

Planting the Seeds of Legacy

Keshia Chanté

My maternal family emigrated from Portugal, while my paternal roots trace back to Trinidad. Both sets of grandparents made significant sacrifices, leaving behind familiarity for an unknown country. They faced different climates, languages and uncertainties, yet persevered to sow the seeds of a better life for their families. I am incredibly grateful for the fruits of their labor. I have immense gratitude for their hard work and determination that laid the foundation that allows me to now enjoy the fruits of their sacrifices.

Legacy, to me, embodies the profound impact of past generations' deliberate choices to improve the world for those to come. The power of handing something down from one generation to the next. Money, property, values, traditions, but even bigger and more long lasting—their impact and influence. Martin Luther King Jr.'s actions were pivotal in social justice and civil rights, making key contributions to our society, profoundly affecting the direction of our lives. He painted a vision of a future in black and white, and today, we have the privilege of seeing it come to life in full color.

> *Legacy, to me, embodies the profound impact of past generations' deliberate choices to improve the world for those to come.*

Starting my career at thirteen, I had my own struggles, planting seeds in soil that wasn't very rich. I encountered challenges in a field where opportunities were scarce for a young R & B artist like myself. Breaking barriers and overcoming numerous rejections required resilience. All of which felt lonely and isolating, until I shared my story and leaned on my community for support—a crucial reminder of the power of solidarity in achieving success.

Honoring my gratitude is what defines my legacy—a tribute to those who came before by paying it forward, ensuring future generations also benefit from the seeds sown by our ancestors. This empathy for humanity fuels my purpose and amplifies my desire to contribute meaningfully to society. In my career endeavors, I strive to create opportunities not only for myself but for others who face similar challenges. Whether in the world of music, television or business, I prioritize inclusivity and fairness, advocating for diverse representation behind the scenes and actively opening doors for aspiring talents.

My role as a voter for the Golden Globe Awards is part of that, too—being there to represent those who haven't been represented before. I believe that true impact requires active engagement and advocacy—an example set by Dr. King. I'm putting my energy into making sure I make contributions to the next generation so they can enjoy the fruits of my labor and have rich soil, sunshine and water to grow seeds of their own.

Keshia Chanté *is an R & B artist who launched a successful music career at age thirteen. Since, she has become a popular TV host and motivational speaker, as well as an international voter for the Golden Globe Awards. A compassionate philanthropist, Chanté is active in numerous charities and causes, including mental health and AIDS research.*

REVERSING AND REBUILDING
THE LEGACIES OF TRAUMA

Sadly, it's impossible to be born human in this world and not have inherited the emotional and physical impacts of trauma. But where other legacies leave us with gifts, traits and ways of understanding the world around us, the legacy of trauma mostly leaves us with wounds and places of disconnection that need our healing.

Just as many of the legacies we inherit come to us through family, so too do many of our traumas. Martin speaks openly about the traumas he inherited that come from his family's tragedies and persecution. He has borne the scars of the family's trauma all his life—his father's assassination and much more. Although still quite young, Martin was nevertheless aware of the frequent death threats, harassing phone calls to their Atlanta home, and crosses burned on their King family front lawn. The harassment continued long after his father's death.

Martin's mother, Coretta, once reflected on the impact of his assassination on her children: "For my children, the way was not easy. They each had to wrestle with and endure major problems. The loss of their father to an assassin's bullet was catastrophic. The riots and the looting that followed were so at odds with our principles of nonviolence that they were deeply confused. All of them had questions. They could not understand why their father, the prophet of nonviolence, had met such a violent end. They wondered if that same fate would take me from them."[94]

Coretta went on to ask: "How do you get children to love and trust others when they have been confronted with such devastating loss?"[95] Martin has reflected that he could have been a very bitter man, but instead, through the love and support of his mother and his grandfather, and his faith in God and the interconnectedness of all of life, he's been able to choose love and compassion as he crafts his own Living Legacy.

As we discussed in chapter 2, our personal and familial legacy burdens may also stem from collective trauma, handed down over decades and centuries, the enduring impact of historic events like the Holocaust, or slavery and segregation for Black people, or the traumas of colonialism experienced by Indigenous peoples. We noted how the legacies of slavery hang on, subversively manifesting in Black poverty and a plethora of mental and physical health challenges that plague Black Americans.

In Canada, where Marc and Craig were born, the legacy burden of colonialism manifested in the brutality of residential schools. For over one hundred years (the last school closed in 1996), First Nations children were taken from their homes—often by force—and placed into schools where they endured sexual and physical abuse, disease and the erasure of their cultures and languages. The survivors of those schools, and their children and grandchildren, are coming to understand how the intergenerational trauma of that experience has contributed to significant mental health issues like addiction, domestic violence and suicide in their communities.

The many collective legacy burdens of war, poverty, violence, racism, sexism, homophobia and colonialism have been passed on from generation to generation, perpetuating and fueling the permacrisis we are mired in. They are the source of most of the trauma we've inherited in the world—collectively and individually. These trauma legacies are also perpetuating the extremes of disconnection that cause so much suffering.

The legacies we inherit are vast and complicated and can impact us in myriad ways. We can't simply hang "good" and "bad" labels on each inheritance and file them away in the designated folder. Nor should you just accept your legacies as written in stone. Something you're stuck with for life. Because the important thing about legacies is that while they make up who you are, they don't define what you can become.

Returning to epigenetics and how the experiences of your ancestors can affect the systems that control how your genes express themselves: Scientists are now exploring whether changing the way you live can potentially cause epigenetic changes within yourself—and how those changes in your epigenetics can, in turn, be passed on to your descendants. The scientific hypothesis is still a long way from definitively proven. But the working theory is that you have the power to significantly impact and even alter what's coded in your cells. How empowering is that?

We believe the same hypothesis applies to the collective legacies we've inherited that have created such disconnection from ourselves and others. Each of us has the power to impact and change the genetic code of our culture. Living your legacy in conscious everyday ways is not only an opportunity to heal and transcend the personal legacies that hold you back from connection with yourself and others. It's also the chance to heal and transcend the collective legacy burdens that are hurting us all and holding us back from the Beloved Community.

This is the point of getting you to think about the familial and collective legacies you've inherited. It's not what you've got, it's not about deciding whether what you've inherited is "good" or "bad." It's what you do with what you've inherited. You are not responsible for the legacies you and the collective inherited, but you are responsible for what you do with them.

EACH OF US HAS THE POWER
TO IMPACT AND CHANGE
THE GENETIC CODE OF OUR
CULTURE. LIVING YOUR LEGACY
IN CONSCIOUS EVERYDAY WAYS
IS NOT ONLY AN OPPORTUNITY
TO HEAL AND TRANSCEND THE
PERSONAL LEGACIES THAT HOLD
YOU BACK FROM CONNECTION
WITH YOURSELF AND OTHERS.
IT'S ALSO THE CHANCE TO
HEAL AND TRANSCEND THE
COLLECTIVE LEGACY BURDENS
THAT ARE HURTING US ALL
AND HOLDING US BACK FROM
THE BELOVED COMMUNITY.

CHAPTER 9

What Do We Keep and What Do We Transform?

ARNDREA'S PARENTS, ARNOLD WATERS AND Gladys Howard, were childhood sweethearts. They met while attending a segregated all-Black high school in Live Oak, Florida. It was a town known for its timber, a chicken factory, watermelon—and its history of slavery and racism. There was a time when robed Ku Klux Klansmen marched down Main Street to show force and lynchings were common. Growing up, Arndrea's parents played with children of the survivors of the 1923 massacre in the nearby town of Rosewood. That predominantly African American community had been destroyed by a white mob; as many as eighty residents were murdered in cold blood. Many of the survivors ended up in Live Oak.

So it wasn't surprising that, beneath the town's pleasant veneer, racial tensions boiled. When Arndrea was still young, her parents moved to Tallahassee, where they continued to work hard to overcome the legacy of racism. As Jehovah's Witnesses, they took seriously their religious obligation to be humble and serve others. Gladys was the first nurse at the hospital where she worked to be named "Nurse of the Year," even as she endured racism from doctors, other nurses and even patients, some who refused to be treated by her.

In the early days of the HIV/AIDS epidemic, when infection

was a death sentence and many doctors and nurses refused even to touch HIV patients, Gladys was one of the few nurses to step up and voluntarily work in HIV wards. Gladys also wrote and produced teaching materials for other nurses to help them understand how to care for HIV-infected patients more humanely while still staying safe. Gladys and Arnold were impressive by any measure. But while they worked hard to serve and do the best job they possibly could, the inherent fear associated with the legacy of racism made them understandably cautious.

WE INHERIT SO MUCH FROM OUR FAMILIES AND CULTURE, AND EACH LEGACY CANNOT BE CLASSIFIED AS SIMPLY "GOOD" OR "BAD."

In grade school, Arndrea was selected to be tested for the school's gifted program. Her mother refused to sign the permission form. A lifetime later, Arndrea wishes she could go back and ask her mother why she said no. It could have been she worried about the potential added cost of having a child in a special program. Or the possibility the program would have required Gladys to do extra volunteer time at the school—time she couldn't afford. But Arndrea suspects a major driving reason was the fear it would call too much attention to Arndrea. Having been raised around the descendants of Rosewood, Gladys knew the potential danger of a Black person drawing attention to themselves.

Arndrea was raised always to serve others and never to be too much. She was consciously or subconsciously told not to stand out. Not to shine. Arndrea now believes this parental injunction to keep her head down was rooted in part in her parents' religious beliefs—and especially her mother's adherence to the values of humility and selflessness. But it was also rooted in the collective legacy of racism they had inherited and, indeed, had experienced firsthand.

Arndrea's story is a living illustration of what we talked about in the last chapter: Legacies are complicated. We inherit so much from our families and culture, and each legacy cannot be classified as simply "good" or "bad." From her parents, Arndrea inherited a legacy of humility and service, but also a pressure to hold herself back.

So what does Arndrea keep and what does she transform to create her Living Legacy?

She made a conscious decision to carry forward the legacies of humility and service but to transform them so they lived differently in her family. From the time Yolanda was very young and came to know of her iconic lineage, Arndrea instilled in her daughter the importance of being humble and respectful of the legendary legacy she inherited. Arndrea likes to tell the story of when she and Martin brought Yolanda to the White House for the fiftieth anniversary of Dr. King's "I Have a Dream" speech. During the event Yolanda met former presidents Jimmy Carter, George W. Bush and Bill Clinton. When President Barack Obama knelt to greet Yolanda and meet the stuffed animal she was holding—the news photographers went into a frenzy. The following day, that moment appeared in almost every major newspaper in the US. Yolanda knew she was meeting the president of the United States. She knew he had placed his hand on her grandfather's Bible when he took his oath of office. She knew she'd met three other presidents and even Oprah was there! She saw her picture in all the newspapers. But on Monday, when her kindergarten teacher prompted Yolanda to tell the class what she did last weekend, Yolanda cheerfully replied, "I stayed at a hotel and swam in an indoor pool."

For Arndrea, the delight in that story is twofold. First, Yolanda didn't brag, though she certainly had the right to do so. To this day, Yolanda remains humble about her legacy and never boasts, even though now she may spend her school break addressing the United Nations General Assembly or meeting the Dalai Lama.

The second delight is that Yolanda was able to just be a little girl who was thrilled with the novelty of swimming indoors. While Arndrea wants Yolanda to humbly honor the enormous legacy she inherited, she still wants Yolanda to become her brightest, most joyful, authentic self. She wants her to shine, just as Arndrea has learned to shine. One of Arndrea's life-guiding quotes is from the author and politician Marianne Williamson: "Who am I to be brilliant, gorgeous, talented, fabulous? Actually, who are you *not* to be? You are a child of God. Your playing small doesn't serve the world."[96]

SORTING THROUGH OUR LEGACIES AND MAKING CHOICES

Arndrea's examples of how she's sifted through her legacies and made decisions about how she wants to live them show us what's possible when we begin to sort through and update our own legacies. Each of us has done this kind of assessment. And each of us assures you we are not done. This is an ongoing process—recognizing the legacies we carry and making daily choices to continue or transform them.

The four of us know the importance of recognizing the familial legacies we've inherited that have infused traits we are proud of and draw our strength from. Martin and Arndrea can tick them off automatically—a commitment to social justice, racial equity, nonviolence, being in service to humanity and most of all, agape love. Marc and Craig likewise draw constantly on the legacies of their forebearers. Our familial legacies are unique, but the fact that the four of us inherited positive ones is not. Most of us can find at least one story of courage, character or charm that was passed down through the generations. Even if we never know any of the life stories that shaped us, we all have inherited strengths from our ancestors. We all inherited the will to survive and the skills to do so—otherwise, we wouldn't be here. We are all descended from people who lived and loved and mostly did the best they could within the world and circumstances they inherited.

WE ALL INHERITED THE WILL TO SURVIVE AND THE SKILLS TO DO SO—OTHERWISE, WE WOULDN'T BE HERE.

In recognizing and being grateful for the legacies of endurance, survival and, perhaps, the precious legacies of love and nurturance that we inherited, we can trust that they live on within us and can guide and sustain us onward. These are resources we have in the bank that help us live the fulfilling Living Legacies we yearn for.

Prioritizing Impact Guarantees Legacy

Yara Shahidi

I was eighteen when I excitedly got "'63" tattooed on my arm. Only three characters, but a world of meaning. Representing the year 1963—a pivotal year of the civil rights movement. When I look at my arm I am reminded of the March on Washington, the release of James Baldwin's *The Fire Next Time*, the bombing of the Birmingham church (which shaped the trajectory of a young Angela Davis), the assassination of Medgar Evers, the first woman in space and the passing of the Clean Air Act. And while the history is heavy, that year helped define my understanding of legacy.

To know me is to know I have *always* been a history nerd. I inherited it honestly from my papa and Gramps. Since before I can remember, I turned to history books, intergenerational dialogue and family dinner conversations to make sense of the world and my place in it. Luckily, my parents and family leaned in and honored my curiosities, helping me become a global citizen by intentionally introducing international reading lists, folklore and experiences. I could appreciate the universality of the human experience and the beauty of our cultural differences.

This type of growing up was a perfect primer from which my social and political consciousness blossomed. Being raised to appreciate our expansive community as a part of one whole, and understanding we are all responsible for one another, translated into a deep passion to be of service. (I think this was my parents' plan all along.) The power of curiosity and care can make the most "convoluted" of political issues just that simple: *Why is this happening? How can I help?*

In tandem with this unique childhood, my equally unique career path was unfolding before me. Even though I never watched much TV, I was moved by the creativity and power of storytelling. Gratefully, my first proper foray into television, *Black-ish*, was a show that unabashedly took its place in a lineage of shows that sought to have real conversations on racial, social and political realities.

Through *Black-ish* and *Grown-ish* (my college spin-off) we discussed police brutality and mental health, honored legends such as Prince and helped make Juneteenth a federal holiday. This experience only further cemented what artist-activists such as Sidney Poitier, Josephine Baker, Lena Horne and Harry Belafonte had taught us: that art helps *redefine* culture. Artistic endeavors can powerfully create the right social climate and prime our communities for positive change.

This perspective serves as a constant anchor. It defines the work myself and my mother and business partner, Keri Shahidi, do at our production company, 7th Sun. From supporting writers and telling underrepresented stories, to ensuring we are advocating for the causes that matter to us in every room we are lucky enough to be in.

Even though my work has been rooted in my values of curiosity and care, the entertainment industry is often more than any actor and artist signs up for (myself included). Even the once-in-a-lifetime experiences and award ceremonies in fancy gowns can feel detached from our reality. In such a public-facing environment we can often be guilty of thinking of our own legacies too soon and trying to control how we are perceived for years to come.

That's why my little arm tattoo means so much to me.

So, 1963 is more than a year. It is a reminder of the generations who fought for a future they were not guaranteed but knew was essential. They dreamed of new futures but could not have known about my tattoo, how we share clips of their speeches, convene to their music and take on after their struggle. In short, *prioritizing impact guarantees legacy.*

Yara Shahidi *is an actor and producer who rose to fame with the ABC sitcom* Black-ish *and its spin-off,* Grown-ish. *A graduate of Harvard University, Shahidi has been named one of* Time's *"30 Most Influential Teens of 2016"; a 2019* Glamour *"Woman of the Year" and one of* Forbes's *"30 Under 30" in 2018.*

YOU ARE NOT RESPONSIBLE FOR THE LEGACIES YOU INHERIT, BUT YOU ARE RESPONSIBLE FOR WHAT YOU DO WITH THEM.

There are, however, legacies we've inherited that, on the surface, seem to give us a leg up. And maybe our family historically used them that way, like intergenerational wealth that has been passed on for ages. Obviously, money helps provide safety, security and opportunities, among other objectives. But we have also seen that passing down wealth to the next generation without much conversation or guidance can sometimes create challenges, such as a sense of entitlement or a lack of incentive to find Inner Purpose and Outer Purpose, resulting in a lack of connection to oneself and others. As legacy architects, Marc and Craig have come to work with people of means who are seeking to find ways to generate greater family fulfillment and social impact with their wealth. The brothers know a lot about social entrepreneurism, the practice of using resources, rigor and creative thinking to solve a community's problems. They have written about using business profits as a force for social good, including writing the international bestselling book *WEconomy* together with Dr. Holly Branson, chief purpose and vision officer of Virgin, and chair of the Virgin Unite charitable foundation.

As they work with families who will be handing down a legacy of wealth, they often ask important questions to first consider before passing on a large check or establishing a trust fund. The positive implications and the unintentional consequences are equally considered. The framework they use is how wealth can serve their

Inner Purpose and Outer Purpose and enhance greater connection within their family and the world instead of hindering it.

You may also have inherited another kind of legacy that seems to give you a leg up—the legacy of privilege. Those who inherited privilege are often told to "check your privilege." That does not mean leaving it behind, because privilege is not something one *can* just choose to drop and forget about. Like it or not, if we've inherited the legacy of privilege in the culture we live in, we carry that legacy within us always. What we can do, though, is notice it as a legacy and decide what we want to do with it. Again, you are not responsible for the legacies you inherit, but you are responsible for what you do with them.

Understanding the legacies of privilege we may have internalized is essential for understanding ourselves and our place in the world. As white men born in Canada, Marc and Craig attended predominantly white schools, and lived in reasonably affluent and predominantly white suburban neighborhoods in a country that, like the US, has been dominated throughout its history by a white majority population. Craig recalls traveling through Asia as a preteen to learn about and help fight child labor. Despite his age, in developing communities, people often deferred to him because he was white. It was the awakening of his awareness about the privilege he enjoyed as a white person. Looking back years later, Craig realized he trusted the police he encountered on those travels without giving it a second thought—a trust not shared by many in the developing communities where Marc and Craig have worked in the years since or, for that matter, by many in non-white communities here in North America.

If you've inherited legacies that give you any degree of privilege, they are yours to leverage however you choose. But what we do know is that those legacies only seem to give us fulfillment when we use them in ways that meaningfully connect us with others and reflect our Inner Purpose and Outer Purpose.

Other familial legacies may not have given you access to privilege but may still have driven your family's moral or ethical coding that was unquestioned and passed down for generations. Your parents may have adhered to traditional gender roles in work and home life that don't reflect who you are inside, your innate gifts, or how you truly want to contribute to your family and society. Perhaps you inherited familial legacies of overt or unconscious racism, homophobia and sexism. Or extremist religious or political views that don't align with yours.

Here's the thing to remember: Acknowledging you've inherited privilege or oppressive beliefs such as racism or homophobia is not about self-shame. If we collapse into shame, we hinder our capacity to see and name the legacy burdens we carry within us that the collective needs us to dismantle and live differently. If a legacy is holding you back from connecting with and loving yourself and others, the world needs you to transform it. As Arndrea likes to say, this reflection shouldn't come from a place of collective guilt but collective responsibility.

Because we often think of these inheritances as ingrained in us, it may seem daunting to imagine living them differently. But keep in mind, values, beliefs and even the epigenetics we spoke of—these legacies from your family as well as the collective—have plasticity. They can be transformed and lived differently once identified as legacies, not just how we are.

TRANSFORMING LEGACY BURDENS

We return to trauma because the legacies of trauma can have the greatest impact on our lives and be the most challenging to face, heal and transform. We now know that so much of the perma-crisis we're struggling with comes through the legacies of familial as well as collective trauma. When we explored the source of per-macrisis, we touched on the collective legacies that are rooted in disconnection and have inflicted so much harm upon the world, such as racism, slavery, genocide and other impacts of colonial-ism. But here, we'd like to explore how Living Legacy can help us heal and transcend these burdens.

Every one of us has inherited familial and collective legacy traumas of the past. The symptoms of these legacies manifest in so many of the inner crises that perpetuate permacrisis—depression, anxiety, substance abuse, violence and extreme disconnection with oneself and others. Healing the aftereffects of these legacy burdens may mean seeking professional assistance. Fortunately, more and more therapeutic models are recognizing and address-ing the impact of collective as well as familial legacy burdens. While no one's path to healing the symptoms of traumatic leg-acies will be the same, we do know that consciously choosing to live and leave new legacies of love and connection can help us and the world heal from them.

Both Martin and Arndrea offer us powerful examples of how this can be done. As Martin shared in his personal reflection in chapter 8, the trauma of that inheritance will always be a part of him, and it's part of what makes him the man he is today.

Still, inheriting and transcending legacy burdens this large hasn't been easy. Every day, Martin actively chooses to lay down the hatred and bitterness he might carry—common symptoms of the kind of trauma he inherited—and instead chooses a different kind of legacy for himself and the world. He finds that consciously living his legacy like this day by day is a balm that helps heal and soothe the emotional burdens of the traumas he was handed.

Understanding Legacy: A Perspective from Richard and Dr. Holly Branson

What does "living a legacy" mean to you?

Richard Branson: For me, the concept of legacy is intrinsically linked to using my influence to make the world a better place. Living a legacy means standing for something significant. When faced with injustice, I choose not to look the other way. Instead, I challenge unacceptable issues and use my energy and resources to help make wrongs right.

Everyone can live a legacy in their own unique way. My father's motto—Isn't life wonderful?—reflected his relentless optimism, which touched everyone he knew. I strive to pursue my passions, share my values and be kind to everyone I meet, because you never know how it might impact them.

Holly Branson: I see legacy as stemming from a life filled with purpose. When you find what makes you feel truly fulfilled, you should channel all your energy into pursuing it. If you dig deep, you'll often find that your purpose is rarely self-centered. A legacy will only endure if it lifts people up. Find your purpose, and your legacy will naturally follow.

How can you manifest your legacy in your daily life and work?

Holly: If you want to make your working life more meaningful, start by looking at your workplace's purpose, mission, objectives, vision and impact. Reflect on whether these align with your own beliefs and what drives you. If they do, consider how your skills, responsibilities and passions can best bring your company's purpose to life and inspire your colleagues to embrace it, too.

If there is a misalignment, address your concerns with management. Guide them toward a more purpose-driven path or consider finding a role in a company that aligns more closely with your values. Alternatively, you might choose to become an entrepreneur and build a business with your purpose at its core.

Richard: Additionally, finding wonderful people who share your purpose to work alongside can make all the difference between success and failure—and it's a lot more fun!

Of course, everyone has their own vision for what their legacy should and will be. How do you manage that within a family like yours, one that's driven by so many causes?

Holly: We are incredibly fortunate to have a close family bond, not just within our immediate family but also within our large, joyful and curious extended family. All of us are passionate about making a positive impact in the world. We love engaging in debates and discussing our mutual causes and personal areas of passion. Dad has never been one to stifle anyone's interests or ideas, so we each focus on our specific areas and support each other's causes.

For instance, education is a major passion that my brother, Sam, and I share. Over the past decade, we've led our education charity, Big Change, with Dad being our biggest cheerleader from day one. Whether it's dressing up as a giant butterfly to run the London Marathon with us to raise funds or participating in grueling endurance events for the Strive Challenge, his support is unwavering.

Richard: I love seeing how passionate Holly and Sam are about their causes, and I always try to support them. This collaboration allows us to cover much more ground than I could ever do alone. From Sam's dedication to the environment to Holly's commitment to responsible business, and my passions for ending the death penalty, protecting the oceans, ending the war on drugs and upholding human rights, the variety gives our family and our Virgin companies a broad spectrum to work with.

*Serial entrepreneur and adventurer **Richard Branson** is the founder of the Virgin Group. Daughter **Holly Branson** is the chief purpose and vision officer on the Virgin leadership team, chair of Virgin Unite and the founder and trustee of Big Change. In 2018, she published her first book, coauthored with Marc and Craig Kielburger, the international bestseller* WEconomy: You Can Find Meaning, Make a Living, and Change the World.

EVERY ONE OF US HAS INHERITED FAMILIAL AND COLLECTIVE LEGACY TRAUMAS OF THE PAST.

Together, Martin and Arndrea have made many conscious choices about how they want to live and transform the collective trauma legacies they've inherited. They've both chosen not to try to forget or get past the legacy burden of racial injustice that has impacted their family history. Instead, they've decided to carry it forward to use as fuel, giving them motivation and purpose to fight racism like their parents did.

We showed you how Arndrea chose to transform the symptom of collective racism that caused her mother to fear Arndrea's standing out. Instead, she decided that being her most powerful and authentic self was a way she could transform and transcend that legacy—for herself and for Yolanda. She and Martin also put careful thought into other ways they can change the coding of the legacy burden of racism for the next generation. They wanted Yolanda to understand the legacy of being Black as a source of pride, not of pain and victimization. They made sure Yolanda learned about Africa before she learned about slavery in school so that slavery was not the first story she ever heard about her African heritage. They read her books and told her stories about the history of Africa and how it was the birthplace of humanity. When the history lessons got to the story of slavery, they taught her not to feel shame but to take pride in the strength of all her ancestors who endured, survived and even resisted despite the price for doing so.

All of us have the power to live new legacies for ourselves and the world. But it begins with seeing them as legacies, not the way things are. From there we can start transforming and healing them. In this way we not only heal the past, we also heal the future. But first, we have to go upstream and see the legacies of disconnection that started the crises. We look within our families and sort through the legacies we inherited and make choices for how we want to live new legacies that nourish love and connection from now on. We do the same with the collective legacy burdens we've inherited fueling so many of our crises.

ALL OF US HAVE THE POWER TO LIVE NEW LEGACIES FOR OURSELVES AND THE WORLD. BUT IT BEGINS WITH SEEING THEM AS LEGACIES, NOT THE WAY THINGS ARE.

Unfortunately, the headlines and TV news that highlight our permacrisis rarely help us with this. Instead, the media mostly presents information about issues of global and local crises without investigating the legacies of disconnection that created the crises in the first place. Nor does it suggest ways to live differently to help generate new legacies of connection. Because of this, many of us are left feeling fearful and helpless about the catastrophic events or situations that are happening now. We think it's not a coincidence that so many antidepressants and antianxiety pharmaceuticals are advertised on television news shows.

Developing Human Skills to Live Your Legacy

Simon Sinek

Think back to your school days and think of a teacher or a coach who had a unique impact on you. Perhaps they saw something in you that no one else did. Perhaps they believed in you and pushed you more than others. Whatever it was, who you are today is due, in part, to that person. I am sure you can recall their name easily. Now tell me the names of all the other teachers you had during the same time. You can't.

This is what it means to have a legacy. The lessons we have passed on to others, the impact or influence we have had in their lives, will live on long after we are gone.

Legacies are not created by trying to have one. It's not about having your name on a building. Buildings can be torn down. Legacies are built by giving in a way that will help those around us rise. True legacies live on through people. And those people will pass on what they learned from us to see those around them rise . . . and in so doing . . . we can live forever.

There is an entire industry designed to help us be better leaders and parents. There are industries designed to show us how to work out, eat better and sleep better.

But there is no industry that exists to teach us how to be better at being human.

Legacies are not created by trying to have one.

We all want to feel seen, heard and understood, and the first step to making that happen is to learn the skills that make others feel seen, heard and understood. The more we model the behavior, the more others will follow our example (indeed, that's what leadership is). We have to learn to listen actively, practice patience, resolve conflict peacefully, have uncomfortable conversations and learn other human skills.

The more we learn and practice human skills, the more the goodness will ripple from relationship to relationship for a very simple reason . . . someone who is treated with humanity is biologically more likely to treat the next person with humanity. And if that happens enough, the result could very well be . . . world peace.

Simon Sinek *is the* New York Times *bestselling author of* Start with Why, Leaders Eat Last, Together Is Better *and* Find Your Why. *As an inspirational speaker, his TED Talk on the concept of "why" has been viewed more than sixty million times. He currently serves as "chief optimist" at Optimism Press, an imprint of Penguin Random House.*

Here's another way we can receive the news. We can become curious about the legacies that may have created the latest crisis. We can recognize the disconnection at the upriver source of these legacies. We can then choose specific ways to live our legacies that stop reinforcing the disconnection that led to these troubling legacies in the first place. This is the most empowered and effective response-ability that we can imagine.

Craig tells the story of when he was a young man, feeling overwhelmed by the ever-worsening state of the world. Around this time, he fortuitously first crossed paths with Archbishop Desmond Tutu. When Craig confided the despair and powerlessness he was beginning to feel, the archbishop said to him, "You're thinking about this the wrong way, college boy." He then told Craig that, in all the terrible news headlines he reads, he sees his "to-do list from God."

This kind of "to-do" list may seem overwhelming, but when we turn it into Living Legacy, we can break it down into small, doable steps. Our daily actions, aligned with Inner Purpose and Outer Purpose, have the power to change the headlines and the world. Now and onward. We can actively choose the legacies of connection we carry forward, trusting in how they will leave an everlasting imprint on the world. In this way, we absolutely have the alchemical power to change the collective legacies we inherit.

We want you to know you do not have to take on this Living Legacy "to-do" list alone. What we know with absolute certainty is that cultivating healthy human relationships is an essential part of the process. Our best inner and outer healing comes through meaningfully connecting with or helping others. There is a considerable body of scientific evidence that backs us up in this belief.

For instance, engaging in activities that help others, like volunteering, can be potent medicine for healing yourself and your trauma. One of Craig's friends and mentors, Sheryl Sandberg, the former COO of Facebook, gave him a piece of wisdom that he quotes often. They were having a wrenching heart-to-heart talk about the sudden loss of her husband, David Goldberg, a successful CEO and loving husband and father. She told Craig: "Grief doesn't get smaller, life gets bigger." What she meant was the pain of loss or trauma may never entirely go away, but the bigger you make your life by connecting with and helping others, the less that pain will be felt compared to the ever-growing positive experiences of your life.

We'll share more about the transformative power of connection in the next chapter. But for now, we hope you will look at all the legacies you've inherited, especially the legacy burdens that are causing so many crises, and trust in yourself to transform them. Legacy may have gotten us here, but your Living Legacy will get us out.

CHAPTER 10

Living My Legacy Every Day

MORE THAN FIFTY YEARS AGO, Martin came upon a quotation from Horace Mann, the father of the American public education system and a slavery abolitionist. Drawn from an address Mann made the year he died, 1859, this quotation profoundly shaped Martin's Living Legacy from that day forward, as well as his understanding of how we can build the Beloved Community step-by-step.

> Be ashamed to die until you have won some victory
> for humanity.

Martin was a teenager visiting Antioch College in Yellow Springs, Ohio, with his mother, who was being honored as a distinguished alumnus. Before the ceremony, Coretta took him on a tour of her old campus. Together, they stood at the foot of an imposing bronze statue of Mann, the school's first president. The inscription beneath, the quotation that profoundly impacted Martin, bears repeating: "Be ashamed to die until you have won some victory for humanity."

Martin found it rousing and a little intense. Despite the achievements of his parents, for mere mortals, winning a victory for humanity seemed so daunting. He turned that statement over and over in his mind. He had many questions about what he read: How do you engage with humanity as an individual? What does victory look like? While an institution can reach hundreds of thousands, if not millions of people, how does an individual make a thundering impact?

Many times throughout his life, Martin has thought about Mann's quote as if it were a dare—challenging Martin to do something important. Being a realist, Martin broke down Mann's insistent message. While we can't all win monumental victories for humanity, Martin thought, we can all tackle smaller aspects of the goal to improve the circumstances of people or our planet.

We can probably get a victory on our street, Martin thought. Maybe we can come together as a neighborhood to clean up a local park or gather food for those who don't have enough to eat. Maybe we can win a victory in our school—by getting elected to student council, running for school board or even being a wonderful teacher. We can certainly win a victory in our places of worship, joining together in service or helping congregants in times of adversity. There are so many possibilities if we just start small. Some of us may win victories for humanity in our cities, like Martin endeavored to do as an elected municipal official in Fulton County. Others may win victories at the state or national level. Collectively, we can win victories for the world, and for humanity.

Mann's message has long guided Martin's work in the world—one action, one victory at a time—as he trusts that, ultimately, it all adds up to a victory for humanity.

The essence of this takeaway is also the essence of Living Legacy. We cannot emphasize enough how important it is for all of us to recognize the impact of our daily actions. This is not a lofty belief; this is a fact: every action, every decision, every choice of words, every act of kindness and every victory for humanity (no matter how small) has a ripple effect in the world. And those ripples are our own Living Legacy. You don't need all

Love is the greatest force in the universe. It is the heartbeat of the moral cosmos. He who loves is a participant in the being of God.

Best Wishes
Martin L. King Jr.

Handwritten letter by Dr. King that is framed in Martin and Arndrea's home: "Love is the greatest force in the universe. It is the heartbeat of the moral cosmos. He who loves is a participant in the being of God."

Yolanda at a rally for voting rights in 2021. Martin, Arndrea and Yolanda are outspoken activists in support of democracy and voting access for all.

Martin and Rev. Al Sharpton in conversation on the fifty-eighth anniversary of Bloody Sunday, referring to the 1965 Selma, Alabama, march for voting rights on the Edmund Pettus Bridge. Marchers were protesting Jim Crow–era laws that blocked access for Black Americans to vote. Law enforcement officers attacked six hundred unarmed marchers, beating them with billy clubs and spraying them with tear gas.

Martin, Arndrea and Yolanda carry Dr. King's torch, organizing and leading marches and rallies to protect voting rights. Here is a 2022 march in Washington, DC, with participation from the National Action Network and Drum Major Institute.

One of Marc and Craig's Legacy+ core values is elevating the health and well-being of impoverished communities. Here they opened a new water kiosk in Kenya, providing access to clean water, which local women are using for the first time.

Legacy+ Baraka Hospital staff deworming students at Enoosoito Elementary School.

Marc and Craig Kielburger at WE Day. From top left: Shiza Shahid, cofounder and former CEO of the Malala Fund; Malala Yousafzai; Prince Harry; Ziauddin Yousafzai; Craig Kielburger. Bottom: Marc Kielburger; Holly Branson and her father, Sir Richard Branson.

Baby Yolanda's first family portrait. She is the only grandchild of Dr. King, a legacy her parents help her honor and carry while staying true to herself.

Martin on the road in his youth. Even as he grappled with the magnitude of the legacy he inherited, he took on leadership roles in politics and nonviolent activism as soon as he reached adulthood.

Yolanda visiting the White House with her parents to commemorate the fiftieth anniversary of her grandfather's "I Have a Dream" speech. When President Obama knelt to meet Yolanda's stuffed animal, the news photographers went wild. The moment appeared in major newspapers across the country.

Arndrea in front of the US Capitol building in Washington, DC, speaking on behalf of voting rights with Martin and civil rights icon and activist Rev. Al Sharpton.

Martin joining grassroots initiatives that support civil rights in the US. In fulfilling the dream of the Beloved Community, Martin and Arndrea emphasize the importance of all races, ethnicities and communities being equally honored, protected and represented.

Martin in front of the National Museum of African American History and Culture's Martin Luther King Jr. "I Have a Dream" exhibit, Washington, DC, in 2022. Martin has listened to that speech many times in his life. He says, "Every time, it brings tears to my eyes."

Yolanda, Arndrea and Martin at the National Museum of African American History and Culture's Martin Luther King Jr. "I Have a Dream" exhibit in Washington, DC, in 2022.

Arndrea's parents, Arnold Waters and Gladys Howard, during Grandparents' Day at Yolanda's school. Arndrea likes to say she inherited a tough head and a tender heart from her parents. Though Gladys is no longer with us, Arndrea says she remains her most admired role model.

In 2024, the Kings and the Kielburgers traveled to the home of the Dalai Lama to learn and speak about the power of love and connection.

The first meeting in Atlanta during the pandemic, when Martin and Arndrea asked Marc and Craig to join forces with them to Realize the Dream. Left to right: Craig, Arndrea, Martin, Jennifer Gold (Martin and Arndrea's chief of staff) and Marc.

Martin and Arndrea speaking about service being good for the soul with John Hope Bryant, the CEO of Operation HOPE, at the 2024 Lake Nona Impact Forum in Florida. The annual event gathers representatives of leading universities, hospitals and research institutions to discuss innovations in health and well-being.

Legacy College in Kenya was built through Marc and Craig's charity leadership in the region. Their educational work began with providing elementary and secondary schooling, but when the students graduated, they needed a place where they could receive a college education. Legacy College's programs include Entrepreneurship, Tourism, Agriculture and Mechanics. The college also offers degrees in Nursing and Clinical Medicine, with students able to practice at the nearby hospital. Photos, left to right: Chancellors Dr. Steve Mainda, Martin Luther King III, Arndrea Waters King, Simon Sinek, Marc Kielburger, Craig Kielburger and Provost Carol Moraa.

Legacy College chancellors. Left to right: Marc Kielburger, Martin Luther King III, Arndrea Waters King, Simon Sinek and Craig Kielburger visiting the Kenya campus in July 2024.

When Martin visited the Legacy College in Kenya in 2024, the students made it clear how inspired they are by the legacy of his father. They even treated him and Arndrea to a stirring presentation of Dr. King's "I Have a Dream" speech.

Arndrea's mother became the first Black nurse to work at the local hospital in her hometown of Live Oak, Florida. Arndrea drew on inspiration from her mother, her most admired role model, to speak to nursing students at Legacy College.

On the Wild Card weekend of 2024, the National Football League kicked off its five-year commitment to help Realize the Dream of one hundred million service hours by January 15, 2029, the one hundredth anniversary of Dr. King's birth. For the entire weekend, all the players wore this message on their helmets in honor of the Beloved Community.

At the launching of the National Football League's commitment to Realize the Dream, Yolanda, Martin, Arndrea and Craig were invited onto the field for the coin toss. NFC Championship game between the Tampa Bay Buccaneers and Philadelphia Eagles at Raymond James Stadium in Tampa, Florida, on January 15, 2024.

Yolanda Renee King speaking at the United Nations General Assembly in 2024 about her legacy and the quest to Realize the Dream.

Arndrea, Yolanda and Martin share a laugh with Cincinnati Reds mascot Rosie Red after Martin threw the first pitch at a game in August 2024. The Reds are one of several sports teams that have committed to supporting Realize the Dream.

Martin and Arndrea presenting the Dreamer Award for extraordinary service work to Steve Ballmer (former CEO of Microsoft) and philanthropist Connie Ballmer, cofounders of the Ballmer Group. The Ballmer Group focuses on inspiring economic opportunities for children and their families in the United States, especially in communities where systemic inequities create barriers.

Martin Luther King III and members of Legacy+ staff kick off Realize the Dream at Legacy+ headquarters in 2023.

the answers to begin living your legacy in ways that create victories for humanity, but an open mind and an open heart help. So does a road map.

COLLECTIVELY, WE CAN WIN VICTORIES FOR THE WORLD, AND FOR HUMANITY.

In this final chapter, we recap the journey we've been on, as well as explore the concrete actions—the small victories—you can all make to help fulfill Dr. King's dream of a Beloved Community.

WHERE DO WE GO FROM HERE?

We began our journey to Living Legacy by assessing the sorry state of the world and the fragile state of the King Dream. We're a world stuck in permacrisis, overwhelmed by crises of war, of violence, of cost of living, of loneliness, of climate change, of purpose, of meaning. And all these crises make the King Dream more elusive than ever.

Yet, Living Legacy holds the power to heal and transcend our permacrisis. We begin with understanding the legacies we've inherited, as well as those that permeate our culture and have shaped us, and we continue by having courage enough to change them.

In this book, we have traveled inward to find the core values and beliefs that make us who we are. We traveled back in time, through our hereditary familial and collective histories, to determine which legacies to carry forward and which to transform and live differently. Along the way, we have explored Inner Purpose and Outer Purpose, all to create a Living Legacy that will help us meaningfully connect with ourselves, others and the world.

As you know, Living Legacy is a mindset and a state of being. We have seen the power of this philosophy firsthand. It has changed our own lives, and it has the power to change yours and change the world.

Thinking back to Dr. King's prophetic "Drum Major Instinct" speech, he didn't say he wanted to be known for accomplishing all that he set out to do. He said, "I'd like somebody to mention that [I] tried to give [my] life serving others." Your actions may or may not lead to the big results you hope to see in your lifetime. But your Living Legacy represents both the positive steps you have taken and your daily dedication to love and connection. These are the most significant kinds of legacies that you can live for your children and for all the children of the world and their children onward. The Haudenosaunee (Iroquois) people call it the Seventh Generation Principle. Make every decision and action in your life today while thinking about how it will make an impact now, and for the next seven generations.[97]

Each victory, large or small, matters. Just 25 percent of a group can influence large-scale social change. That number—one-quarter—is the "social tipping point," according to researchers from the University of Pennsylvania.[98] In their study, ten groups of twenty participants were each given financial incentives to adopt a linguistic norm, an agreed-upon way to communicate. Once the norm was established, activists rallied to change it. When that activist minority was below 25 percent of the group, efforts failed. However, as soon as the disruptors reached 25 percent, there was an abrupt change in group dynamics. Lead researcher Damon Centola has said, "remarkably, just by adding one more person, and getting above the 25 percent tipping point, [group] efforts can have rapid success in changing the entire population's opinion."

It is easy to dismiss academic studies for not reflecting the real world, but our experiences building movements prove this one's truth. Just sixty years ago, Black and white people weren't allowed to drink from the same water fountain or swim in the same pool, but a solid minority of dedicated people fought to change a racist system. A small group with big voices has the power to make change. More importantly, just one person can help a whole population reach critical mass.

So, how many people need to speak out against racial injustice? How many need to make more environmentally friendly choices? How many have to vote to change political tides? The number, 25 percent, seems manageable whether you want to change workplace standards, local bylaws or the hearts and minds of a whole population. Collectively, our Living Legacies can amount to large-scale positive impact. Purpose-driven daily actions connecting us with ourselves, others and the world will help us reach a state of love and fulfillment. This is how we heal the past and co-create the world and the future together. And this is how Living Legacy becomes a movement.

LIVING LEGACY IS A MINDSET AND A STATE OF BEING.

To reach the Beloved Community, we don't need to change everyone's mind right away. But we do need readers like you to think carefully about the daily actions that make up your Living Legacy.

Living Legacy Through the Transformative Power of Agape Love

Rev. Dr. Michael Bernard Beckwith

I was just a young boy when I met Dr. Martin Luther King Jr. at Holman Methodist Church in Los Angeles. Dr. King was on the West Coast, speaking and raising funds for the Southern Christian Leadership Conference. My mother, understanding the gravity of the moment, took me to meet him. When I shook Dr. King's hand, I remember remarking to my mom, "His hands are so soft." She smiled and said, "That's because he does a different kind of work, baby."

Later in life, I came to truly understand the profound nature of his work—a work rooted in agape love.

Dr. King said, in substance, that agape is the love of God operating in the human heart. This understanding of love transcends the mere sentimentality of loving only folks we like, those who look like us or those who are of the same nationality. Agape calls us to a higher state of consciousness, one where we recognize the God-presence in every being and love them unconditionally.

> ## Dr. King said, in substance, that agape is the love of God operating in the human heart.

Agape love is the foundation of the Beloved Community, and spirituality is the key. Without transformed and enlightened people, you cannot have an enlightened society. In his Nobel Peace Prize acceptance speech, Dr. King said, "Civilization and violence are antithetical concepts."[115] The spiritual practices of meditation, self-reflection, daily forgiveness of self and others, conscious compassion, life visioning, authentic affirmative prayer and conscious generosity awaken us to our inner peace and potential and provide the way for all of us to become aware of our better nature and to make choices from that state.

When I consider Living Legacy, I think of living my life knowing that my thoughts, words and actions affect everyone I meet and even carry a vibration to those I will never meet. When we live with intention, vision and purpose and consistently ask ourselves, "How can I make a positive difference in the world?" we become receptive to the inner guidance that leads us to the right action.

My Living Legacy is an ever-evolving spiritual community that is an example of the Beloved Community. Beyond philosophy and intellectual understanding, we are working to build a living community that the world can see and participate in that encourages the activation of the highest and the best within us all.

Legacy may be what we leave behind, but living our lives in ways that make a positive difference now makes our legacy alive in this moment and able to ripple out forever.

Michael Bernard Beckwith is the founder and spiritual director of the Agape International Spiritual Center in Los Angeles. In the '70s, he began an inward journey into the teachings of East and West, and today he teaches universal truth principles found in the traditions of spirituality. He speaks to a congregation of more than nine thousand people weekly at Agape.

How would you live differently if you knew you were the tipping point to fulfill Dr. King's dream?

BUILDING THE BELOVED COMMUNITY

The Beloved Community has been described in many ways—as a phrase, an idea, a place and an attainable goal where everyone, no matter their origin, is welcome and interconnected.

To Martin's mom, Coretta, "the Beloved Community is a state of heart and mind, a spirit of hope and goodwill that transcends all boundaries and barriers and embraces all creation . . . the Beloved Community is an engine of reconciliation."[99] And Dr. King said this of the Beloved Community: "It is this type of understanding goodwill that will transform the deep gloom of the old age into the exuberant gladness of the new age. It is this love which will bring about miracles."[100] His vision of the Beloved Community was a place energized by a love-centered way of thinking, speaking, acting and engaging that led to personal, cultural and societal transformation.

Even though there is no formal definition of the Beloved Community, Martin, Arndrea and many others have agreed that one of the main tenets of the Beloved Community is connection. Dr. King shared the vision of an interconnected, shared humanity, for all. He saw that we existed in a fractured state, where people of different ethnicities, socioeconomic statuses and politics lived in silos.

Dr. King did not precisely explain how to achieve his vision of the Beloved Community. He did not lay out a framework or seven-point plan. He did, however, establish a clear goal and vision. In doing so, he inspired a nation, and gave his own life in the process. He wanted to see this vision come to be. Dr. King's final book, *Where Do We Go from Here: Chaos or Community?*, outlined his most expansive vision for an inclusive, diverse and equitable world.

We hope our book can make at least a small contribution to taking up the torch from where Dr. King's 1967 book left off. While Dr. King asked whether it was chaos or community, many years later, we are asking whether it is chaos or connection, the latter of which will enable us to build the Beloved Community. At a time when there are so many tension points in our world—politically, culturally and personally—we have never been more disconnected from ourselves and those around us. We now have an opportunity to build connections with ourselves and others as we realize the dream.

We know that we cannot go forward in isolation. We cannot continue to be so fractured by political, economic, racial, ethnic or cultural lines. We are not going to get through today's myriad problems in silos, cut off from others, or if we exclude certain groups. We need to nurture connections and get through today's challenges together.

As a reminder, Dr. King taught us that we are not powerless. Nor are we condemned to isolation, loneliness and despair. These past years of convulsions—Covid, racial injustice, insurrection, war—have opened our eyes to the challenges ahead. The answer lies in healing the disconnection that isolates each of us. And the work begins when we take important steps to foster deep and true connections with ourselves and others.

Dr. King—Martin's father—continues to call us.

CONNECTION AND COMMUNITY

There are many ways we can answer the call. We'll share some of the ways that have helped us generate more love and connection in our Living Legacies. When connecting with existing and new friends, we try to be authentic and vulnerable and share our true selves, including our failures and the insights we've gleaned from them. We try to embrace our imperfections and allow others to see who we really are. For the four of us, we've found that vulnerability has been essential for deep connection.

Other ways that have helped us: when engaging with family members, be honest about your past actions and any mistakes you may have made. Being truthful builds trust, which is essential for family bonding. Like Martin's granddaddy, we've found that offering forgiveness soothes our souls and makes it possible for family rifts to heal. Similarly, we try to let go of expectations and recognize that every family member is unique. We accept who they are and focus on creating positive experiences together. Finally, we suggest creating new traditions that bring your family closer together. This can include volunteering, exploring new activities or simply having regular family dinners.

To connect to your work, we encourage you to understand why you work and whether your work gives you meaning and purpose. Ask yourself how your work challenges you. How does your work contribute to your community, to your clients, to your team or organization? And how could your work make a greater positive difference for others? Similarly, reflect on what motivates you. Finally, create a personal connection through your work—especially for those who work from home—by looking for ways to make your efforts personal, such as mentoring a colleague or assisting a team member in need. Small acts of kindness and support can replenish your sense of Outer Purpose.

To connect to your community, we encourage you to pay attention to all the communities you are part of. Sometimes, we just don't see how many potential connections we have. Leverage existing communities to make a positive impact. Our neighborhoods, children's schools, faith communities, sports teams, book clubs, choirs and theatre troupes, networking groups, professional associations, to name just a few—all are places we can transform, uplift and empower as we try to fulfill Dr. King's dream of a Beloved Community.

Maybe you don't yet belong to a community group. You can still perform an act of service or an act of kindness. Nothing is more rewarding than making (or rebuilding) connections and using them to contribute to something greater than oneself.

Love is also an important way this larger movement takes shape. Love is feeling a deep sense of connection with someone or something higher than yourself. It could be your children, your family, your best friend, your God, your spiritual self, nature, the universe or a complete stranger. We equally believe love is how you rid the world of the triple evils of poverty, hate and inequality that we are working to eradicate. Love is how you heal our planet. Love is also how you heal yourself.

Dr. King spoke and wrote about the importance of love. He shared that there were different forms of love, including agape love, which we've spoken of throughout this book.

As Arndrea explains, agape love is based on a foundational belief of the interrelation of each one of us. It is an acknowledgment of the underlying unity of all of humanity. To go a step further, we are not only interconnected but also interdependent upon each other. Martin reminds us that we all must nurture agape love from within and find ways to deposit it into the world.

To connect with the world through agape love means recognizing that we are all natural beings. Nature is part of us, and we are part of nature. When we destroy nature, we destroy ourselves. Part of so much of our suffering is that, as humans, we've become disconnected from nature. Our planet is facing huge challenges right now—climate change, deforestation and declining biodiversity. We can address these challenges by changing our daily habits to make more sustainable choices. We can support and encourage businesses that prioritize good environmental stewardship. We can engage in activism to demand environmental protection from governments and corporations. It's not like we've never heard these suggestions before, but when we think of them in terms of the real and lasting impact of legacy, we have a greater incentive to do them.

Each of these things alone may seem small, but your new Living Legacy mindset changes everything. You will see the world differently when you treat every engagement as an opportunity for connection. Specific actions in the above areas of your life will manifest according to the core values and beliefs you've established and the legacies you choose to carry with you.

REALIZING THE DREAM

We have a final suggestion—well, more like an invitation—for how your Living Legacy can help us build the Beloved Community. But first, we want to set the stage.

On what would have been his father's ninety-fifth birthday—January 15, 2024—Martin found himself surrounded by football players and fans, being peppered with questions about his dad's athletic chops. He was in Tampa, Florida, at Raymond James Stadium (with Arndrea, Yolanda, Marc and Craig), explaining that his dad had played basketball, ridden bikes and, yes, played football. "He could jump super high," Martin told reporters. Martin wasn't there to boast about his dad's athleticism, but—in the words of one journalist—to give his dad's legacy a "quantum leap."[101]

This appearance at a Wild Card game coincided with the

National Football League's announcement of a five-year commitment to Realize the Dream—a collaboration between the Martin Luther King III Foundation and Legacy+, calling for one hundred million hours of service by Jan. 15, 2029, the one hundredth anniversary of Dr. King's birth.

"I believe we'll be a much better nation after that, and it will help us get closer to realizing the dream," Martin told those assembled. "It's really just about making the world better for all of God's children."

Arndrea infused the moment with hope: "I know what happens when good people come together," she said. "This is not something that is just theoretical. So, what we really believe is that by five years of coming together, serving together, that we really will be closer to realizing the dream. We really will build that table of brotherhood and sisterhood with this initiative."

Dr. King was a unifier. Realize the Dream is a unifier. Sports are also a unifier, bringing people together from every walk of life.

Also joining are hundreds of nonprofit organizations and corporations, as well as over two hundred thousand teachers, the American Federation of Teachers, and College Board.

Realize the Dream is a vehicle for us all to live the ideas contained in this book; it is an invitation for us to live our legacy. Realize the Dream is the plan to build the Beloved Community.

We hope that each individual action, taken together, will grow the Beloved Community. The four coauthors are voracious readers, and we've lamented how let down we feel when an inspiring book concludes without the support to put a book's principles into action. We are committed to supporting you. And Realize the Dream is our promise to you and others. We provide the following resources to you as both a thank-you and a gift.

Through Realize the Dream, we envision a volunteer base of

millions of people from diverse backgrounds and life experiences packed with unique talents, skills and perspectives. How you serve is based on what you care about, what communities you belong to and your vision for those communities. We have created extensive online content and resources so you can align your Inner Purpose with your Outer Purpose to live your legacy. You don't need to wonder how to get involved; we show you how by providing a personalized way to live your legacy through meaningful actions. We have a free online portal at RealizeTheDream.org for you to pair the causes you care about and your geographic location to find tens of thousands of service opportunities. It also comes with a tracking system so you can log and track your contributions to the one hundred million hours.

If you want to get involved through your workplace, volunteering shoulder to shoulder with your colleagues, we've got free resources to help you do that, too. Teachers and youth, through their schools, can find incredible resources to help them get involved in service campaigns. Martin and Arndrea have often said, "service should not be the privilege of the privileged." Service needs to be available to those who don't have access to transportation or a lot of free time, whether they're working two jobs or raising a family. So we've made sure many of the resources and actions are designed to support those closest to you, through mental well-being resources, living tributes and a family action plan.

For Realize the Dream, the four of us have been crisscrossing America to meet with teachers, students and parents. Sometimes, we meet people who marched with Dr. King and who embrace Martin and Arndrea with tears of gratitude in their eyes. Because of his courage and sacrifice, many we have sat with express that they can vote, ride in a bus or sit in a restaurant. While some of these rights seem in jeopardy, it's important to remember how far we've come since Martin's father was born in 1929, but also how far we still need to go to reach the Beloved Community. Many of the students we've met so far have studied Dr. King in school and share how much participating in Realize the Dream means to them. They want to live their legacy by supporting this extraordinary campaign.

WE HOPE THAT EACH INDIVIDUAL ACTION, TAKEN TOGETHER, WILL GROW THE BELOVED COMMUNITY.

The stories of communities already helping to Realize the Dream are deeply inspiring. In Pomona, California, where more than 20 percent of residents live below the poverty line, the Pomona Unified School District has already contributed eighteen thousand hours of service to their community. They have held canned food drives, held hygiene drives for those experiencing homelessness, and collected donations to family support services and even pets in need. The project is led by sixth-grade teacher Joe Shim, who is retiring in 2029, once we celebrate the one hundredth anniversary of Dr. King's birth. This is his legacy project. He says, "No matter where you live, we all want to volunteer time in our community and to see the vision of Dr. King coming together to unify under service."

In his "Drum Major Instinct" sermon, Dr. King said, "everybody can be great, because everybody can serve." In these uncertain times, all of us must make a sincere commitment—through our families and friends, communities, faith groups, work and personal resources—to engage in acts of service as a means of building an inclusive community. When we wake up every morning, asking ourselves, "How can I live my life in service to love and connection today?" we align our Inner Purpose and Outer Purpose and find the fulfillment we all yearn for. We also become members of the Beloved Community.

Approximately 341 million people are living in the US. Imagine the impact if even just one-third of us committed to one hour of volunteer service each week. We can imagine it. That's why we have written this book and are creating this movement. If the messages in this book have moved you to live your legacy, please tell ten friends. Better yet, share this book with them. This is how movements get built: one person living their legacy at a time.

Take it from us, four authors who don't possess outsize wealth or special abilities but are dedicated to living our individual legacies, today and every day. If there is one message we hope you take away from this book, it is that legacy is not about mighty deeds and impressive monuments; it's about building a life of connection, fulfillment and love.

Every action you take creates a victory for humanity and brings us one step closer to building Dr. King's dream of a Beloved Community.

Join us.

ACKNOWLEDGMENTS

ONE OF THE KEY MESSAGES of this book is the importance of connection. This book is a testament to the power of connection—and collaboration. It exemplifies our belief that you can't live a legacy alone. This work is not the product of four authors writing in isolation, but of our collective effort, enriched by the contributions and support of many. To all these people—and to you, the reader—our deepest gratitude. This book is part of our Living Legacy, and we can't live it without all of you!

We wish to thank His Holiness the Dalai Lama for agreeing to provide the foreword, and for his many years of mentorship.

To the many amazing contributors who have shared reflections from the depth of their diverse life experiences: you've shown us all the power of Living Legacy every day. Tracy Anderson, Rev. Dr. Michael Beckwith, Bobby Berk, Dr. Holly Branson and Richard Branson, Dan Buettner, Ken Burns, Pete Carroll, Keshia Chanté, Radhi Devlukia, Melinda French Gates, Dr. Sanjay Gupta, Dr. Vivek H. Murthy, Sr. Theresa Aletheia Noble, Tommy Orange, Billy Porter, Dan Rather, Julia Roberts, Yara Shahidi, Rev. Al Sharpton, Martin Sheen, Jay Shetty, Simon Sinek, and Ciara and Russell Wilson: your words are profoundly inspiring and light the path ahead.

We also wish to thank Dr. David Baum for his wisdom and insight, and for being one of our first readers.

This book is the first step on a five-year journey to helping millions of people craft a legacy through one hundred million hours of service by 2029—a movement called Realize the Dream. We want to thank the leaders who have volunteered to help drive the project as co-chairs: Tom Wilson, Rumi Verjee, Carolyn Everson, Janiece Evans-Page, Robert F. Smith and Jessica Upchurch. A shout-out to the thousands of educators who have already joined in to bring Realize the Dream into classrooms across the country, inspiring a new generation to serve their communities. And an even bigger shout-out to the NFL and NBA, who are going all-in on RTD throughout their organizations, encouraging their players and fans to answer the call to service.

We want to express our deep gratitude to the many businesses, foundations, sports leagues and organizations who are empowering us to make all this happen.

We want to acknowledge the incredible teams at our organizations for the amazing work they do every day, especially the people in leadership, who are our rock and our foundation.

We wish to thank the late Harry Wachtel, a civil rights lawyer who worked closely with Dr. King and who founded the Drum Major Institute more than sixty years ago. We also wish to thank Harry's son, William B. Wachtel, as well as former UN ambassador Andrew Young for continuing to nurture the think tank and community action organization for many years. Both dear friends are on the board of the DMI, along with Daniel Roberti, Eric Gioia, Lisa Gioia, Fred Davie, Norm Ornstein, Scott Rechler, Sec. Jeh Johnson and Verna Cleveland.

To our chiefs of staff, Jennifer Gold and Jackie Pilon, thank you for your incomparable energy, operational and organizational excellence, and friendship. We would be lost without you.

At Legacy+, thank you to Scott Baker, Heather Harkness and the senior leadership team, as well as Dalal Al-Waheidi for coming on board to lead Realize the Dream.

We want to express our gratitude to the talented individuals who helped us turn our passion project into a well-researched thesis. To Gail Hudson for her guidance, thoughtfulness and editing skills. And to Shelley Page, Lisa Lisle, Kieran Green and Katie Hewitt, for your multilayered editorial support, commitment and craft. To Brandon Vieira for wrangling our outreach to contributors, and Lisa McCoy, for your patience in designing our cover. And thank you to the Girl Friday team—Karen McNally Upson, director of sales; Emilie Sandoz-Voyer, publishing director; Abi Pollokoff, production editor; Kristin Duran, publishing manager; the design team of Rachel Marek and Paul Barrett; and Georgie Hockett, marketing strategist—for turning a manuscript into a book.

Thank you to everyone over the years who has believed in our dreams and made them their own, stepping up to provide moral and financial support without which we couldn't have achieved all that we have. We wish we had the space to name you all, but we would particularly like to recognize the contributions of Scott Brickman, Cara France, Joseph Kroetsch and Kristin Uscinski, Jim and Valerie Milostan, Dave Richardson, Mario and Franco Romano, Andy Stillman, Brett and Miranda Tollman, and Jennifer Tory.

For your support in driving the core mission of DMI, thank you to Leigh Brown, Hilary Carr, Beni Ivey, Kent Matlock, Julie Moret, Michael Murphy, Sukey and Mike Novogratz, the S3 Group, Amber and Andrew Salisbury, and Marc Weintraub.

As befits a book about legacy, we acknowledge our parents, Dr. Martin Luther King Jr. and Coretta Scott King, Gladys and Arnold Waters, and Fred and Theresa Kielburger, as well as our siblings, Glynnis Waters, Katha Waters, Arnelia Waters, Bernice King and the late Yolanda Denise King and Dexter Scott King.

We also want to honor and acknowledge our grandparents and all our ancestors who came before and who bequeathed unto us their dreams.

And we want to thank our children, who are the future and to whom we have dedicated this book. May the Dream be realized in their lifetime.

All our gratitude to Craig and Marc's life partners, Leysa and Roxanne, for their unwavering love, patience and support.

Finally, thank you again to you, the reader. Your engagement with this book and spreading its message is what brings our collective vision and the movement to life.

NOTES

1   M. L. King III, interview.

2   M. L. King III, interview.

3   Michael Balsamo, "Hate Crimes in US Reach Highest Level in More than a Decade," Associated Press, November 16, 2020, https://apnews .com/article/hate-crimes-rise-fbi-data-ebbcadca8458aba96575da 905650120d.

4   "In 2022, We Tracked 1,225 Hate and Antigovernment Groups Across the U.S.," Southern Poverty Law Center, https://www.splcenter.org /hate-map?year=2022.

5   David Shariatmadari, "A Year of 'Permacrisis,'" Collins Language Lovers Blog, November 1, 2022, https://blog.collinsdictionary.com /language-lovers/a-year-of-permacrisis/.

6   Collins Dictionary, s.v. "permacrisis," accessed 2023, https://www .collinsdictionary.com/dictionary/english/permacrisis.

7   Brandon Tensley, "America's Long History of Black Voter Suppression: A Timeline of New and Old Efforts to Limit the Political Power of Black Americans and Other Voters of Color," CNN, accessed March 22, 2024, https://www.cnn.com/interactive /2021/05/politics/black-voting-rights-suppression-timeline/.

8   Richard Rothstein, "Modern Segregation," Economic Policy Institute, March 6, 2014, https://www.epi.org/publication/modern-segregation/.

9   Em Shrider, "Poverty Rate for the Black Population Fell Below Pre-Pandemic Levels," US Census Bureau, September 12, 2023, https:// www.census.gov/library/stories/2023/09/black-poverty-rate.html.

10   "Race and Ethnicity," Prison Policy Initiative, accessed March 22, 2024, https://www.prisonpolicy.org/research/race_and_ethnicity/.

11   Kat Stafford, "Why Do So Many Black Women Die in Pregnancy? One Reason: Doctors Don't Take Them Seriously," Associated Press, May 23, 2023, https://projects.apnews.com/features/2023/from -birth-to-death/black-women-maternal-mortality-rate.html.

12   Kat Stafford, "Black Children Are More Likely to Have Asthma. A Lot Comes Down to Where They Live," Associated Press, May 23, 2023, https://projects.apnews.com/features/2023/from-birth-to -death/black-children-asthma-investigation.html.

13   Kat Stafford, "High Blood Pressure Plagues Many Black Americans. Combined with COVID, It's Catastrophic," Associated Press, May 23, 2023, https://projects.apnews.com/features/2023/from-birth-to -death/high-blood-pressure-covid-racism.html.

14   Kat Stafford, "A Lifetime of Racism Makes Alzheimer's More Common in Black Americans," Associated Press, May 23, 2023, https://projects.apnews.com/features/2023/from-birth-to-death /alzheimers-black-americans.html.

15   Dan Witters, "U.S. Depression Rates Reach New Highs," Gallup, May 17, 2023, https://news.gallup.com/poll/505745/depression-rates -reach-new-highs.aspx.

16   "WHO Launches Commission to Foster Social Connection," World Health Organization, November 15, 2023, https://www.who.int /news/item/15-11-2023-who-launches-commission-to-foster-social -connection.

17   Vivek H. Murthy, "Our Epidemic of Loneliness and Isolation: The U.S. Surgeon General's Advisory on the Healing Effects of Social Connection and Community," US Department of Health and Human Services, May 2023, https://www.hhs.gov/sites/default/files /surgeon-general-social-connection-advisory.pdf.

18   Aaron Zitner, "America Pulls Back from Values That Once Defined It, WSJ-NORC Poll Finds: Patriotism, Religion and Hard Work Hold Less Importance," Wall Street Journal, March 27, 2023, https://www .wsj.com/articles/americans-pull-back-from-values-that-once-defined -u-s-wsj-norc-poll-finds-df8534cd.

19   Murthy, "Epidemic of Loneliness."

20   Tawfiq S. Rangwala, What WE Lost: Inside the Attack on Canada's Largest Children's Charity (Toronto: Optimum, 2022), 59–74.

21 Rangwala, What WE Lost, 86–92.

22 Rangwala, What WE Lost, 94–106.

23 Mario Dion, Trudeau III Report (Ottawa: Office of the Conflict of Interest and Ethics Commissioner, May 2021), https://ciec-ccie.parl .gc.ca/en/investigations-enquetes/Pages/Trudeau3Report.aspx.

24 Dion, Trudeau III Report.

25 Rangwala, What WE Lost, 342–354.

26 Justice E. M. Morgan of the Ontario Superior Court of Justice determined in Kielburger v. Canadaland Inc. that "There is reason to believe that there is substantial merit in the claim against Brown and Canadaland based on the restatement of the Money Passage; in addition, there is no reason to believe that Brown and Canadaland have any valid defence." In his May 8, 2024, decision, Justice Morgan also referred to the journalist as "callous," "high handed and oppressive." Kielburger v. Canadaland Inc., 2024 ONSC 2622 (CanLII), https:// canlii.ca/t/k4jx2.

    The United States District Court for the District of Columbia has denied the Canadian Broadcasting Corporation's (CBC) motion to dismiss WE Charity's defamation lawsuit against the outlet. The failed motion to dismiss was the CBC's only response to WE Charity's defamation claim. Jack Queen, "Canadian Broadcasting Corp Must Face WE Charity Defamation Lawsuit, U.S. Court Rules," Reuters, June 28, 2023, https://www.reuters.com/legal/canadian -broadcasting-corp-must-face-we-charity-defamation-lawsuit-us -court-2023-06-28/.

27 Brett Waggoner, Jesse M. Bering, and Jamin Halberstadt, "The Desire to Be Remembered: A Review and Analysis of Legacy Motivations and Behaviors," New Ideas in Psychology 69 (April 2023): 101005, https://doi.org/10.1016/j.newideapsych.2022.101005.

28 Brett Waggoner, "Legacy: Motivations and Mechanisms for a Desire to Be Remembered" (doctoral thesis, University of Otago, 2022), 186, https://ourarchive.otago.ac.nz/esploro/outputs/doctoral/Legacy -Motivations-and-mechanisms-for-a/9926478891101891.

29 J.D. Capelouto, "At Least 20 Institutions Have Now Dropped the Sackler Name," Semafor, May 16, 2023, https://www.semafor.com /article/05/16/2023/20-institutions-drop-sackler-name.

30 Stephen B. Oates, Let the Trumpet Sound: A Life of Martin Luther King, Jr. (New York: HarperCollins, 1983), 10.

31 Martin Luther King Jr., The Autobiography of Martin Luther King, Jr., ed. Clayborne Carson (New York: IPM in association with Grand Central, 2001), 12.

32 Rebecca Hamlin, s.v. "Montgomery Bus Boycott," Encyclopaedia Britannica, accessed April 17, 2024, https://www.britannica.com /event/Montgomery-bus-boycott.

33 Coretta Scott King and Barbara A. Reynolds, Coretta: My Life, My Love, My Legacy (New York: Henry Holt, 2017), chap. 5, Kindle.

34 King and Reynolds, chap. 5, Kindle.

35 King and Reynolds, chap. 5, Kindle.

36 King and Reynolds, chap. 6, Kindle.

37 King and Reynolds, Kindle.

38 King and Reynolds, Kindle.

39 King and Reynolds, introduction, Kindle.

40 Sanya Mansoor, "Georgia Approves Hate Crimes Law, but Critics Say It Could Be Tainted by Pending Bill That Adds Protections for Police," Time, June 26, 2020, https://time.com/5857282/georgia-hate-crimes/.

41 Selena Gomez: My Mind & Me, directed by Alek Keshishian, written by Alek Keshishian and Paul Marchand (United States: Lighthouse Management & Media and Interscope Films, 2022), Apple TV+.

42 Selena Gomez: My Mind & Me, directed by Alek Keshishian, written by Alek Keshishian and Paul Marchand (United States: Lighthouse Management & Media and Interscope Films, 2022), Apple TV+.

43 Vocabulary.com, s.v. "legacy," https://www.vocabulary.com /dictionary/legacy.

44 "How's Life?" OECD Better Life Index, 2020, https://www.oecdbetter lifeindex.org/.

45 "World Happiness Report 2024," World Happiness Report, 2024, https://worldhappiness.report/.

46 Chris Lee, "Latest Federal Data Show That Young People Are More Likely Than Older Adults to Be Experiencing Symptoms of Anxiety or Depression," KFF, March 20, 2023, https://www.kff.org/mental -health/press-release/latest-federal-data-show-that-young-people-are -more-likely-than-older-adults-to-be-experiencing-symptoms-of- anxiety-or-depression/; Witters, "Depression Rates." Joe Pindar,

"Depression Statistics UK: 2023," Champion Health, https://champion health.co.uk/insights/depression-statistics/.

47 Oliver Balch, "Can a Chief Happiness Officer Improve Workplace Morale?" Financial Times, March 11, 2024, https://www.ft.com /content/4601acca-12c8-4c14-9eec-7ceeb61a0cce.

48 Gregory Scott Brown, "Happiness Is Fleeting. Aim for Fulfillment," Washington Post, May 19, 2023, https://www.washingtonpost.com /wellness/2023/05/19/fulfilled-life-happiness-strategies/.

49 Gregory Scott Brown, "Happiness Is Fleeting. Aim for Fulfillment," Washington Post, May 19, 2023, https://www.washingtonpost.com /wellness/2023/05/19/fulfilled-life-happiness-strategies/.

50 Gregory Scott Brown, "Happiness Is Fleeting. Aim for Fulfillment," Washington Post, May 19, 2023, https://www.washingtonpost.com /wellness/2023/05/19/fulfilled-life-happiness-strategies/.

51 Doris Baumann, "How Can You Live a Healthy and Fulfilled Life? New study shares tips," World Economic Forum, January 20, 2022, https://www.weforum.org/agenda/2022/01/fullfillment-mental-health -study-ageing/.

52 Baumann, "Fulfilled Life."

53 Baumann, "Fulfilled Life."

54 Doris Baumann and Willibald Ruch, "Measuring What Counts in Life: The Development and Initial Validation of the Fulfilled Life Scale (FLS)," Frontiers in Psychology, January 10, 2022, https://www.frontiers in.org/journals/psychology/articles/10.3389/fpsyg.2021.795931/full.

55 "Fidelity Investments 2022 Investor Insights Study." The study was conducted during the period August 8 through September 2, 2022. It surveyed a total of 2,490 investors, including 673 millionaires and 1,520 investors with advisors. The study was conducted via an online survey, with the sample provided by Brookmark, a third-party firm not affiliated with Fidelity. Respondents were screened for a mini- mum level of fifty thousand dollars in investable assets (excluding retirement assets and primary residence), with additional quotas by age and affluence levels.

56 "Activating the Advice Value Stack," Fidelity, March 16, 2023, https:// institutional.fidelity.com/app/item/RD_9889363/activating-the-advice -value-stack.html.

57 "5 Steps to Stand Out in Every Environment" (white paper, Fidelity,

March 16, 2023), https://clearingcustody.fidelity.com/app/proxy
/content?literatureURL=/9909384.PDF.

58 King, Autobiography, 15.

59 Martin Luther King Jr., "The Three Dimensions of a Complete Life,"
partial transcript of the sermon delivered at New Covenant Baptist
Church in Chicago on April 9, 1967, published in the Seattle Times,
https://projects.seattletimes.com/mlk/words-life.html.

60 Learn more about Dr. King's 1967 book here: https://kinginstitute
.sites.stanford.edu/where-do-we-go-here-chaos-or-community.

61 "The Beloved Community," The King Center, https://thekingcenter
.org/about-tkc/the-king-philosophy/.

62 As mentioned, much has been written about Dr. King's sermon, and
we appreciated the insights of Dagmawi Woubshet, "Revisiting One
of King's Final and Most Haunting Sermons," The Atlantic, April 1,
2018, https://www.theatlantic.com/entertainment/archive/2018/04
/revisiting-martin-luther-king-jrs-most-haunting-sermon/556277/.

63 Listen to a recording of "The Drum Major Instinct" at https://www
.youtube.com/watch?v=Mefbog-b4-4. Or read more about it at the
Martin Luther King, Jr. Research and Education Institute at Stanford
University https://kinginstitute.stanford.edu/encyclopedia/drum
-major-instinct.

64 King, Autobiography.

65 Mark Alfano, Andrew Higgins, and Jacob Levernier, "Identifying
Virtues and Values Through Obituary Data-Mining," Journal of
Value Inquiry 52, no. 1 (2018): 59–79, https://doi.org/10.1007/s10790
-017-9602-0.

66 Alfano, Higgins, and Levernier, "Identifying Virtues."

67 Alex Traub, "Christine King Farris, Last Sibling Of Martin Luther
King Jr., Dies at 95," New York Times, June 29, 2023, https://www
.nytimes.com/2023/06/29/us/christine-king-farris-dead.html.
Associated Press, "Christine King Farris, Martin Luther King's Last
Living Sibling, Dies Aged 95," Guardian, June 29, 2023, https://www
.theguardian.com/us-news/2023/jun/29/christine-king-farris-dead
-95-martin-luther-king-sister.

68 Monique Rojas, "Remembering Christine King Farris," Atlanta

History Center, July 10, 2023, https://www.atlantahistorycenter.com /blog/remembering-christine-king-farris.

69   Victor J. Strecher. Life on Purpose: How Living for What Matters Most Changes Everything (New York: HarperOne, 2016), 7.

70   Strecher, Life on Purpose, 7.

71   Strecher, Life on Purpose, 43.

72   "Text of Dr. King's Statement on Viet Nam," Civil Rights Movement Archive, August 12, 1965, https://www.crmvet.org/docs/6508_mlk _vietnam.pdf.

73   Haja Yazdiha, "Martin Luther King Jr.'s Moral Stance Against Vietnam War Offers Lessons for the Middle East," Indiana Capital Chronicle, January 15, 2024, https://indianacapitalchronicle.com/2024 /01/15/martin-luther-king-jr-s-moral-stance-against-vietnam-war -offers-lessons-for-the-middle-east/.

74   King, Autobiography, 342.

75   Brené Brown, Dare to Lead: Brave Work. Tough Conversations. Whole Hearts. (New York: Random House, 2018), Kindle.

76   Grant A. Pignatiello, Richard J. Martin, and Ronald L. Hickman Jr., "Decision Fatigue: A Conceptual Analysis," *Journal of Health Psychology* 25, no. 1 (January 25, 2020), https://www.ncbi.nlm.nih.gov/pmc/articles /PMC6119549/.

77   Brown, Dare to Lead, part 2.

78   April Ryan, "Martin Luther King III Arrested, Later Released After Voting Rights Protest Outside White House," TheGrio, November 3, 2021, https://thegrio.com/2021/11/03/martin-luther-king-iii-arrested -voting-rights-protest-white-house/.

79   Britannica Dictionary, s.v. "value," https://www.britannica.com /dictionary/value.

80   Stanford Encyclopedia of Philosophy, s.v. "Confucius," accessed June 14, 2023, https://plato.stanford.edu/entries/confucius/.

81   For Aristotle, "magnificence" meant spending money on great works that would be of benefit to society. Today he would probably use the word "philanthropy." Strecher, Life on Purpose, chap. 3, Kindle.

82   P. Alex Linley et al., "Children's Intrinsic and Extrinsic Values: Sources of Internalization and Implications for Well-Being"

(unpublished manuscript, 2009, Centre for Applied Positive Psychology), https://www.pprc.gg/uploads/intrinsic.pdf.

83 George Monbiot, "To Beat Trump, We Need to Know Why Americans Keep Voting for Him. Psychologists May Have the Answer," Guardian, January 29, 2024, https://www.theguardian.com/commentisfree/2024/jan/29/donald-trump-americans-us-culture-republican.

84 Ron Carucci, "Why Success Doesn't Lead to Satisfaction," Harvard Business Review, January 25, 2023, https://hbr.org/2023/01/why-success-doesnt-lead-to-satisfaction.

85 "Maya Angelou: America's Renaissance Woman," Academy of Achievement Interview, January 22, 1997, https://achievement.org/achiever/maya-angelou/#interview.

86 King, Autobiography, 4–8.

87 Coretta Scott King and Barbara A. Reynolds, Coretta: My Life, My Love, My Legacy (New York: Picador, 2018), 11.

88 King and Reynolds, Coretta, 28.

89 King and Reynolds, Coretta, 98.

90 "What Is Epigenetics?" National Library of Medicine MedlinePlus, accessed June 13, 2024, https://medlineplus.gov/genetics/understanding/howgeneswork/epigenome/.

91 "Epigenetics and Child Development: How Children's Experiences Affect Their Genes," Harvard University Center on the Developing Child, accessed June 13, 2024, https://developingchild.harvard.edu/resources/what-is-epigenetics-and-how-does-it-relate-to-child-development/.

92 Rachel Yehuda and Amy Lehrner, "Intergenerational Transmission of Trauma Effects: Putative Role of Epigenetic Mechanisms," World Psychiatry 17, no. 3 (October 2018): 243–57.

93 W. Thomas Boyce, The Orchid and the Dandelion: Why Some Children Struggle and How All Can Thrive (Toronto: Penguin Canada, 2019): 207.

94 King and Reynolds, Coretta, 173.

95 King and Reynolds, Coretta, 174.

96 Marianne Williamson, A Return to Love: Reflections on the Principles of a "Course in Miracles" (Pymble, NSW: HarperCollins, 2007), chap. 7, Kindle.

97   "Values," Haudenosaunee Confederacy, June 9, 2021, https://www
     .haudenosauneeconfederacy.com/values/.

98   Michele W. Berger and Julie Sloane, "Tipping Point for Large-Scale
     Social Change? Just 25 Percent," Penn Today, June 7, 2018, https://
     penntoday.upenn.edu/news/damon-centola-tipping-point-large-scale
     -social-change.

99   "Nonviolence Toolkit: Beloved Community," Center for Applied
     Nonviolence, accessed June 2, 2024, https://nonviolencetoolkit.com
     /nonviolence-toolkit-way-of-life-beloved-community.

100 Martin Luther King Jr., "Facing the Challenge of a New Age" (ad-
     dress delivered at the First Annual Institute on Nonviolence and
     Social Change, Montgomery, Alabama, Dec. 3, 1956).

101 Joey Knight, "Family of Martin Luther King Jr. Aligns with NFL to
     Carry on 'Dream,'" Tampa Bay Times, January 15, 2024, https://
     www.tampabay.com/sports/bucs/2024/01/15/martin-luther-king-iii
     -nfc-wild-card-arndrea-waters-yolanda-renee/.

102 Coretta Scott King, "1968 Interview with MLK's Family," interview
     by Mike Wallace, 60 Minutes, December 24, 1968, https://www
     .cbsnews.com/news/60-minutes-1968-interview-with-martin-luther
     -king-jr-family/.

103 Read more about the March for Our Lives movement here: https://
     marchforourlives.com/.

104 NBC10 Boston (@NBC10Boston), "@AyannaPressley: 'Yolanda I was
     going to say if you lived in Boston you might be coming for my seat,
     but I think you might skip Congress altogether and head straight
     for the White House,'" Twitter post and video, January 13, 2023,
     https://x.com/NBC10Boston/status/1613987758862929920.

105 Learn more about Lifebook at https://www.mindvalley.com/lifebook.

106 The Martin Luther King Jr. Research and Education Institute, "I've
     Been to the Mountaintop," Stanford, https://kinginstitute.stanford
     .edu/ive-been-mountaintop.

107 Robert Bierstedt, *American Sociological Theory* (New York:
     Academic Press, 1981), 98.

108 Bernard Lefkowitz, "Church School in Atlanta Rejects Rev. King's
     Son," New York Post, March 18, 1963, https://www.episcopalarchives
     .org/church-awakens/exhibits/show/escru/item/147.

109 "1965: Dr. King's Children Enroll in White School," International
     Herald Tribune, August 31, 1965, reprinted in New York Times,
     August 30, 2015, https://archive.nytimes.com/iht-retrospective
     .blogs.nytimes.com/2015/08/30/1965-dr-kings-children-enroll-in
     -white-school/.

110 Martin Luther King Jr., *Strength to Love* (Minneapolis: Fortress
     Press, 1981).

111 Helen Taylor Greene and Shaun L. Gabbidon, *Encyclopedia of Race
     and Crime* (Thousand Oaks, CA: SAGE, 2009).

112 Martin Luther King Jr., "Letter from a Birmingham Jail," April 16,
     1963, African Studies Center, University of Pennsylvania, https://
     www.africa.upenn.edu/Articles_Gen/Letter_Birmingham.html.

113 King and Reynolds, Coretta, chap. 15, Kindle.

114 Martin Luther King Jr., "Remaining Awake Through a Great
     Revolution," Oberlin College Archives, https://www2.oberlin.edu
     /external/EOG/BlackHistoryMonth/MLK/CommAddress.html.

115 Martin Luther King Jr., "Acceptance Speech," Nobel Prize, accessed
     July 15, 2024, https://www.nobelprize.org/prizes/peace/1964/king
     /acceptance-speech/.

ABOUT THE AUTHORS

Martin Luther King III is a global human rights advocate and the eldest son of Dr. Martin Luther King Jr. and Coretta Scott King. A champion for nonviolence and social justice, he has inspired millions, advised heads of state, and led civil rights initiatives on nearly every continent. Martin served two terms on the Fulton County Board of Commissioners before leading the Southern Christian Leadership Conference, which was founded by his father. He continues his father's legacy through his work with the Drum Major Institute, focusing on poverty, racism and militarism.

Arndrea Waters King is president of the Drum Major Institute and a passionate advocate for social justice and equality. She organized the first National Conference on Hate Crimes and Hate Violence, partnering with over one hundred national organizations. Arndrea's work with the Center for Democratic Renewal (formerly known as the National Anti-Klan Network) and civil rights icon Dr. C. T. Vivian, a lieutenant of Dr. Martin Luther King Jr., has been instrumental in advancing civil rights. She coauthored *When Hate Comes to Town: Faith-Based Edition* and has written numerous articles and publications. She has spoken before mass crowds as a champion of democracy, justice and human dignity.

Marc Kielburger is a *New York Times* bestselling author, Harvard graduate, Rhodes Scholar and Oxford-trained lawyer. With thirty years as a movement builder and social entrepreneur, he's collaborated with leaders like Oprah Winfrey and brands like Virgin Group, headlining over 130 live events to inspire millions. A member of the Order of Canada and recipient of ten honorary doctorates, Marc has been named Canada's Most Admired CEO in the public sector.

Craig Kielburger is a *New York Times* bestselling author, humanitarian and social entrepreneur. An expert at driving movements for scalable social change and building mission-driven brands, he cofounded Legacy+ with his brother. Craig has received the Nelson Mandela human rights award and the World's Children's Prize and is a member of the Order of Canada. He holds fifteen honorary doctorates and remains a leading voice in global social change.

MYLEGACY

My Legacy is a vibrant global community that empowers individuals to live their best lives and lives larger than themselves. Our connection platform offers an array of tools, resources, education and inspiration designed to light a path toward the most sought-after yet elusive state of being: fulfillment.

From books and podcasts to educational courses, training programs and immersive travel experiences, My Legacy provides the knowledge and skills needed to build a meaningful and impactful life. Our exclusive events are designed to spark inspiration and foster deep connections, offering unforgettable experiences that celebrate personal growth and collective achievement.

 Join the My Legacy community.

REALIZE
the DREAM

Realize the Dream is a bold movement to rally communities to perform one hundred million hours of service by the one hundredth anniversary of Martin Luther King Jr.'s birth. It's a call for us all to reach out to people and causes in need—and make a difference through acts of love, compassion and goodwill.

Get started at RealizeTheDream.org.

PEACE ★ JUSTICE ★ EQUITY

Founded in 1961 on Dr. King's vision of a world free of racism, poverty and violence, the Drum Major Institute carries Dr. King's work and vision of radical nonviolence into the twenty-first century, democratizing it for all people. DMI leads through collaboration by convening leaders and organizations to identify common-sense solutions to our most pressing problems. DMI strives to inspire people to embrace their role in the King legacy, to empower them to build the Beloved Community and take action to promote peace, justice and equity for all.

Learn more at DrumMajorInst.org.

LEGACY+

Legacy+ is a foundry of strategists, designers, creators, storytellers and innovators that brings purpose to life for companies, foundations and individuals. It builds real movements and legacy-driven projects with life-changing impacts for people and communities around the world. They have partnered with globally renowned thought leaders, activists, CEOs, entertainers, athletes, celebrities and more to inspire millions.

Learn more at LegacyPlus.org.